Europe Inc.

D1280913

Belén Balanyá, Ann Doherty, Olivier Hoedeman
Adam Ma'anit and Erik Wesselius

Europe Inc.
Regional and Global Restructuring and the Rise of Corporate Power

Pluto Press
LONDON • STERLING, VIRGINIA

in association with

Corporate Europe Observatory (CEO)

First published 2000 by Pluto Press
345 Archway Road, London N6 5AA
and 22883 Quicksilver Drive,
Sterling, VA 20166–2012, USA

The right of Belén Balanyá, Ann Doherty, Olivier Hoedeman,
Adam Ma'anit and Erik Wesselius to be identified as the authors
of this work has been asserted by them in accordance with
the Copyright, Designs and Patents Act 1988

British Library Cataloguing in Publication Data
A catalogue record for this book is available from
the British Library

ISBN 0 7453 1496 1 hbk

Library of Congress Cataloging in Publication Data
Europe Inc. / Belén Balanyá ... [et al.]
       p.   cm.
    ISBN 0–7453–1496–1
    1. Trade associations—Europe. 2. International trade—Societies
etc. 3. International business enterprises—Europe. 4. Big
business—Political aspects—Europe. 5. Pressure groups—Europe.
6. World Trade Organization. 7. European Roundtable (Brussels,
Belgium) 8. UNICE. 9. Europe—Commercial policy. 10. Europe–
–Foreign economic relations. 11. Democracy—Europe. I. Balanyá,
Belén.
HD2429.E87E94   2000
382'.094—dc21   99–040487
                                                              CIP

Designed and produced for Pluto Press by
Chase Production Services, Chadlington, OX7 3LN
Typeset from disk by Stanford DTP Services, Northampton
Printed in the European Union by TJ International, Padstow

Contents

Figures

Abbreviations

ABB	Asea Brown Boveri
ACEA	Association des Constructeurs Européens d'Automobiles (European Automobile Manufacturers Association)
AFL–CIO	American Federation of Labor – Congress of Industrial Organizations
AmCham	EU Committee of American Chamber of Commerce
AMUE	The Association for the Monetary Union of Europe
API	American Petroleum Institute
BCSD	Business Council for Sustainable Development
BECs	Business Enlargement Councils
BIAC	Business and Industry Advisory Council (to the OECD)
BP	British Petroleum
BRT	Business Roundtable
BT	British Telecom
CAG	Competitiveness Advisory Group
CBD	Convention on Biodiversity
CDM	Clean Development Mechanism
CEE	Central and Eastern Europe
CEFIC	Council of European Chemical Industry Association
CEO	Chief Executive Officer, or Corporate Europe Observatory
CEPS	Centre for European Policy Studies
CNI	Community Nutrition Institute
CSA	Community Supported Agriculture
COP	Conference of the Parties
COREPER	Committee of Permanent Representatives
DG	Directorate General
EAGS	European Alliance of Genetic Support Groups
EC	European Commission
ECB	European Central Bank
ECIS	European Centre for Infrastructure Studies
ECST	European Coalition for Sustainable Transport
EFPIA	European Federation of Pharmaceutical Industry Associations

EMU	European Monetary Union
EP	European Parliament
EPC	European Policy Center
EPE	European Partners for the Environment
ERT	European Roundtable of Industrialists
ESLG	European Service Leaders Group
ESN	European Services Network
ESNBA	European Secretariat for National Bioindustry Associations
ETUC	European Trade Union Confederation
EU	European Union
FAO	Food and Agriculture Organization (UN)
FDI	Foreign Direct Investment
FEBC	Forum for European Bioindustry Coordination
FIEC	European Construction Industry Federation
FLG	Financial Leaders Group
GATS	General Agreement on Trade in Services
GATT	General Agreement on Tariffs and Trade
GCC	Global Climate Coalition
GCIP	Global Climate Information Project
GDP	Gross Domestic Product
GIG	Genetic Interest Group
GM	Genetically Modified
GMA	Grocery Manufacurers of America
GMOs	Genetically Modified Organisms
GSDF	Global Sustainable Development Facility
ICC	International Chamber of Commerce
ICE	Information Council for the Environment
IGC	Intergovernmental Conference (EU)
IMF	International Monetary Fund
IN	Investment Network
IPC	Intellectual Property Committee
IPCC	International Panel on Climate Change
IRF	International Road Federation
JI	Joint Implementation
LDCs	Less Developed Countries
LETS	Local Exchange and Trade Scheme
MAI	Multilateral Agreement on Investment
MEAs	Multilateral Environmental Agreements
MEP	Member of the European Parliament
MIA	Multilateral Investment Agreement
MRA	Mutual Recognition Agreement
NAFTA	North Atlantic Free Trade Agreement
NFTC	National Foreign Trade Council
NGOs	Non-governmental Organisations
NTM	New Transatlantic Marketplace

OECD	Organization for Economic Cooperation and Development
PR	Public Relations
SACTRA	Standing Advisory Committee on Trunk Road Assessment
SAGB	Senior Advisory Group on Biotechnology
SEIA	Strategic Environmental Impact Assessment
SM	Single Market
SMEs	Small and Medium-sized Enterprises
TABD	Transatlantic Business Dialogue
TENs	Trans-European Networks
TEP	Transatlantic Economic Partnership
TERN	Trans-European Roads Network
TNCs	Transnational Corporations
TRAC	Transnational Resource and Action Center
TRIPs	Trade-Related Aspects of Intellectual Property Rights
TUAC	Trade Union Advisory Council (to the OECD)
UEAPME	Union Européenne de l'Artisanat et des Petites et Moyennes Enterprises (European Union for Artisans and Small and Medium-sized Enterprises)
UN	United Nations
UNCED	United Nations Conference on Environment and Development (the Rio Earth Summit)
UNCTAD	United Nations Conference on Trade And Development
UNCTC	United Nations Centre on Transnational Corporations
UNDP	United Nations Development Programme
UNICE	Union of Industrial and Employers' Confederations of Europe
US	United States
USCIB	United States Council for International Business
WBCSD	World Business Council for Sustainable Development
WEF	World Economic Forum
WICE	World Industry Council for the Environment
WTO	World Trade Organization

Foreword

by George Monbiot

The most important conflict of the twenty-first century will be the battle between corporations and democracy. As companies tighten their grip on national governments and international institutions, ordinary people will discover that, unless they are prepared to confront big business, their residual democratic rights will disappear.

The critical weapon in this battle will be information: those who know most will win. Our power lies in our ability to expose the machinations of society's corporate enemies, to embarrass the governments which have surrendered to them, and to use our knowledge to wage incisive, informed campaigns against both the companies themselves and, even more importantly, the institutional failures which have allowed them to hold sway. We must arm ourselves with as much information as we can lay hands on.

There could scarcely be a better place to start than *Europe Inc.* This new edition, updated and expanded, will prove to be one of the most useful guides to the murky world of international corporate politics ever published. It exposes the colonisation of Europe's public institutions by bodies seeking to run them for strictly private purposes.

Europe Inc. is the result of years of investigation and analysis, by researchers who have come to understand how Europe really works perhaps better than anyone else on earth. Every chapter is fully referenced and sourced: the claims it makes are demonstrable and sound. This is a terrifying account, but it is also an inspiring one. The first shot in the twenty-first century's information war, it will smash a massive hole in the corporate defences, through which we, the disenfranchised, can pour. No one who reads this book will ever be naked on the information battlefield again.

Preface

This book is a collective undertaking by Corporate Europe Observatory (CEO), a research and campaign group based in Amsterdam, the Netherlands. CEO exposes the threats to democracy, equity, social justice and the environment posed by the economic and political power exercised by corporations and their lobby groups. We disseminate our research into the ambitions, activities and influence of industry *vis-à-vis* national and international politics through reports, briefings and a regular newsletter. No less important, CEO endeavours to support progressive groups whose interests are threatened by corporate conduct. The five members of CEO and authors of this book are Belén Balanyá, Ann Doherty, Olivier Hoedeman, Adam Ma'anit and Erik Wesselius.

This book is the product of over six years of increasingly intensive investigation into the activities and influence of corporate lobby groups. As environmental and international solidarity campaigners, we found ourselves time after time facing the challenge of countering European Union policies with a strong corporate bias. The shocking plan for 12,000 kilometres of new motorways announced in 1991 – part of the EU's megalomanic and unsustainable Trans-European Networks (TENs) scheme – was an early catalyst. We quickly discovered that the TENs had been placed on the political agenda by the European Roundtable of Industrialists (ERT), a club of some 45 captains of industry from the largest European transnational corporations. Further research exposed the far wider ambitions of the ERT for accelerating the process of European unification and the simultaneous fundamental reshaping of European societies in the interests of industry. We wrote our first articles and briefings on the Roundtable and the malevolent impacts of its influence in 1993.

In the following years, as critical observers of the process of European unification, we witnessed a continual series of successes won by the ERT and other lobby groups in promoting socially and environmentally controversial projects such as the single currency, the promotion of genetically modified seeds and products, the restructuring of educational

policies, and so forth. We were frustrated and concerned that the ERT
was able to perform this role without attracting either critical media
attention or opposition from citizens' groups. In 1996, when EU
governments initiated negotiations which resulted in the Amsterdam
Treaty the following year, we were amazed to see that the ERT's lobbying
apparatus was in operation from the very beginning. We found this an
opportune moment to document and report on the privileged access to
EU decision makers enjoyed by the ERT and other corporate groupings in
Brussels, and the impacts of their lobbying. In this way, we hoped to
spark a debate on the disproportionate influence of corporations on EU
politics and the resulting biased nature of EU treaties and policies.

Relatively few Europeans are aware of the systematic way in which
transnational corporations, through bodies like the ERT, have succeeded
in influencing a wide range of EU policies. No analysis of the EU's current
neoliberal economic strategies – which involve promoting deregulation
and privatisation in virtually all areas and subordinating every policy
field to the objective of international competitiveness – can ignore the
activities of corporate lobby groups. Yet the problematic nature of
corporate influence on EU policies was virtually ignored during the
debate around the revision of the Maastricht Treaty and the future of the
European Union. In May 1997, a month before the crucial EU Summit in
Amsterdam, CEO published the 72-page report *Europe, Inc.: Dangerous
Liaisons Between EU Institutions and Industry*. The report examined the
major corporate actors in Europe and provided information about their
overall strategies and successes, as well as their specific activities around
the negotiations in the treaty revision process.

This book is an updated and significantly expanded version of that
1997 report. While still focusing on corporate influence on EU policies,
it also deals with increasing corporate power within other international
institutions, such as the OECD, the World Trade Organization and the
United Nations. In the past decades, elite networks of individuals from
national governments, international institutions and the corporate
sector have crafted and carried out policies facilitating economic globalisation. This has come to pass largely unnoticed and without much
public discourse, and has further strengthened the position of transnational corporations. In this book, we describe major fora for elite
consensus building and the institutional arrangements created to
facilitate and accelerate the process of economic globalisation.

The first section of the book provides an introduction to the major
corporate lobby groups in the EU, and describes how they have
contributed to the current neoliberal character of EU legislation and
policies. The exact extent to which corporate lobby organisations shape
specific political decisions is difficult to assess. EU decision-making

procedures are complex, involving numerous national and European actors. The institutions of the EU itself – the Council, Commission and Parliament – are obviously far from monolithic. Excessive corporate power is certainly not just a Brussels phenomenon: corporations and their coalitions lobby at every level of the complex EU system. One of the main lobbying targets are the member state governments. These national governments increasingly tend to equate corporate interests with those of society at large. This first section also includes case studies on corporate influence upon transport and biotechnology policies.

The second section describes the EU's role in promoting economic globalisation, a model of global restructuring of economies and societies around corporate interests. We examine the liaisons between corporate lobby groups and the most powerful governments and blocs, such as the EU, and their combined influence over key economic globalisation institutions and projects like the World Trade Organization, and the Transatlantic Economic Partnership. Furthermore, we look at how progressive movements, questioning economic globalisation and the whittling away of democracy and demanding equitable and sustainable international economic relations, are gaining ground.

In the third section, we introduce the most important corporate groupings operating on the global level. The International Chamber of Commerce's bold attempts to gain control over UN institutions is one example. The book ends with a number of recommendations for how corporate political and economic power can be rolled back in order to create space for progressive policies and for the democratisation of our societies.

A starting point for the authors is that the current model of economic globalisation does not work in the interest of the majority of Europeans, let alone for those in the increasingly marginalised South. Further deregulation of the global market will unleash ever fiercer competition and downward pressure on wages and social and environmental protection. In the process, the ability of local, national and supranational governments to intervene and regulate the workings of the market in the public interest is undermined. Women in particular pay a high toll for the neoliberal restructuring of societies, suffering specifically from the resulting higher unemployment rates, lower quality jobs and reduced salaries. The dismantling of the welfare state also has a greater impact on women, as they predominantly bear the burden of providing what were previously governmental functions within their families.

According to 'The Environmental Impacts of Economic Globalisation', a forthcoming study conducted by the International Forum on Globalization in San Francisco, economic globalisation poses a fundamental threat to ecosystems at the local, regional and global level through numerous combined impacts. To feed highly unsustainable production and consumption patterns, initially in the rich industrialised countries but now becoming rapidly globalised, corporations continue to exploit valuable and irreplaceable natural resources in the remaining pristine corners of the world. Intensive and destructive agricultural and fishery practices are replicated worldwide, causing huge environmental damage and threatening local food security. Sky-rocketing volumes of transport, fuelled by ever-increasing distances between producers and consumers, are a major contributor to health-threatening pollution and dangerous climate change.

Certain beneficiaries of this truly irresponsible economic experiment are the transnational corporations that hold European and global economies in an ever-tightening grip. The increased economic dominance of large corporations is a matter of great concern. Flexible and footloose, TNCs profit from economies of scale: they centralise and automate production, and relocate to regions with lower wages and more relaxed regulations. They are champions of increasing production while destroying jobs. In a globalised economy, governments have little choice but to attract investments. This entails adapting regulations and freeing up economic resources to serve the needs of corporations at the expense of people and the environment. Corporate lobby groups are working expeditiously in order to instruct politicians how to best go about this.

Although corporate influence is definitely not the result of secretive conspiracies, it is by nature elusive and difficult to trace. Therefore, this book shows only the tip of the iceberg. We hope that our work will inspire journalists to dive into these matters; they have gone unnoticed by the media for far too long. We also hope to spark a reaction from those politicians who are seriously committed to democratic processes. And most importantly, we hope that it catalyses action by groups working for social and environmental justice. This action should not only be directed at the undemocratic structures that have permitted and stimulated the prominent role of corporate lobbies, but should also target the negative impacts of corporate power.

We would like to thank Christian Wolter, Aart van de Hoek, Johan Frijns, Stephanie Howard (and the rest of the A SEED Europe Office), and Iza Kruzewska for reading our manuscript as well as other essential support. Our thanks also go to George Monbiot who wrote the preface for this book, and to Susan George, Joshua Karliner, Ramón Fernández Durán, Thomas Wallgren, Martin Khor, Iza Kruzewska, Colin Hines and Ralitsa Panayotova (CEO's advisory board) for their continued input and support during the writing. Centro Nuovo Modelo di Sviluppo, Coordi-nation against Bayer-Dangers, Corporate Watch, the Critical

Shareholders Association, Ethical Consumer, IBFAN, Oilwatch Europe,
Norwatch and others have been essential resources for information on
the social and environmental records of corporations active within the
ERT. All of those who have supported our work over the past years are
now too numerous to list, but we are deeply grateful. Finally, thanks to
the people at Pluto Press for their interest, encouragement and patience.

June 1999

Corporate Europe Observatory
Paulus Potterstraat 20
1071 DA Amsterdam
The Netherlands
Tel/fax: +31-20-6127023
E-mail: ceo@xs4all.nl
http://www.xs4all.nl/~ceo/

Part I

Corporate Europe

Welcome to Corporate Europe

Transnational corporations (TNCs), working both individually and within various lobby groups, have become significant political actors in European Union decision making. Over the past 15 years, European unification has entered the fast lane with the completion of the Single Market, the adoption of a single currency and the overall empowerment of the EU institutions. This process has been expedited by the European Roundtable of Industrialists and other lobby groups representing the largest transnational corporations in Europe. Section I of this book provides an overview of some of the most influential corporate players in Brussels and presents case studies of EU policies which have been (mis)shaped by corporate lobbying.

Today's Brussels teems with lobbyists. Over ten thousand professional lobbyists roam the halls of the Commission, Council and Parliament buildings, the vast majority of them from PR firms, industry lobby groups and individual companies.[1] Following the example of Washington DC, the birthplace of intensive corporate lobbying, Brussels has become home to rising numbers of corporate government affairs offices, lobby groups, think-tanks, political consultancies and PR agencies.[2]

The burgeoning lobbying industry was established in the late 1980s and early 1990s, a period during which the European Commission was busy drafting some 300 single market directives which would form the skeleton of a single European market. Corporations jumped at the chance to shape this massive harmonisation exercise to their interests, and began to focus more of their energies on Brussels.[3] Currently, more than two hundred large corporations have European government affairs offices in Brussels, among them many US and Japanese corporations.[4] They are reinforced by no less than five hundred corporate lobby groups, varying from large and powerful groups like the European chemical industry federation CEFIC and the European Roundtable of Industrialists to more specialised groupings like the European Candle Manufacturers.[5] This book will introduce a number of the most influential European corporate groups, but due to the sheer magnitude of the phenomenon only the tip of the lobbying iceberg can be shown.

Relations between the European Commission and large corporations have changed dramatically over the last 25 years. In 1973, reacting to widespread concerns about corporate power, then Industry Commissioner Altiero Spinelli launched a proposal 'to address the economic and social problems raised by the activities of the multinationals'.[6] The European Community's more critical approach towards TNCs throughout the 1970s has, however, gradually been transformed into the current virtual symbiosis between the EU's key political and economic actors.

The Commission began to engage industry in strategic alliances in the 1980s, and has since actively encouraged the involvement of large corporations and pan-European industry associations in the Brussels political apparatus. These partnerships add weight to EU initiatives, and they tend to strengthen the Commission's position *vis-à-vis* member state governments; moreover, such corporate-political alliances are already well-established at the national level in most countries. The number and intensity of connections with business varies within different Commission directorates, but the phenomenon appears only to be increasing. Corporations and their lobby groups also often provide useful information for the understaffed and disconnected Commission bureaucracy. In fact, it can be said that corporate lobby groups act as a replacement for the citizen-based constituency which the Commission lacks.

The EU political system is a wonderful place for corporate lobby groups to do business: decisions with far-reaching effects are made behind closed doors and in secretive committees, invisible to and far removed from those affected by the resulting deals. Despite slight improvements in the treaties of Maastricht and Amsterdam, the European Commission and the Council of Ministers remain largely unaccountable to voters, and control by both European and national parliaments is insufficient.

In early 1999, a parliamentary committee investigating allegations of fraud in the European Commission arrived at the harsh verdict that it was difficult to find a responsible civil servant within that institution. In fact, the European Council is even more opaque than the Commission. It tends to shroud itself in secrecy, often even refusing to release agendas of its meetings to the public. Important decisions to be taken by Ministers are pre-cooked by non-transparent committees of national diplomats operating deep inside the Brussels labyrinth.

While social movements have stepped up their presence in Brussels in recent years, the playing field remains fundamentally unbalanced. The complexity of the EU system means that substantial resources and expertise are needed to keep abreast of political developments. Whereas companies can pay thousands of lobbyists to represent their interests in

Brussels, European coalitions of citizens' organisations and trade unions are relatively poor, understaffed and lacking in resources.

No less critical is the enormous gap in access to decision makers. The centralisation of power in Brussels, which has developed at the expense of democracy on the national level, has provided large corporations with an enormous advantage in the European political arena. Organisations like the European Roundtable of Industrialists (ERT) are clearly in an extremely privileged situation, as the prestigious leaders of their powerful member corporations are granted easy access to Commissioners and high-level government officials. The absence of public opinion or discussion on the European level makes it easy for shady corporate front groups and think-tanks to slide into the gap and to orchestrate virtual, decidedly non-democratic debates.

The social movements that often constitute a real countervailing force to corporate pressure groups on the local and national levels are comparatively weak at the European level. As a result, they have lost numerous battles. The Single Market (SM) and Economic and Monetary Union (EMU) are examples of projects in which social, environmental and democratic concerns have largely been bypassed. Trade unionists and the social and environmental movements are now racing to catch up, but they are hindered by their lack of European constituencies.

Whereas the powers of the European Parliament (EP) were expanded in both the Maastricht and Amsterdam treaties, the body is still comparatively weaker than national parliaments in EU member states. None the less, the EP's new competences have attracted throngs of corporate lobbyists. UK Member of European Parliament (MEP) Glyn Ford explains, '80 per cent of the European Parliament's amendments are accepted in whole or in part by the Commission and the Council of Ministers.'[7] Today, the Parliament is lobbied by an estimated 3,000 people, most of them directly employed by industry: this averages out to five lobbyists for each MEP. Although to the untrained eye this lobbying may appear overly focused on minuscule details, Ford explains that for corporations, 'the dots, the commas, the decimal points are worth millions of pounds'. This section will provide examples of Parliament-directed corporate lobbying that 'successfully' targeted issues with major ethical and environmental implications, such as the EU's *Life Patents Directive* (see Chapter 9).

Special attention will be given to four of the main corporate groupings on the EU political scene. Of these, the European Roundtable of Industrialists (ERT, see Chapter 3) is without doubt the most influential, bringing together some 45 captains of industry from Europe's largest TNCs. Since the early 1980s, the ERT has performed an agenda-setting role at the EU level, pushing for deregulation, liberalisation and other measures to increase the international competitiveness of European industry. Through its privileged access to both governments and the

European Commission, the Roundtable has managed to catapult several of its projects onto the EU's agenda. ERT members are frequently represented in high-level Commission working groups, such as the Competitiveness Advisory Group (CAG, see Chapter 3). These close contacts are consolidated through an active 'revolving door' phenomenon, with Commissioners regularly leaving their positions to join the private sector and vice versa. For example, prominent business elite like Etienne Davignon (Société Générale) and Peter Sutherland (British Petroleum and Goldman Sachs) are former Commissioners, and Ricardo Perissich (Pirelli) was formerly Director-General of Industry.[8]

The corporate elite united in the ERT have formed a number of other groupings in order to create optimal political pressure for their shared agenda. The European Centre for Infrastructure Studies (ECIS, see Chapter 8) and the Association for the Monetary Union in Europe (AMUE, see Chapter 6) provide prime examples of this tactic. Furthermore, the ERT's message is reinforced by a chorus of other corporate lobby groups in Brussels, led by the European employers' organisation UNICE (see Chapter 4) and the EU Committee of the American Chamber of Commerce (AmCham, see Chapter 5). Although less proactive than the ERT, UNICE and AmCham have also succeeded in sculpting the emerging body of European law by closely monitoring and advocating for or against EU policies relevant to business.

Industry lobby groups leapt to the occasion to provide direction to the revision of the Maastricht Treaty in 1996 and 1997. Their major demands – including the strengthening of the Commission's powers, acceleration of the European Monetary Union and expansion of the EU towards Central and Eastern Europe – were largely fulfilled. Furthermore, the corporate lobby succeeded in eliminating any serious threats to the EU's comprehensive agenda for competitiveness, for instance with their siege upon a far-ranging chapter on employment in the new Amsterdam Treaty.

Business lobby groups have also played a major role in charting the direction of EU transport policy, which has the overriding goal of facilitating the growth in commercial transport resulting from the EU's free trade policies. The centrepiece of the EU's transport programme is an ambitious scheme for new trans-European transport infrastructure networks (TENs, see Chapter 8) criss-crossing the EU and extending to Central and Eastern Europe.

European Union policies on genetic engineering provide yet another example of how ecological, social and ethical concerns are sacrificed in pursuit of free trade and international competitiveness. 'Life science' corporations, efficiently organised in groupings like EuropaBio (see Chapter 9), have worked closely with the European Commission in promoting biotechnology in Europe despite broad public opposition. After a £15 million lobbying campaign in 1997 and 1998, the European Parliament finally succumbed to the biotech industry's demands and allowed the patenting of life forms.

How Low Can You Go?

'This is really the moment of truth. Globalisation has brought one shock after another. Yet Germany has refused to adapt. A new generation of business leaders in Germany is demanding nothing short of a revolution, and the government will have to respond or companies will flee and the economy will gradually sink.'
Thomas Mayer, managing director of the Frankfurt office of Goldman Sachs, commenting on industry's revolt against the German government's plans for tax reform.[9]

Demands by TNCs and their lobby groups that international competitiveness be established as the main priority for decision makers is a recurring theme in this book. In many cases, these demands are backed by threats of relocation to more 'business-friendly' regions. Although TNCs are not completely footloose or 'stateless', decades of trade and investment liberalisation have increased their mobility and they have been able to employ the threat to relocate with devastating success. Thus, in the manic logic of the deregulated global marketplace that holds European decision makers in a firm grip, maintaining international competitiveness has become a matter of political survival.

The pursuit of competitiveness has driven EU countries into a downward spiral of tax competition. To attract investments or to keep disgruntled industries from fleeing, governments are reducing corporate taxes or handing out tempting subsidies in the forms of free infrastructure and tax holidays. While taxes on labour have gradually increased in most EU member states over the past two decades, corporate taxes continue to decrease. This shift of the tax burden to labour has had extremely negative impacts on employment; companies relocating to more accommodating climates leave unemployed people in their wake and usually create insecure, lower-paid jobs in their new locales.

In 1998 and 1999, Ericsson and many other large corporations announced their intentions to shut down their Swedish headquarters if corporate and other taxes were not lowered. The centre-left government – elected for its promises to preserve the welfare state – is expected to bow to the pressure and introduce tax cuts over the coming years.[10] In the first months of 1999, German businesses launched a full-scale offensive against the red-green government's plans for a new round of social and ecological tax reform.[11] Some twenty corporate heavyweights took the lead, threatening a mass exodus if the German government withdrew its generous tax reliefs and subsidies. Germany has lost close to a million jobs since 1995, as Siemens, DaimlerChrysler, Hoechst, Volkswagen and other large corporations have transferred operations to countries with lower wages and tax rates.[12] In March 1999, Finance Minister Oskar Lafontaine, who had been the main architect of progressive tax reform as well as the target of the corporate campaign, announced his resignation.[13] Commenting upon these events, the leading German weekly *Die Zeit* ran the headline question: 'Who Rules the Republic?'[14] Lafontaine was replaced by the more right-wing Hans Eichel, who recruited the head of Bayer's tax department to become his secretary of state, responsible for the German tax reform. Manfred Schneider, Bayer's CEO, commented: 'We sent our best man and briefed him, so all will be okay.'[15]

Ireland, with its low industrial tax rates, is the European Union's current corporate darling. With a corporate tax rate as low as 10 per cent for the manufacturing and services industries, Ireland has successfully lured investors away from more expensive EU member states. Despite pressure from its EU partners and the European Commission, the Irish government refuses to raise its corporate taxes, which have contributed to growth rates of up to 7 per cent per year.[16]

The ability of large corporations to vote with their feet has been further increased through Economic and Monetary Union. Companies can now shift their operations or headquarters to other euro-zone countries with lower wages and more business-friendly government regulations without incurring exchange risks. In a world of free capital flows, business carries a very large stick.

The Restructuring of Corporate Europe

With European and global markets under the control of an increasingly small number of mega-corporations, the concentration of economic and political power has reached a level at which it seriously endangers democracy. Markets in virtually every sector of the new EU economy are controlled by the five largest corporations in that sector. Despite the Commission's self-styled image as trust buster, since the 1980s it has in fact actively promoted a set of policies encouraging corporate mergers and the squeezing out of smaller, local companies. The negative 'side-effects' of this process, including huge losses in local economic activity and increased unemployment in many regions of Europe, are either ignored or presented as inevitable consequences of 'progress'.

Free trade policies in Europe have contributed to the deepening divide between rich and poor regions. Less-favoured regions have lost out to a limited number of booming, highly-industrialised economic centres from which large corporations supply the entire European market. A significant number of the EU's more than 20 million unemployed are situated in these numerous 'peripheral' regions, which are trapped in a state of perpetual economic crisis. Rigid EU regional disciplines (for example, banning pro-local subsidies, public investment and procurement policies) leave these weaker regions with few options for economic development besides increasing their attractiveness to international investors. The EU funnels large sums of money into high-speed transport infrastructure, which often worsens the economic position of 'less favoured' or peripheral regions by encouraging the centralisation of production.

In the 1980s, the European Commission's industrial policy had the explicit goal of turning large corporations into 'European champions' that could easily compete with US and Japanese competitors. To achieve this, research and development subsidies and other forms of corporate welfare were generously distributed. In addition, the new 'free' trade rules of the Single Market discourage policies protecting local economies, thus favouring TNCs over companies producing for local markets. On top of this, the standard-setting process for products to be marketed in the EU's free trade area was completely dominated by large TNCs during the late 1980s and early 1990s.[17] Assisted by a sharp increase in mergers, the Euro-champions nourished by the EU have now become global corporate giants.

Mergermania

Since the late 1980s, EU liberalisation, deregulation and privatisation policies have facilitated the waves of mergers and acquisitions which have resulted in corporate concentration. Today, as the 1990s draw to a close, European corporations are racing ever more frantically to either buy up or merge with competitors in order to achieve further economies of scale. The 1997 record of US$384 billion spent in European mergers – an increase of almost 50 per cent in one year – was topped by even higher levels and an unprecedented number of crossborder mergers in 1998.[18] These mergers are instigated by Single Market competition, which grows increasingly fiercer as the remaining barriers to trade are dismantled one by one. The single currency has further accelerated the concentration of economic power in a limited number of mega-corporations (see Chapter 6). The latest trend is a steep increase in transatlantic mergers and acquisitions between EU- and US-based corporations, reaching a record of US$256.5 billion in 1998 – almost four times the rate in 1995.[19]

Alongside the detrimental social, economic and ecological aspects of this ongoing corporate monopolisation and concentration, the process threatens to further undermine democracy in Europe. The mega-mergers – which create European and global corporate Goliaths overnight –

further increase the disproportionate bargaining powers held by TNCs, and thereby corporate dominance in political decision making. The following chapters will expand upon how 'European' TNCs have succeeded in occupying the political as well as the economic realms in order to gain optimal influence and profits.

Laying the Foundations: European PR Agencies and Think-Tanks

The novelty of the political construct of 'Europe' has led to the recent upsurge in Brussels of two important US exports: public relations/public affairs agencies and consultancies,[1] and corporate think-tanks. The Brussels public relations (PR) apparatus has emerged over the past decade, following closely on the heels of the European corporate lobby groups which sprouted up in Europe's 'capital' city. PR agencies have sniffed out a lucrative business lurking within the complex Brussels bureaucracy, and they provide lobbying, public relations, information gathering, media and consultancy services to large corporations and their lobby groups. Beyond that, the PR industry is skilled in the transformation, manipulation and even creation of information and images to benefit its corporate clients. Think-tanks funded by large corporations also play an important agenda-setting role by promoting various aspects of European unification to policy makers, the media and the public.

Thriving in Brussels

Spawned in the United States, the PR sector has quickly managed to create a comfortable niche for itself in Brussels' unique lobbying climate. The lack of transparency connected with lobbying in the EU, as well as complicated and often undemocratic decision-making systems in Brussels, provide fertile ground not just for corporate lobbyists but also for their faithful servants in the PR industry. 'Lobbying consultancies', as Brussels PR companies often refer to themselves, do a brisk and booming business assisting their clients in making important connections, navigating the Brussels apparatus, and understanding the important cultural subtleties of the European Union. The laxity of rules and regulations for Brussels lobbyists encourages practices which would be considered underhanded and unacceptable in the US or in other European capitals. For example, PR agencies are not required to record the identity of their clients when on official business in the Commission or Parliament, and thus can wear a different corporate hat each day if they so choose. 'In Brussels, a public affairs consultancy can very easily say we lobby,' according to Laurentien Brinkhorst, Deputy Managing Director of public affairs agency Edelman Europe. 'There's no dirty feeling about it.'[2]

The astronomical fees charged by PR agencies – senior staff members charge some £500 per hour for their expertise[3] – means that their services are affordable nearly exclusively by large companies. Social and environmental actors, which generally represent public rather than private interests, cannot hope to match the financial and organisational power flaunted by industry lobbies and PR agencies in political hotspots like Brussels and Washington, DC.

The Mechanics of PR

Lobbying assistance is just one of the services that the public relations industry offers to its corporate clients. Leading US PR critics Stauber and Rampton describe the industry as deliberately designed to 'alter perception, reshape reality and manufacture consent'.[4] PR agencies are often called in to help with the creation and transformation of corporate images and consumer loyalty. When public concern about a specific company or product is awakened, the PR industry may perform 'crisis management' to quell the criticism and boost the company's profile. Media services and Internet advice are also offered by most major PR companies.

In the United States, the PR industry has been well established for several decades. In the 1970s, when the 'green' movement succeeded in enacting a new wave of environmental legislation, disgruntled companies began to work in coalitions in order to quash these unwelcome threats to their economic interests. Bodies such the US Business Roundtable were created, and existing groups like the US Chamber of Commerce invigorated.[5] These coalitions joined forces with the PR industry to weaken the new regulations in what has proven to be an ongoing and highly successful display of teamwork.

In the US and elsewhere, the PR industry has scored multiple successes over the years – most recently by 'greenwashing' corporate images to make them appear more environmentally-friendly and socially conscious. PR companies have also mastered the art of slinging mud at the critics of corporations and economic liberalisation. Some of the dirtier tactics used include 'anti-publicity' campaigns to sabotage environmental, progressive, health-related or anti-corporate initiatives and the deliberate promotion of scientific misinformation. US-based PR companies wage phoney, high-tech 'grassroots' citizens' campaigns for their corporate clients which 'lobby' on legislation of interest to industry. To facilitate these 'astroturf' campaigns, the PR industry has helped to create powerful, well-funded corporate front groups on issues ranging from food and chemicals to climate change and toxic waste disposal. For example, the American Council on Science and Health is largely funded by the chemical industry, and PR giant Burson-Marsteller created the National Smokers Alliance on behalf of the Philip Morris tobacco company. The anti-environmental Global Climate Information Project, set up by PR firm Shandwick at the request of major oil and mining companies, was responsible for a multi-billion dollar advertising campaign to spread disinformation about climate change in 1997.

Europe Here We Come!

Although many of these strategies are not yet common in Europe, they will without doubt increasingly make their way across the ocean as the PR industry continues to deepen its roots in Brussels. German energy companies, for example, with the help of PR agencies, have already set up phoney local activist groups that 'campaign' against the construction of windmills.[6] And the European waste industry has created a fake lobby group called 'Waste to Energy' which unsuccessfully 'fought like lions' to convince the European Commission to redefine waste as sustainable energy.[7]

Today, there are several hundred public relations agencies in the European 'capital', and PR staff levels have doubled in the past five years.[8] All of the major players have emigrated from North America and other European capitals – including Burson-Marsteller, Shandwick, Hill & Knowlton, and Edelman – and the number of smaller rivals is increasing. Corporations and PR firms have established a cosy club in the small world of Brussels, where for example Unilever shares an office building with Burson-Marsteller and Hill & Knowlton.

Brussels, however, 'still has an element of mystery', according to one public affairs specialist,[9] and this has allowed the PR industry to capitalise on the provision of lobbying, information and media services. How does a public relations agency help its clients to navigate the Brussels bureaucracy? Professor Alan Watson, European Chairman of PR consultancy Burson-Marsteller and a former Commission employee, provides some insight about where a company with a cause should begin:

First of all they've got to start by knowing how the system works. That probably means they will come to a company like Burson-Marsteller which can it explain to them. It's no good for them just to go and talk to their local MP ... He or she will only have a *very* limited perspective and virtually no influence on what happens in that area ... We will certainly suggest for instance [that] there is the chairman of this particular committee in Strasbourg, in the parliament, you must go and talk to that person. We can advise them on how they should put their argument on paper. We can advise them on which people in the committee would be interested and they should go and talk to. So in a way you build a map for them, a sort of road map of where they need to go, who they need to talk to and what they need to know ... We don't do the lobbying ... What we do is to give the company the information so that they can actually go and make the case themselves.[10]

PR agencies invest enormous time and resources in tracking all of the legislation which shuttles between the Commission, the Parliament, the Council and the various committees – a task that even the largest of companies find daunting. Michael Berendt, of Burson-Marsteller, explains: 'Brussels after all is very remote for many people and it is also remote for many companies. Companies find it quite difficult to know what's going on, what is going to affect them, what they should do to influence it and how they should respond themselves. And that's where we come in.'[11] Like the more influential industry lobby groups, PR companies are well aware that the Commission is where the most important action unfolds. 'What we try to do in our business is to know as early as possible what the Commission is thinking of doing, even before something has been finalised as a proposal,' continues Berendt. 'You have to know where things are in the system, who is responsible at different stages in the system and then ... find the entry point, the pressure points and the places where you can influence policy.'[12] Personal contact is key: 'Of course we get to know people. We know people personally. We talk with them and find what information we can.'[13]

Burson-Marsteller, the world's largest PR agency with 60 offices in 32 countries, claims to specialise in 'perception management'.[14] Some of its more notable past successes have included 'crisis management' for Union Carbide following the Bhopal disaster in India and for Exxon after the Exxon Valdez oil spill, and it has assisted in upgrading the images of dictatorial governments in Indonesia, Argentina and South Korea. The agency has also been involved in what has been one of the most expensive corporate lobby efforts in Europe to date: a massive and successful disinformation campaign to convince policy makers to legislate in favour of biotechnology and life patenting. In 1998, Burson-Marsteller came up with a PR strategy for the industry lobby group EuropaBio which was aimed at soothing public fears about the new biotechnologies and at manipulating political sympathies in Brussels. Its tactics provide a revealing insight into the workings of a true propaganda machine (see Chapter 9).

Edelman is another booming public affairs agency with offices in Brussels. Established in 1995, the company's clients are US and increasingly European transnational corporations, and its main activity in Brussels is 'mostly high-level lobbying'.[15] Laurentien Brinkhorst, Edelman's deputy managing director in Brussels,[16] stresses how complex lobbying has become in the EU:

> It used to be that if you knew the commissioner or you knew the Director General that was enough. Now it's a lot more complex ... There are a lot more players involved. You have a multi-layered approach, you've got interest groups, such as industry associations ... you've got NGOs, who play a very important role, you have companies, you've got trade unions ... And the EU is now competent in many more areas than it used to be ... The media plays an incredibly important role. Twenty years ago, there was no real need for media relations.[17]

Edelman's specialities include complicated issues 'where companies are still completely in the dark'.[18] The agency carefully tracks the activities of the World Trade Organization (WTO) and, most extraordinarily, claims to have access to the secretive Article 133 committee (formerly known as Article 113) in which EU member states formulate trade policies.[19] Edelman represented Fuji when the United States, spurred on by Kodak, took Japan before the WTO alleging that the Japanese film company unfairly dominated its home market. Although Edelman, Fuji and Japan ultimately won the case, the PR company did not lose the opportunity to ingratiate itself to the EU, which sided with the US ('partly for broader political reasons'[20]) by keeping the Commission up to date. 'We did inform the Commission, even though they were on the other side, on a regular basis,' said Edelman's Brinkhorst. 'They very much appreciated that. We often had the information much before they did.'[21] Brinkhorst is firmly convinced of the power of sharing information: 'If you do a good job you can actually help formulate policy. I think that many members of the European Parliament would not be able to do their job so well if they hadn't had the information that they get from lobbyists.'[22]

Another area in which Edelman claims to excel is in what they term 'corporate citizenship', or helping 'multinationals understand NGOs and trade unions better'.[23] This involves polishing the tarnished images of certain companies: 'We have worked, and we still work with a number of US multinationals which have been taken as an example of bad corporate citizenship, for example on the issues of labour rights and factory conditions and environmental behaviour.'[24] Edelman, which claims to take both the concerns and the influence of NGOs and trade unions very seriously, has carved out a niche for itself in the facilitation of 'dialogues' between the corporate and non-governmental sectors.

Pressure Politics

Other PR firms, however, take a different approach in their dealings with social and environmental actors. In June 1998, for example, the Brussels-based public PR group Entente International Communication co-organised a conference with the *European Voice* newspaper with the sinister-sounding title 'Pressure Politics: Industry's Response to the Pressure Group Challenge'. According to the invitation, 'Pressure groups are exploiting the perceived democratic deficit in European society, increasingly to mobilise Europe's citizens on a range of consumer and environmental issues, often with damaging commercial implications for companies.'[25] Participants and speakers were from well-known companies (including Exxon, Ford Europe, Hoechst, McDonald's, Mitsubishi, Monsanto, Nestlé, Petrofina, Philips, Price Waterhouse, Rio Tinto, Shell and SmithKline Beecham), PR agencies (including Edelman, Shandwick, the Communications Group and Master Media) and from the European Commission and Parliament.

The cynical observer might draw the conclusion that the 'Pressure Politics' conference was little more than an attempt by Entente, one of the leading public affairs agencies in Brussels, to drum up some work by exploiting a new market opportunity. In fact, according to Maria Laplev, director of consultancy firm GPC Market Access Europe, 'The increasing supply of political advice and lobbying has caused stronger competition within the Brussels PR industry. Consultancies are therefore doing more aggressive outreach to get contracts to lobby for corporations.'[26]

There is no doubt that in recent years clashes between corporations and activist groups have increased in frequency and intensity. Shell, for example, has been hard hit by the wave of negative publicity prompted by the Brent Spar episode and its role in Nigeria's Ogoniland, and the reputation of McDonald's was seriously tarnished during the McLibel trial in the UK.[27] As a result, many companies have been prompted to adopt the tactic of 'dialogue' with NGOs and civil society, and have sought the guidance of PR agencies in doing so.

With this conference, however, Entente was clearly less interested in negotiation and joint solution finding than in sowing seeds of concern among industry representatives. The agency's fearmongering was apparent in the unsettling questions put on the agenda by Entente; for example, whether the growing number of activists 'clamouring and sometimes physically demonstrating for attention' would 'eventually lead to bedlam, chaos, even anarchy'.[28] The company's overwhelming message to corporate participants that the lack of a strategy to deal with pressure groups is a '"bunker-like" approach, and failure to use external and experienced help is surprising – and potentially dangerous'[29] was clearly profit motivated. But even more disturbingly, such PR propaganda fuels misperceptions about the goals and tactics of activist groups.

Corporate Think-Tanks

'We are action-oriented and we believe that business must be more involved in public policy.'
Stanley Crossick, Chairman, European Policy Centre.[30]

Right-wing think-tanks funded by industry have been a common phenomenon in North America since the 1970s. Institutes like the Heritage Foundation and the American Enterprise Institute, though ostensibly of a more neutral nature than conventional corporate lobby groups, have played a major role in shaping the public debate and government policies in the interests of their corporate sponsors. Think-tanks focused on European unification, some of which are no more than corporate front groups, have also found friendly turf in Brussels: again, the centralisation of political power in the still far-from-democratic European Union and the lack of a truly European public debate provide ideal working conditions. To a large degree, their influence and authority is derived from the ample coverage they receive in the European media. The Centre for European Policy Studies and the European Policy Centre are two examples of European think-tanks with different tactics but similar goals.

The Centre for European Policy Studies (CEPS), founded in 1982, is one of the most effective and most senior think-tanks in Brussels. It has a network of chapters in a number of European countries, 40 employees working from its Brussels headquarters, and an annual turnover of approximately 4 million euro.[31] Annual membership fees start at 24,000 euro for ordinary corporate membership, and are as high as 60,000 euro for exclusive 'Inner Circle' members.[32]

CEPS organises elite gatherings of CEOs, top EU decision makers and conservative academics, and produces hard-hitting reports on various timely EU topics. On its web site, the group proclaims that its 'policy papers and working parties on EMU, CAP [Common Agricultural Policy] reform, fiscal policy, institutional reform and enlargement have contributed ideas that have been adopted by the policy makers in the Commission, the Council and the European Parliament and in the governments of the member states'.[33] Connections are key, as Director Peter Ludlow explains: 'CEPS is seen as an insiders' institute and this is crucial. We set out to establish that we are here to talk at the highest level.'[34]

A relative newcomer to Brussels is the European Policy Centre, established in January 1997 by the trio of Stanley Crossick, godfather of Brussels lobbying;[35] Max Kohnstamm, former vice-president of the Jean Monnet Action Committee; and John Palmer, former European editor of the *Guardian*. The EPC defines its mission as 'contributing to the con-struction of Europe'.[36] Its industry bias is reflected in the composition of its advisory board, which includes corporate directors from Philips and

Mars, influential industrialists such as Peter Sutherland (former European commissioner and GATT director and current chairman of British Petroleum and Goldman Sachs International Associate); the former and current European Roundtable of Industrialists (ERT) Secretary-Generals Keith Richardson[37] and Wim Philippa; UNICE Secretary-General Dirk Hudig, a European Central Bank executive board member; six European parliamentarians, five former directors-general and a vice-president of the European Commission, and journalists from newspapers such as *Le Monde* and the *Financial Times*. The EPC enjoys significant financial support from its corporate members, which include ERT members BAT, BP, British Telecom and Solvay as well as Dow, Du Pont, Philip Morris and SmithKline Beecham. In exchange, these corporate donors are provided services such as regular contact with decision makers.

Industrialists attend EPC conferences to discuss themes of common interest, which currently include the Economic and Monetary Union (EMU), EU enlargement and European taxation policies. The EPC publishes reports and briefings on these and other relevant issues, including the June 1998 EU Cardiff Summit which pleased the EPC with its commitments to complete the Single Market and to promote 'a range of business friendly policies'.[38] Another EPC scheme is the creation of a European industry strategy for the WTO negotiations: in other words, how to most efficiently push for further trade and investment liberalisation.[39] Studies are also carried out on behalf of and with the financial support of the European Commission.

The Tip of the Iceberg

The think-tanks and PR agencies described in this chapter give a flavour of the immense support network for the implementation of corporate dreams that has been created and continues to grow in Brussels. For the most part, the unearthing and laying bare of this sturdy foundation, which assists TNCs and their lobby groups in the implementation of competitive, neoliberal policies, is *terra nova* for NGOs and social movements. Much work needs to be done in identifying the main players and exposing their operations to the mass public. Without public awareness about the biased roles played by major PR agencies and conservative think-tanks in the European Union, hopes for genuine democracy, transparency, and access in Brussels decision making are illusory.

3

Writing the Script: The European Roundtable of Industrialists

> Access means being able to phone Helmut Kohl and recommend that he read a report. Access also means John Major phoning to thank the ERT for its viewpoints, or having lunch with the Swedish Prime Minister just prior to the Swedish decision to apply for EC membership.
> *Keith Richardson, former ERT Secretary-General*[1]

Although largely unknown to the general public, the European Roundtable of Industrialists (ERT) has been one of the main political forces on the European scene for well over a decade. Its unhampered access to top politicians at both the European and national levels is key to the Roundtable's amazing success in helping to set the EU's political agenda. The results of the ERT's influence are unmistakable: a gradual shift towards European policies which increasingly favour large corporations and economic globalisation.

This shift was most pronounced in the late 1980s and early 1990s, when the ERT's wishes for a Single Market and Trans-European Networks (TENs) of transport infrastructure were fulfilled. Roundtable fingerprints are also clearly visible on the 1991 Maastricht Treaty, which laid the groundwork for European Monetary Union. The group has proven remarkably flexible in adapting to new circumstances, birthing offspring such as ECIS (the European Centre for Infrastructure Studies, see Chapter 8) and AMUE (the Association for the Monetary Union of Europe, see Chapter 6) to better channel particular messages.

In recent years, the ERT has jumped on the EU's enlargement bandwagon, eagerly prescribing structural adjustment for potential member countries from Central and Eastern Europe. In 1995, its informal access to the EU's decision-making structures was institutionalised through the creation of the Competitiveness Advisory Group (CAG), which effectively duplicates the ERT's voice. And today, the ERT continues its competitiveness crusade with the triumphant promotion of ideas like 'benchmarking' and 'innovation' as fundamental principles in EU policy making. Behind these technical-sounding concepts lies the ERT's chilling strategy to subvert all levels of society to market forces and the increasing pressures of global economic competition.

The ERT Unveiled

The ERT, founded in 1983, consists of some 45 'captains of industry' from European multinational corporations with a 'significant manufacturing and technological presence worldwide'.[2] Membership is personal rather than corporate, and strictly by invitation only. Companies currently represented in the ERT include Investor AB, Bayer, British Petroleum, DaimlerChrysler, Ericsson, Fiat, Nestlé, Nokia, Petrofina, Philips, Renault, Shell, Siemens, Solvay, Total and Unilever (see Appendix 3 for a full listing).

More than just another industry pressure group trying to benefit from European integration, the ERT was formed with the express intention of reviving the unification process and shaping it to the preferences of European corporations. It pushes relentlessly to 'change the way that Europe is managed', claiming that 'industry is entitled to a system that delivers results: an EU which functions like an integrated economic system with a single centre of overall decision making.'[3] Over the past 15 years, the ERT has consistently supported the strengthening of the European Union through the removal of national veto powers and other causes of 'fragmentation'. 'The problem is that in the individual countries the politicians have to gather votes,' explains ERT Assistant Secretary-General Caroline Walcot. 'But in the EU they can see the whole picture.'[4]

Unlike most other corporate lobby groups in Brussels, the ERT has never bothered to lobby on detailed legislation. Instead, it concentrates on painting the big picture, and filling the EU's agenda with sizeable new projects. According to former ERT Secretary-General Keith Richardson: 'We don't deal with sectoral issues. We don't deal with national issues. We only talk about the overall questions.'[5] The ERT's access to European commissioners is unchallenged, and it also enjoys privileged connections with members of the increasingly powerful European Parliament. In combination with long-standing linkages between member companies and their national governments, this access to the Brussels bureaucracy has been a critical element of the ERT's lobbying successes.

The Founding Fathers

In the early 1980s, the European Community appeared unable to respond to the prevalent economic crisis brought about by a decade of high inflation, rising unemployment and declining growth. In 1982, this impasse drove Pehr Gyllenhammar, then CEO of Swedish car manufacturer Volvo, to ring the alarm bell and to start campaigning for an overall scheme 'to spur growth, and to build industry and infrastructure'[6] in Europe. In close consultation with Etienne Davignon, then Commissioner for Industry, and with the support of Umberto Agnelli of Fiat and Wisse Dekker of Philips, Gyllenhammar drew together a cross-sectoral group of leading European CEOs. Modelled on the influential US Business Roundtable,[7] this elite new industrial body had the ambitious objective of 'relaunching Europe'.[8] The ERT's[9] inaugural meeting, held in April 1983, gathered 17 leading European industrialists as well as EC commissioners Davignon and François Xavier Ortoli (Finance).[10]

Giving Birth to the Single Market

This novel alliance between the European Commission and the ERT played a historic role during the process leading up to the 1986 Single European Act. In the autumn of 1984, the Commission had put forth a package of proposals to remove trade barriers within the European Community. Member states, worried about a possible loss of sovereignty, were not overly enthusiastic, and business leaders also considered the Commission proposals 'unwieldy' and lacking 'a precise time-table'.[11] In January 1985, just after the installation of a new European Commission, ERT chairman Wisse Dekker launched a far more ambitious proposal for a five-year plan to eliminate trade barriers, harmonise regulations and abolish fiscal frontiers. The Dekker proposal, *Europe 1990: An Agenda for Action*, was featured in the ERT document *Changing Scales*, which was sent to European heads of state and government and numerous other high-level officials.[12]

This pressure from industrial leaders for the unification of European markets was precisely the momentum towards further integration that the Commission had been seeking. Three days after Wisse Dekker presented his *Europe 1990* initiative, the newly appointed president of the European Commission, Jacques Delors, delivered a speech in the European Parliament which closely paralleled Dekker's proposal. Some months later, Industry Commissioner Lord Cockfield published his White Paper, which became the basis of the 1986 Single European Act, the legal framework of the Single Market. The only rather trivial difference between the ERT report and the White Paper was the postponement of the ERT's overly optimistic 1990 deadline for internal market completion to 1992.

The codification of Delors' corporate-inspired proposals of early 1985 was propelled by an intensive ERT campaign in which Roundtable members vigorously lobbied undecided national government leaders. According to Richardson, 'Wisse Dekker of Philips made it [the Single Market] his main priority for four years. Bearing in mind that when it was first launched governments were not very keen, we helped a lot to push it through.'[13] After the Single European Act came into force in July 1987, the ERT concentrated on ensuring its speedy implementation. Between 1987 and 1992, members of the ERT's Internal Market Support Committee had a profusion of meetings with government and Commission representatives.[14] The ERT's role in these striking new developments on the European level should not be underestimated. Lord Cockfield eventually admitted that the White Paper was influenced by the ERT's action plan,[15] and in a 1993 television interview, Delors recognised the 'continuing pressure' of the ERT, claiming that it was 'one of the main driving forces behind the Single Market'.[16]

In their eagerness to comply with industry's agenda for the Single Market, commissioners ignored other voices, including critical reports from within their own ranks. In 1989, for example, the Commission ordered an examination of the impacts of the Single Market upon the environment. The resulting Task Force Report listed an ominous inventory of possible negative effects, including large-scale waste transport, the obligatory acceptance of less stringently controlled products, diminished opportunity for environmental taxes on the national level, and increased road traffic and resulting emissions. Although many of these warnings have come true after more than six years of the Single Market, the report fell upon deaf ears at the time of its release. In the end, the ERT got its free trade zone with 340 million consumers and the Commission saw the relaunch of European integration that it desired.

Missing Links, Missing Networks

The triumphant ERT turned then to its next priority: the development of 'Europe's infrastructure ... A single interacting system or mega-network with a single output: mobility'.[17] Claiming that existing infrastructure formed a barrier to the unrestricted flow of goods in the Single Market and thus hindered economic growth, the ERT argued side by side with the Commission for the adoption of the environmentally controversial Trans-European Networks (TENs).

TENs is the largest transport infrastructure plan in history. It includes a number of built and unbuilt monsters: the Channel Tunnel, the Øresund Bridge connecting Denmark and Sweden, a series of high-speed train links, numerous airport expansions and 12,000 kilometres of new motorways. The ERT's ambitious infrastructure plans were unveiled in reports like *Missing Links* (1984) and *Missing Networks* (1991). Through an intensive lobby campaign which specifically targeted national transport ministers, the ERT contributed to placing the TENs squarely on the EU's agenda. The icing on the Roundtable's cake was the inclusion of the Trans-European Networks in the 1991 Maastricht Treaty.

The next step was to push for additional funding for the implementation of the projects. In *Missing Networks*, the ERT had heralded its creation of a body which would 'place infrastructure at the top of the political agenda' and 'act as a friendly watch dog over European, national and municipal authorities'. The European Centre for Infrastructure Studies (ECIS) was established in 1993, and most of the ERT's work on infrastructure was transferred to this new public-private hybrid infrastructure lobby group. Until 1997, ECIS worked in concert with the Commission to remove the final obstacles to various large infrastructure plans. Today, a huge majority of the TENs projects have either been completed or are under construction (see Chapter 8).

The Maastricht Treaty and the EMU

The ERT was very active during the negotiation of the Maastricht Treaty in the 1990–91 Intergovernmental Conference, meeting regularly with commissioners such as Vice-President Frans Andriessen (External Trade), Ray MacSharry (Agriculture), Leon Brittan (Competition) and Commission President Jacques Delors.[18] Meanwhile, individual Roundtable members also met with powerful national policy makers in their respective countries.

For the ERT, one of the most tangible results of the Maastricht Treaty was the project for European Monetary Union (EMU). As early as 1985, the ERT had argued that the Internal Market must be completed with a single currency. In its 1991 report *Reshaping Europe*, the Roundtable proposed a timetable for EMU implementation that bears remarkable similarity to the one incorporated in the Maastricht Treaty a few months later. The potent triangle between industrial leaders, national governments and commissioners had clearly been fruitful. Keith Richardson elaborates:

> We wrote a formal letter to all heads of government saying: 'When you meet at the Madrid Summit, will you please decide for once and for all that monetary union will start on the day agreed at Maastricht and with the criteria agreed at Maastricht.' We wrote to them, we asked them to do that. And they did it. They put out an announcement in Madrid and said exactly that: 'We will do it.'[19]

However, the main work preparing the ground for the EMU was done not by the ERT, but rather by the Association for the Monetary Union of Europe (AMUE, see Chapter 6). The AMUE was founded in 1987 by five transnational corporations, each of which was also represented in the ERT.

The ERT, Delors and the White Paper

Perhaps the most noteworthy example of cosy collaboration between the ERT and a Commission President is Delors's famous 1993 White Paper on Growth, Competitiveness and Employment. The White Paper, endorsed by heads of state and government at the EU Council in Brussels at the end of 1993, was prepared in close cooperation with members of the Roundtable. During the autumn of that year, the ERT was busy preparing its report *Beating the Crisis*, and drafts of this text and the White Paper regularly changed hands. At the media launch for the White Paper, Jacques Delors thanked the ERT for its support in the preparations;[20] just a week earlier, he had taken part in the ERT press launch for *Beating the Crisis*. Not surprisingly, the ERT report bears a striking similarity to the Commission paper, both in the analysis of the problems facing the European Union and in the recommended solutions: deregulation, flexible labour markets, transport infrastructure investments and international competitiveness.

Turning Tides for Transnationals

This close cooperation between the ERT and the Commission was not accidental. Whereas there had been little contact between multinational corporations and the European Commission throughout the 1970s, a dramatic transformation occurred in the 1980s. During the presidency of Jacques Delors, relations between Europe's industrial leaders and commissioners became closely entwined. According to the ERT's appreciative Assistant Secretary-General, 'The Commission is the motor in Europe. An internal revolution has taken place under Delors. It is less bureaucratic now. It listens more'.[21]

Whereas the ERT of the 1980s was split between two factions, one preferring the nurturing of Euro-champions via protectionist industrial policies and the other preferring global free trade, today's Roundtable members push unanimously for the opening of markets around the world. Predictably, the ERT was an ardent supporter of the Uruguay Round negotiations of the General Agreement on Tariffs and Trade (GATT). According to the ERT's Caroline Walcot in 1993: 'We have spoken to everybody. We have made press statements. We have written to Prime Ministers. We have done *everything* we can *think* of to try and press for the end of the Uruguay Round.'[22] ERT pressure tactics included regular meetings with national government leaders, including a luncheon held with French Prime Minister Balladur in September 1993 where 14 ERT members urged him to drop his opposition so that the trade negotiations could be completed.[23]

Relations with Santer

The good relations and regular meetings between the Roundtable and the Commission established during the decade-long presidency of Jacques Delors were maintained under the weaker Commission of Jacques Santer. 'There is a good relationship, because in many ways we have a common interest,' explained former ERT Secretary-General Richardson. 'By and large, our main priorities are the same. We cooperate, we discuss subjects with the Commission, from time to time we meet them, and from time to time we send them papers in order to ensure that they know what we think. And I think they know very well what our concerns are.'[24] Through a request for access to information at the Commission Secretariat, Corporate Europe Observatory obtained eight letters sent by President Santer to the ERT between 1995 and 1998 (see Chapter 19). These letters, written in warm, friendly tones, demonstrate how highly ERT opinions are valued by the Commission president: 'I would like to repeat again, following our last meeting, how much I have appreciated your outstanding chairmanship of the European Roundtable.'[25] The letters reveal that this is even the case regarding matters in which the ERT would not appear to be the Commission's most likely ally: for example, on improving the economic and financial perspectives of Small and Medium Enterprises (SMEs).[26]

The symbiotic relationship between the ERT and the Commission continues to bear fruit. Various Commission initiatives have gained momentum thanks to the active support of industrial leaders for further European integration and a more powerful Commission. And the Roundtable's access to EU decision-making structures has become increasingly institutionalised. This has happened mainly through its participation in EU working groups, some of which have been created upon the ERT's own recommendation. The most noteworthy example is the Competitiveness Advisory Group (CAG, see below), a group with official status which effectively amplifies the ERT's voice. Yet the ERT's strong grip on the CAG is not an anomaly. When Industry Commissioner Bangemann set up a working group on telecommunications in February 1994, six of the twenty members were from the ERT.[27] Among these twenty members was not a single representative of consumer groups, trade unions, or small and medium-sized companies.

CEOs at Work

Although the ERT's 45 members come from huge corporations with a combined turnover of 800 billion euro and more than 4 million employees worldwide, the ERT office in central Brussels is fairly modestly staffed by seven employees.[28] The secretariat has an administrative and coordinating function, and in fact is little more than a contact point for Roundtable membership. The ERT derives its strength from its prestigious members, highly influential industrialists with established access to both national and European decision makers. The organisation also mentions 'the substantial resources which ERT companies can mobilise' as one of its assets.[29] 'The ERT is basically a club of individuals. And these individuals are committed to working in the interest of the European economy and European competitiveness,' explains current ERT Secretary-General Wim Philippa. 'That means they are prepared to put their organisation behind certain actions that improve an actual situation.'[30]

A steering committee, formed by the ERT chair, the two vice-chairs and five other elected members, coordinates the organisation's work and points to new priorities.[31] This committee reviews ERT activities and makes proposals to the biannual plenary sessions, which are often organised in the member state holding the EU presidency. The plenaries decide upon the ERT's general priorities, work programme and budget, and approve reports and proposals prepared by the issue-based working groups. All decisions are taken by consensus.[32] Much of the nitty-gritty business is done by the eleven working groups on issues ranging from accounting standards, education, employment and social policy to foreign economic relations.[33] Each working group is chaired by an ERT member and staffed by experts from ERT companies; external consultants are also frequently brought on board.[34]

Current ERT Priorities

After securing the Single Market, Trans-European Networks and the single currency, the ERT has more recently focused on the mainstreaming of complementary policies encouraging competitiveness, public policy benchmarking, and its new buzzword, 'innovation'. Meanwhile, the lure of new markets has proven irresistible, and the ERT has launched a concerted lobby effort directed at EU enlargement in Central and Eastern Europe.

Competitiveness Crusade

Strengthening European industrial competitiveness within the global economy has always been the ERT's main objective, and it lobbies for the promotion of Europe-wide competition and competitiveness through the development of the Single Market into a steadily more integrated economic system. The Roundtable argues that this powerful economic bloc will then have the capacity to stimulate investment, increase production and create new jobs.[35]

Impressively, the bulk of ERT demands for 'completion of the Single Market' were written into the Single Market Action Plan adopted by the EU Council in 1997 in Amsterdam, and are now being implemented by the EU member states. In February 1997, more than three months before the Amsterdam Summit, ERT Secretary-General Richardson was already confident that this Action Plan would be adopted: 'The Commission is very keen to launch a new initiative – it will do this in Amsterdam, parallel to the Intergovernmental Conference – on completing the Single Market. This is immensely important to industry, and we are talking to them about how we can combine forces.'[36] The implementation of the Single Market Action Plan has led to further liberalisation of the telecommunications, transport and energy markets, the patenting of life, the granting of monopolies to biotech companies for products developed with biotechnological techniques, and movement towards the harmonisation of corporate taxation in Europe.

The Benchmarking Bible

For the ERT, nearly everything ultimately boils down to competitiveness, including environmental and social policy. This is why the group has been promoting the 'benchmarking', or the quantitative comparison, of the effects of policies on competitiveness as a tool for policy makers. Benchmarking, as the ERT explains, means 'scanning the world to see what is the very best that anybody else anywhere is achieving, and then finding a way to do as well or better'.[37]

The benchmarking gospel has also been spread through the Competitiveness Advisory Group, and the concept has been embraced by the European Commission.[38] As Santer explains in a 1996 letter addressed to Solvay President and ERT member Baron Daniel Janssen,[39] the Commission is prepared to use benchmarking as a tool to improve industrial competitiveness. The letter encourages further collaboration between the ERT and the Commission on the benchmarking issue, and specifically mentions Industry Commissioner Bangemann's commitment to this end. These sentiments proved sincere, and Bangemann shortly afterwards set up a special working group with the mission of introducing benchmarking as a leading principle in EU policy making. The implications are far-reaching: international competitiveness is institutionalised as the primary criterion for decision making, and policy is adopted along technical specifications rather than through political deliberation.

Benchmarking as proposed by the ERT can be applied to virtually every imaginable area. ERT Secretary-General Richardson compares the EMU criteria with a benchmarking exercise. The strict EMU targets put enormous pressure on all EU governments 'to bring their finances in better order and to keep them there'.[40] Benchmarking is also used to promote further trade and investment liberalisation. In 1996, before the financial crisis, the ERT was busily conveying the message that Europe's economy was less competitive than the economies of some southern countries. Such deliberate scare tactics serve to bully European governments into an endless competitive race with southern countries.

For example, in its November 1996 report *Investment in the Developing World: New Openings and Challenges for European Industry*, the ERT concludes that Europe is falling behind in the benchmarking race:

> Countries in the developing world have realised to what extent the impediments to private foreign and local investment were hurting their own competitiveness. Policy changes, providing better market access for foreign investors and more room for manoeuvre for local business people, are now transforming earlier weaknesses into a formidable competitive challenge. The competitive challenge becomes even more powerful through the fact that in more and more cases these countries move ahead of Europe.[41]

The point that Europe is lagging dangerously behind in the competitiveness race is further reinforced through examples of how privatisation in southern countries has resulted in 'virtually unrestricted access to markets of supply of infrastructure services, like water treatment, sewage systems or telecoms.'[42]

One dangerous byproduct of increasing global free trade is policy competition between regions, countries and trade blocs in areas including social and environmental protection. The consequence is a high-speed race to deregulate, and the primary beneficiaries are large corporations like the ones represented in the ERT. To the Roundtable, of course, deregulation competition is the equivalent of dream fulfilment: 'Competition on rules and benchmarking have proven to be among the most effective drivers of the present process of opening the economy, deregulating and modernising the institutions for private business investment.'[43] The nightmarish aspects of this unregulated global free trade – a free-for-all global arena with lowered social and environmental standards in which only the fittest survive – are not part of the ERT's concerns.

Moving Eastward

Since the collapse of Central and Eastern European communist regimes, the ERT has promoted the expeditious integration of these newly market-oriented economies into the European Union. An enormous supply of high-skilled, low-wage workers and the addition of some 150 million consumers to the Single Market makes the prospect of enlargement wildly exciting to ERT companies. In Richardson's view, 'It is as if we had discovered a new South-east Asia on our doorstep.'[44]

In 1997, the ERT stepped up its activities in this field by creating a special working group on enlargement, chaired by ERT veteran Percy Barnevik of the Swedish company Investor AB. In December of that year, the ERT presented its enlargement action plan to the EU Summit in Luxembourg, inciting leaders to quickly 'integrate all the candidate countries into a larger, more competitive and reinvigorated European Union'.[45] ERT demands included 'radical economic transformation within the candidate countries'; to facilitate this, it announced that its member companies would 'cooperate directly with the Commission and in Business Advisory Councils which are being set up within the candidate countries'.[46]

In February 1999, the ERT's enlargement working group published *The East–West Win–Win Business Experience*. In confident ERT-speak, the report aims at 'fostering integration' and inspiring actions to strengthen economic relations between East and West. A number of so-called 'win–win' case studies, drawn from the experiences of ERT companies in Central and Eastern European (CEE) countries, are provided to support the thesis that investment by Western companies will bring only benefits for both the EU and host countries.[47]

However, this rosy presentation is based on flawed case studies, and declines to mention the negative impacts on employment and environment that dependency on foreign investments has already had in CEE societies.[48] In Hungary, for instance, TNCs currently account for up to 30 per cent of Gross Domestic Product (GDP). Local companies throughout the region struggle – often unsuccessfully – to compete with large corporations, which benefit from enormous advantages of scale, access to cheaper capital, superior technology and massive advertising budgets. That TNCs are able to produce greater quantities at less expense and with fewer employees gives them a distinct advantage, but creates the legacy of increased unemployment.

Unilever and Procter & Gamble are two examples of Western companies that have profited from the unequal playing field in Europe. They have basically divided the CEE market for personal care products markets between them, shutting down national companies in the process. While it is true that TNCs often use cleaner technology in their Western operations, they do not automatically introduce the best available technology in their operations in CEE or elsewhere. There are numerous examples of TNCs using dirtier technology and lower production standards in Central and Eastern Europe than in Western Europe.

In general, the negative environmental impacts of TNC investments are often substantial, as lower emissions per product unit are often cancelled out by hugely increased production volumes. Western investments in CEE countries are currently multiplying rapidly, with current annual foreign direct investment flows to the region totalling nine billion euro.[49] ERT companies have been particularly active, with exports to the region totalling 70 million euro in 1996.[50]

ERT Business Enlargement Councils (BECs) have already been established in Hungary, Romania and Bulgaria under the leadership of Shell, Lyonnaise des Eaux and Solvay, respectively. More of these bodies, which bring together business leaders from multinational and local companies and senior government officials, are soon to follow. Member companies 'of course have a certain commercial interest in doing it,' according to ERT Secretary-General Wim Philippa. Beyond this, however, 'It's an education process, where with the close involvement and support of national governments we are guiding, training and leading the national industries in a quick way to a situation where they can enter the European Union.'[51]

The BECs will spread the ERT's competitiveness message, focusing on the need for structural adjustment in CEE countries in order to attract foreign investment. The ERT's cherished recipe includes market liberalisation in the energy, transport and telecommunications sectors and increased public investment in transport infrastructure. 'Input from the business community can ensure that funds are targeted towards priority needs,' explains Asea Brown Boveri President Eberhard von Koerber.[52] This approach basically mirrors the model prescribed by the EU for countries awaiting membership, as well as the way EU funding has been channelled through the controversial Phare Programme. This EU programme has been heavily criticised for benefiting Western European corporations and consultants more than its recipient countries in Central and Eastern Europe.[53]

The CEE countries lining up for membership are subjected to a rigorous ordeal, as the complete adoption of the EU's free trade model of economic development is a necessary prerequisite. This involves the restructuring of economies and infrastructure, the adoption of the complete body of EU legislation, a reduction in the role of the state, and an increased dependence upon foreign direct investment. Although the desirability of this model with its inevitable economic dominance by Western TNCs is the subject of debate in CEE countries, the negotiations with the EU leave no room for alternatives. This is no doubt a sobering experience for those in the region who envisioned a more sustainable democratic economy following the fall of the Iron Curtain.

Although the ERT admits that the drastic restructuring of societies will cause problems, these are downplayed as facts of life in a globalising world:

Structural change inevitably means changes in employment patterns; jobs are destroyed in some areas but protected and created in others. Any adverse short-term effects within the EU and the CEE are likely to be similar to those resulting from recent restructuring of industry, as a consequence of changes in technology and globalisation.[54]

At any rate, enlargement woes are of no concern to the ERT, as Keith Richardson explains: 'Our job is to say that the potential gains are much more important ... It is not for us to make speeches about the political unity of Europe.'[55] Currently, Western investments in CEE countries are rapidly multiplying, with annual foreign direct investment (FDI) flows to the region totalling nine billion euro in 1997.[56] EU companies took the largest share, and in 1997 accounted for two-thirds of FDI flows into Hungary and the Czech Republic and half of those into Poland.[57] EU exports to CEE now top 80 billion euro – treble the level of a decade ago,[58] with ERT companies playing a particularly active role.

Innovation: Restructuring Europe

Decision makers at both the European and national levels have been very receptive to the corporate mantra that international competitiveness is the true path to job creation. And the ERT now claims to have found the fastest path to employment nirvana through the concept of 'innovation'. In November 1998, the ERT's working group on competitiveness, chaired by Solvay's Baron Janssen, produced a new report entitled *Job Creation and Competitiveness through Innovation*. The report portrays the world economy as being in turmoil, with an 'irresistible flow of newer, better or cheaper goods or services that is constantly making older products uneconomic or obsolete – along with the jobs attached to them'.[59] Adaptation to this process of creative destruction, according to the ERT, must take place at every level of society, within companies of every size, within governments, and within individuals. 'Fighting against restructuring,' it says, 'is simply to obstruct change and job creation.'[60]

The report drones on with the predictable ERT demands for the creation of the perfect business climate through deregulation, flexibilisation of the labour market and educational reforms. The ERT has historically stressed the need to leave education in the hands of industry instead of with people 'who appear to have no dialogue with, nor understanding of, industry and the path of progress'.[61] The new report again stresses that Europeans should be subjected to 'life-long learning'[62] in order to stay employed amidst the constant changes and restructuring required by ever-fiercer global competition. Decision makers should stimulate and speed up the process of change, and foster innovation by providing finance, education, research and development and business-friendly regulatory conditions. ERT companies have already completely adapted their strategies to this profit-driven process, and present these disruptive prescriptions as incontestable.

The innovation report also calls for financial and regulatory measures to support small and medium-sized enterprises (SMEs). Yet the ERT deems only those SMEs that can withstand the constant changes in global economic conditions worthy of support. Small, innovative high-tech industries such as those found in the biotechnology sector – 'one of the key technologies of the new millennium'[63] – are also considered deserving of special financial treatment by the EU. This unusual display of generosity by the ERT is explained by the trend that large corporations, busy focusing on the most lucrative core ventures, outsource more and more activities to small and medium-sized subcontracting companies.

In the ERT's stunted worldview, policies which are in the immediate interest of the largest transnational corporations are by extension also for the common good. ERT Secretary-General Philippa claims that ERT members 'basically forget about their own company-specific desires, and think macro-economically. What is good for Europe and for European industry, small, medium-sized and big?'[64] Yet the ERT, despite its perpetual babble about employment creation, consistently ignores the fact that large companies are responsible for massive job losses. The centralisation of production and distribution catalysed by the Single Market has allowed corporations to cut costs by significantly reducing their workforces. For example, the Dutch electronics company Philips cut 22 per cent of its staff – some 68,000 jobs – over a five-year period beginning in 1989.[65] Market liberalisation also allowed British Telecom to boast of a reduction in employees from 235,000 to 125,000 between 1985 and 1996.[66]

In the late 1990s, a new boom of mergers, acquisitions and corporate restructuring has again resulted in both record profits and major job cuts. Swedish ERT member company Ericsson, for example, announced plans in early 1999 to eliminate 11,000 jobs, some 10 per cent of its global workforce. Pilkington, the UK-based glass products giant and an ERT member, cut 9,000 jobs in 1998 and eventually plans to employ less than half as many workers as it did in 1990. When announcing the cuts, company CEO Paolo Scaroni explained that the measure was part of a continuing process of 'restructuring' to drive down costs and increase profits. At the same time, he proudly told the press that Pilkington was pocketing a minimum of 20 per cent profit on its capital investments and 12 per cent on sales.[67]

Such figures have become standard as corporations increasingly focus on short-term profits and high shareholder returns. After he reorganised his new company, DaimlerChrysler boss Jürgen Schrempp was nicknamed 'Neutron Jürgen'. This was a flattering reference to General Electric's 'Neutron Jack' Welch, who is infamous for his talent for destroying jobs while leaving buildings intact. Although Schrempp is currently one of the hottest names in European business and Daimler-Chrysler shares are booming, this glory comes at the expense of huge numbers of jobs. The ERT, however, callously views this as part of the process of change to which European society must adapt.

Competitiveness Advisory Group: Doubling the ERT's Voice

The Competitiveness Advisory Group (CAG), baptised by Commission President Santer in February 1995, is one of the more impressive examples of the institutionalisation of ERT access to EU decision-making structures. Its original mandate was to produce a biannual report 'on the state of the Union's competitiveness',[68] and Santer also asked the group to 'advise on economic policy priorities and guidelines with the aim of stimulating competitiveness and reaping its benefits'.[69] Santer hand-picked the 13 CAG members, among them ERT men Floris Maljers (Unilever), Percy Barnevik (Asea Brown Boveri), David Simon (British Petroleum) and J. Olilla (Nokia). The rest were CEOs of other large corporations and banks, the former President of Treuhand,[70] three trade unionists and a number of politicians, including Carlo Ciampi, formerly Italian Prime Minister and Bank of Italy governor.[71] The first CAG was replaced by a new team after its two-year mandate expired.

In the media, the CAG is portrayed as an independent advisory group composed of top industrialists, trade unionists and academics. Although the ERT link is absent in the press, it is impossible to deny. The ERT first proposed the creation of such a body, modelled after US President Clinton's Competitiveness Council, in its December 1993 report *Beating the Crisis*, and repeated the suggestion the following year. As then ERT Secretary-General Richardson explained: 'The original idea was fundamentally put together by Floris Maljers [of Unilever] and me. The first idea was not accepted, so we changed the format and the final idea was accepted at the Essen Summit.'[72]

Chanting the Competitiveness Mantra

During its first two-year mandate, from 1995 to 1996, the CAG produced four reports on the theme of 'enhancing competitiveness', each published just a few weeks before the biannual EU Summits. The waves of new ideas and recommendations for decision makers contained in each report closely resemble the advice given by the ERT. Many of the proposals eventually appeared on the EU's political agenda or otherwise influenced EU decision making.

The first CAG report, published just prior to the June 1995 EU Summit in Cannes, concluded that there was an urgent need to improve overall competitiveness in the EU. Echoing familiar ERT prescriptions, CAG cures included the funding of TENs transport infrastructure through public/private partnerships, the speedy enlargement of the EU eastward, and the introduction of life-long learning and the 'learning society' (the continuous re-educating of employees to enable them to adapt to the changing needs of industry). The second CAG report, released six months later in time for the December 1995 EU Summit in Madrid, recommends a major new role for the state. In the CAG's vision, the government should facilitate the deregulation and privatisation of the public sector, particularly in the areas of energy, transport and telecommunications. For environmental policies, the CAG advises that governments use market-based instruments rather than regulation.

In its third report, issued in June 1996 and discussed at the EU Summit in Florence, the CAG worries about the heated debates on mass unemployment in Europe and calls for social pacts between employers, labour and government 'to counter the threat of disruption'.[73] It proposes the modernisation of the labour market through greater flexibility in working hours, wage moderation and greater mobility between companies, regions, and countries. The CAG also recommends changes in social legislation in the EU member states, making use of 'cost-benefit analysis' which would likely put corporate needs before the public interest.

The fourth and final report of this first CAG, issued in December 1996 before the EU Summit in Dublin, focuses on the EU's position in the globalising world economy. It assesses the Union's international trade and investment performance, particularly in comparison to what were at that time extremely high-growth markets in Asia. It also calls for

Figure 1   45+ members of the European Roundtable of Industrialists gathered to draw up recommendations for the EU Summit in Madrid, December 1995.

continuing liberalisation of trade and investment within the World Trade Organization, the completion of the OECD's Multilateral Agreement on Investment (MAI, see Chapter 12), and the modification of Article 133 of the Maastricht Treaty (the Common Commercial Policy) which would enable the Commission to negotiate on services, intellectual property and foreign direct investment.

More of the Same: the Second CAG

In May 1997, Santer announced the 13 new members of the second Competitiveness Advisory Group. Although the Commission President emphasised that 'once again, there is a broad balance of outstanding politicians, businessmen, trade unionists and academics in the group',[74] a closer look at its members reveals a decidedly non-neutral group of experts. Chaired by former OECD Secretary-General Jean-Claude Paye, it includes ERT member companies British Telecom, Pirelli and Repsol. The two other corporate representatives are from the German employers' organisation and the Portuguese BFE-Investimentos company. Again, three trade unionists, from Italy, the UK and Sweden, are among its ranks.

The new CAG, appointed for another two-year period, produced *Competitiveness for Employment* in November 1997. In this report, released in time for the so-called 'Jobs Summit' in Luxembourg, economic globalisation is enthusiastically defended as an irreversible process that imposes rapid but necessary adjustments on all countries. The numerous proposed measures are largely recycled, and massively biased towards the competitiveness concern despite lip service given to the need to preserve social cohesion. The CAG's proposals for accelerating structural reforms, relaxing the legal environment for business, and more 'individual responsibility' in pension, health and unemployment systems are not exactly recipes for social cohesion. In its later report *Capital Markets for Competitiveness*, published before the Cardiff EU Summit in June 1998, the CAG focuses on reforms of European capital markets in relation with the single currency.

Calling for Competitiveness

Keith Richardson was quite satisfied with the work of the first CAG: 'It has done a lot of good work. It has produced four excellent reports, and now they are preparing a new team for another two years. We have been closely in touch with them all along'.[75] In contrast with the strong ERT presence in the CAG, the European employers' confederation UNICE (see Chapter 4) has not been represented in either group. Former UNICE Secretary-General Zygmunt Tyszkiewicz explained why the confederation did not support the ERT's original proposal: 'We felt very strongly that you needed an undiluted competitiveness message, because Europe was not competitive. It was a serious situation. But we did not want the message to be clouded with a compromise between employers, trade unions, academics and politicians, which is what the CAG ended up being.'[76] Yet UNICE's fears proved unfounded. Commenting on the presence of three trade unionists in the CAG, Richardson notes that 'the fact that they have signed onto the CAG reports gives [the reports] extra weight'.[77]

The CAG has allowed CEOs from the ERT to present their recommendations through a formal body with official EU status. Consequently, industrial competitiveness has *de facto* become the main goal of EU policy making, overriding all other concerns. The ERT's need for exposure has therefore decreased, which could explain why it has launched significantly fewer reports on the general direction of EU policies since the founding of the CAG. The ERT can now continue its work behind the scenes, and can rest assured that its voice is being strengthened by a body with the status of official adviser to the European Union.

UNICE: Industry's Well-oiled Lobby Machine

While the ERT subtly masterminds its grand vision of Europe in collaboration with the European Commission, another Brussels-based European lobby group is busy implementing the less glamorous but equally critical details. Whereas the ERT is quietly proactive, UNICE is a reactive, detail-obsessed, supremely efficient lobby machine. Its working groups dissect every proposal, regulation, directive and article emerging from Brussels before spitting influential position papers back into the policy-making apparatus. Its efforts often result in the adoption of business-friendly initiatives, and the blockage of more socially or environmentally progressive legislation. Despite notably divergent working styles, the ERT and UNICE have a similar goal: increased industrial competitiveness in the European Union.

The Role of UNICE

UNICE (the Union of Industrial and Employers' Confederations of Europe), has been the official voice of industry in the EU since 1958,[1] giving it a *carte blanche* to open, unhampered access to EU institutions. 'Our mission is to influence decision-makers at the European level. Of course the word "lobby" is not used, but that's what it's all about,'[2] confides UNICE's communications director. 'You can see UNICE as a manufacturing plant where we produce documents, and my work here in the communications department is to sell them to decision-makers.'[3] The factory image fits well with the atmosphere in UNICE's Brussels headquarters, where piles of paper fill plain grey rooms.

This 'family' of 33 employers' federations from 25 European countries proudly speaks on behalf of 'millions of small, medium and large companies'.[4] It boasts a lineage of leaders with impressive corporate credentials. Current president George Jacobs worked at the IMF before

joining Belgian chemical/pharmaceutical company UCB Group,
eventually becoming president of its Executive Committee. His
predecessor, François Perigot, was formerly head of Unilever France and
is currently a board member of the Association for Monetary Union in
Europe (AMUE, see Chapter 6). Current UNICE Secretary-General Dirk
Hudig previously worked on EU-government relations for ERT member
company ICI, and was also the European coordinator of the Transatlantic
Business Dialogue's working group on chemicals (TABD, see Chapter 11).

UNICE's detailed, micro-approach to policy making in the EU has
proven effective over the years: 'There are about 19,000 experts in the
Commission, and we send them our position on every possible topic which
matters for business ... Our Secretary-General writes to commissioners,
our directors discuss with the directors of units, and our staff communi-
cates with experts.'[5] According to former Secretary-General Zygmunt
Tyszkiewicz, UNICE gains regular access even to the Commission: 'We
are in touch. It's a very open bureaucracy, the Commission, it is very
approachable. And they feel that we can help them.'[6]

The various UNICE national federations play a special role in buttering
up EU Ministers in their respective countries: 'After they've all been
approached in the same fashion, the hope is that when they get together
in the Council of Ministers to make the final decision they will take
account of what business has been telling them.'[7] A similar decentralised
approach is used to influence Euro-parliamentarians: 'If you want to
influence a Spanish MEP, you would be more efficient doing it in Spanish
through our Spanish federation.'[8] Still, keeping tabs on 626 MEPs as
they shuttle between home, Strasbourg and Brussels is a daunting task,
so UNICE works with a public relations agency to ensure the continual
presence of 'somebody with a UNICE hat in the Parliament'.[9] Courting
the media is also important for UNICE: 'If you want to make your voice
heard, you have to know that politicians read newspapers, and that they
are more influenced by the *Financial Times* than by UNICE.'[10]

Brussels Old Boys' Network

UNICE staff regard the ERT with both admiration and complacency. 'The
ERT selects a few topics where it wants to be proactive – education for
example, even though it is not at all on the agenda of the Commission.
That's how it works, because it is a club of persons,' explains Communications Director Christophe de Callatäy. And then, as if to justify the more
pedantic, decentralised working style of UNICE versus that of the more
elitist ERT: 'We have no room for emotions here. UNICE is very rational,
and we keep a common denominator between all federations which
eventually leads to a style which is difficult to read, not attractive, and not
media friendly at all.' Although the virtues of the ERT's agenda-setting

style are certainly not lost upon UNICE bureaucrats, the group holds claim to its own strengths as well. One of these is the official and thus legitimate status enjoyed by UNICE as one of the EU's partners in the Social Dialogue.[11] 'Being proactive is always a dream,' says de Callatäy, 'but it would be foolish to think that you can be proactive all the time.'[12]

Despite their differences, there is much overlap between the agendas of the two lobby groups, and the president of UNICE and the ERT Secretary-General meet regularly. 'On a daily basis, they are comrades. And of course we call each other when there is a problem,' says de Callatäy.[13] UNICE also networks regularly with the EU Committee of the American Chamber of Commerce (see Chapter 5), with the Transatlantic Business Dialogue (see Chapter 11) and with sectoral groups such as CEFIC, the association of the European chemical industry. 'This networking is very, very important,' according to former UNICE Secretary-General Tyszkiewicz. 'There may be many voices, but the important thing is that they are all carrying the same message.'[14]

This message, of industrial competitiveness in a globalised Europe, is loudly proclaimed by the larger, transnational companies headquartered in the EU member states. Smaller, less international firms benefit less from this agenda, and thus UNICE's relationship with UEAPME, the largest of the lobby groups representing small and medium-sized enterprises (SMEs) in Europe has not been entirely smooth. UEAPME (the European Union for Artisans and Small and Medium-sized Enterprises) has long dreamt of being recognised as an official partner in the EU's Social Dialogue together with the European Trade Union Confederation, the public sector employers' union (CEEP) and UNICE.

In 1998, UEAPME threatened to take UNICE before the European Court of Justice if they were not included in the Social Dialogue, and were only persuaded to drop the case when UNICE promised to integrate their input into every dialogue meeting. 'They pretend that we only represent big business and not small and medium-sized companies, so we had kind of a long dispute,' admits de Callatäy. 'Now UNICE's strategy is to allow them a seat in the Social Dialogue, sitting next to UNICE, and that will allow us to represent business as a whole, which is what we want.'[15] However, UEAPME's 'seat' is not an official one, and it enjoys no real rights in the Social Dialogue.

Although UNICE's Brussels headquarters employs only about 40 staff, Tyszkiewicz claims that it can 'mobilise a thousand people to help it do its work'.[16] In fact, policies and positions are elaborated through a complex web of policy committees[17] and some sixty working groups composed of experts from the various national member federations. Although it doesn't set policy, the UNICE Secretariat plays a crucial role in setting the overall agenda: 'We identify the issues, because we know the Commission's plan of action. We know what the Parliament is doing, we know what the Council is doing, and we know what big issues are coming up. So we feed that back to our federations.'[18] Policy papers drafted by the working groups are sent to UNICE's Executive Committee for final approval. 'Then it is our job, and the job of our federations, to spread that policy around, to talk about it, to explain it, to present it to the political decision-makers,' says Tyszkiewicz.[19]

UNICE's priorities do not differ much from those of the ERT: strengthening European competitiveness, completion of the Single Market and Economic and Monetary Union (EMU), enlargement to the East, benchmarking and liberalisation of world trade and investment.

Benchmarking Competitiveness

UNICE has been chanting the mantra of industrial competitiveness for many years. The message in its reports on competitiveness (1994) and regulatory reforms (1995) is the same: if only public authorities would concentrate on creating a favourable climate for business, Europe would enjoy greater rates of economic growth, employment and social welfare and higher standards of living. One recent report, *Benchmarking Europe's Competitiveness: from Analysis to Action*[20] harps further on structural and regulatory reforms. The report concludes that the gap between analysis and action in the EU is mainly due to the fact that the concept of competitiveness remains largely unexplained to the public, and proposes the benchmarking[21] of 20 basic conditions which affect business activity in Europe. These conditions cover most policy areas, from the completion of the Single Market and the EMU to taxation: 'Action is needed now, not further analysis.'[22]

The Single Market and EMU

Concerning the Single Market, although quite satisfied with its progress, UNICE is still clamouring for full liberalisation of public procurement and the opening up of many services to greater competition. Simultaneously, the group complains vociferously about the introduction of new environment and health regulations which might damage industrial competitiveness.

Now that the Economic and Monetary Union (EMU) is firmly in place, UNICE is calling for structural reforms and flexible markets so that its 'benefits' can be fully reaped. These reforms are meant to achieve a permanent reduction in public spending, 'particularly in the areas of public consumption, pension provision and health care, welfare benefits and state subsidies'.[23] People-friendly policies are by no means a priority for UNICE. 'Try to favour business, that's the point. This is a clear follow up of the EMU,' says de Callatäy.[24] Not surprising, then, that UNICE strongly opposes initiatives such as the one proposed by the Italian government to allow exemptions from the Stability Pact[25] if the expenditures are on job creation: 'We are for a sound public policy and sound financing, which means public deficit should be close to zero. And don't find excuses to create public deficit.'[26]

Taxes and Jobs

UNICE's *Benchmarking* report also calls repeatedly for tax reduction for industry: 'Tax systems should be restructured so as to promote rather than penalise enterprise and employment. In a globalised economy, illusory tax-switching solutions, such as new taxes on energy products or higher taxation on capital, should be rejected, as they would reduce European competitiveness and attractiveness as a place for investment.'[27] The ideal situation for UNICE, as well as for other corporate lobby groups, does not involve social and environmental policies which benefit local economies, but rather minimal corporate and labour taxes: 'Taxation is a threat for business. Now we are very afraid that every proposal coming up from the Commission is the coordination of fiscal measures, but only up to a certain ceiling. We would like to get to the floor.'[28]

UNICE claims that high European unemployment levels can be resolved with the creation of an ever more flexible labour market: 'It has become nearly impossible to create jobs. Labour costs are so huge. It is so difficult to fire people, so you don't want to hire them.'[29] In line with this thinking, UNICE prefers that member states rather than the Commission deal with employment policies for fear that the latter will 'go too far in setting goals, objectives and so on'.[30] Of course the group also strongly rejects the idea of collective bargaining at the European level: 'That's what the unions would like. Employers want to shift bargaining processes to the shop floor, to companies.'[31]

Enlargement: the Bigger the Better

The extension of the EU towards the East, with the corresponding expansion of the Single Market, is a mouth-watering prospect for the various industrialists within UNICE. 'The EU's internal market will be enlarged by more than 100 million consumers with rising incomes. To catch up with the economies of the EU-15, the Central and Eastern countries need huge investment in infrastructure and production equipment. The EU-15 anticipates a trade surplus with the applicant countries for more than the next decade,' is UNICE's predictable line. [32]

Although happy to include as many candidates as possible in enlargement negotiations, UNICE feels *sine qua non* that countries must be able to implement every aspect of the Single Market legislation. Thus, it proposes parallel negotiations with the countries not included in the first round in order to reach an agreement which includes the essential elements of the Single Market. The adoption of the institutional and financial reforms discussed but not agreed upon at the June 1997 Inter-governmental Conference in Amsterdam is also of great concern to UNICE; in particular, it hopes to clarify Article 133 which covers the EU's external commercial policy. In its view, the Commission should gain the full competence to negotiate international agreements on services and intellectual property – otherwise, the unanimity now required for these decisions will be automatically extended to the new members.

To smooth the accession process, UNICE has set up a task force on enlargement. Experts are assigned to each candidate country: 'They go there, [and] they try on the one hand to help our federations or the business representatives in these countries to adapt to the *acquis com-munautaire*, [33] and on the other hand to help the UNICE network to have a better understanding of the problems they meet and to be able to give recommendations to the Commission.' [34] Now, however, UNICE is worried about the enlargement process losing momentum: 'At first you always have a lot of enthusiasm, but now people realise how big it is.' [35]

Sir Leon's Groupies

UNICE is firmly committed to world trade and investment liberalisation, actively supporting initiatives in international fora including the World Trade Organization (WTO, see Chapter 13), the Organization for Economic Cooperation and Development (OECD) and ongoing transatlantic free trade negotiations. Trade Commissioner Sir Leon Brittan has surely found in UNICE one of his biggest fans and a trusty ally in his free trade crusade. 'UNICE has always backed Sir Leon, so whatever he comes up with, UNICE says okay, fine, do it!' [36] says de Callatäy. Yet he also bitterly complains that Brittan's initiatives are always ultimately watered down, citing the failure of the Multilateral Agreement on Investment (MAI) negotiations at the OECD (see Chapter 12) and the New Transatlantic Marketplace (see Chapter 11) as examples.

UNICE has now pinned its hopes on the Transatlantic Economic Partnership (TEP) and the proposed Millennium Round in the WTO. To avoid potential stumbling blocks in the creation of the TEP, it recommends 'a broad information campaign to win over public opinion, stressing the benefits in terms of growth, jobs, consumer health and safety, and sustainable development'.[37] UNICE has also requested that it be 'fully involved in the final decision of the EU proposal, considering that many of the likely components of such an initiative have been identified jointly by European and US companies, and are the object of work in the framework of the TABD'.[38]

As for the next set of negotiations in the WTO, UNICE has made its preference clear for a round which specifically nails down agreements on international investment and intellectual property rights. Furthermore, it hopes that market access, services, agriculture, government procurement and electronic commerce are addressed, and that agreement is reached on trade measures in international environmental agreements and ecological labelling which does not impede liberalisation.[39]

Absolute Monsters

Civil society's successful campaign against the MAI seems to have shaken UNICE's complacency, and since that victory the group has been attempting to integrate NGO concerns into its pro-globalisation demands. For example, UNICE recommends that WTO negotiators secure 'the widest possible endorsement by public opinion' while simultaneously 'reconciling liberalisation of international trade and investment with the realisation of other objectives of general interest, such as economic development of the least-developed countries, application of internationally accepted labour standards and protection of consumers or the environment'.[40]

But at least when it comes to the environment, it is clear that these sentiments are superficial. 'Absolute monsters' is how one Brussels-based environmental lobbyist describes UNICE:

> Their membership is huge, and they are present at virtually any discussion that takes place on water, chemicals, waste and so forth. They take dreadful positions on packaging, incineration and recycling, and say that they consider clean technology a joke. They strongly push voluntary agreements, so that environmental policy can be determined entirely by industry.[41]

UNICE takes global conferences on environmental issues very seriously, flying a delegation of nine to Buenos Aires in November 1998 for the fourth Conference of Parties to the Climate Convention. Its position on climate change (see Chapter 17) is business-as-usual, and in an effort to avoid any regulation which would reduce emissions, the group has been busy promoting voluntary compliance for industry. Yet at the same time,

UNICE has been quick to embrace the economic opportunities implicit in the market-based solutions which industry has successfully lobbied for during the climate negotiations.

On the whole, how successful is UNICE in achieving its goals? Quite, according to Tyszkiewicz: 'There are countless examples of legislation that was either avoided altogether or was quite seriously amended because of the work that UNICE does.'[42] If success can be measured by the extent to which UNICE simultaneously influences EU legislation to the advantage of its industry members and thwarts the attempts of environmental and social groups to place their issues on the agenda, it could be said that UNICE comes through with flying colours.

5

AmCham Chimes in with the Brussels Corporate Choir

Strange as it may seem, one of the most important corporate players on the Brussels political scene – and the first to introduce the US style of corporate lobbying to Brussels – is a lobby group representing US-based corporations. AmCham, or the EU Committee of the American Chamber of Commerce, established its initially somewhat sleepy presence in the European 'capital' in the 1970s. In the early 1980s, it underwent a major renaissance and became one of the first industry lobby groups to systematically monitor and influence European Commission policy making.

Although national corporate identities are increasingly blurred by transatlantic mergers and globalisation, AmCham's membership remains predominantly restricted to 'European companies of American parentage or those with control ultimately resting in the US'.[1] Boeing, Du Pont, Exxon, General Motors, McDonald's, Monsanto and Procter & Gamble are among the 145 plus industrial giants gathered under the lobby group's umbrella. Although large US corporations such as these have enjoyed a steady influx into European markets since the 1960s, the advent of the Single Market and the euro have encouraged new waves of US corporate expansion in Europe. In total, AmCham companies currently have approximately three million employees and US$350 billion worth of investment in Europe.[2]

The Corporate Choir

AmCham works closely with the two most influential 'European' corporate groupings, the employers' confederation UNICE and the European Roundtable of Industrialists (ERT). As AmCham's Manager for European Affairs John Russell[3] explains: 'We exchange a lot of information, have joint meetings and even publish joint papers.'[4] These three corporate groups use what Russell calls 'the choir approach', strategically reinforcing and supplementing each other's positions.[5] He explains: 'It is normally more effective not to say everything together, but to have different people telling the institutions more or less the same thing.'[6]

AmCham, as well as the other corporate choir members, tends to warble on about the urgency of adjusting European societies to be more internationally competitive in the globalising economy. To avoid relocations and create jobs, the EU should strive for 'flexible workforces' and 'further liberalisation and a competitive regulatory environment', according to AmCham Chairman Keith Chapple.[7] 'Europe will feel the squeeze if it lags behind in making itself a truly competitive place to do business',[8] says Chapple, who is also marketing director of semi-conductor giant Intel, a company which has moved substantial parts of its US production to low-wage countries like Indonesia and China. He warns: 'Europe will increasingly be in competition with developing countries which can offer attractive alternative bases for business ... To be competitive in this shrinking world, Europe has to be flexible, drive out unnecessary costs and be open in its trading relationships.'[9] In fact, AmCham rarely passes up the opportunity to stress the threat of corporate relocation in its European lobbying on various issues of interest to its members.

A Lobbying Machine

AmCham offers its members a superbly refined lobbying strategy, and its techniques have been a major source of inspiration for UNICE and other corporate lobby groups in Brussels. In the late 1980s, AmCham established itself as the main clearing house for business requiring EU policy information.[10] The group's mandate, according to Russell, includes monitoring EU policies and processes, furnishing relevant information to members, and providing 'a constructive input into the legislative process, or, one could say, lobbying'.[11]

After identifying juicy EU legislation, AmCham contacts the relevant Commission officials and begins to churn out position papers and specific amendments. In 1998, AmCham produced around sixty policy papers and ten books, and had 'about 350 meetings with the Commission and the Parliament'.[12] AmCham also has access to another powerful political actor in Brussels: the Committee of Permanent Representatives (COREPER), the group of member state 'ambassadors' to the EU which prepares decisions for the Council of Ministers. In addition to regular hobnobs with the Committee, AmCham enjoys special biannual sessions with COREPER representatives from the country holding the EU presidency.[13]

AmCham's secretariat, which has doubled in size since 1990 and currently houses twenty staff members, works closely with the more than 650 individuals from AmCham member companies. Business is conducted mainly through twelve subcommittees which focus on weighty issues like trade, consumer affairs, fiscal initiatives and competition policy, and the details are filled in by some forty specialised working groups. The environment subcommittee, for example, consists of about a hundred companies, and they are split into ten working groups and task forces on specific issues like packaging, liability, waste and eco-taxes. These groups are engaged in an ongoing attempt to modify or destroy EU legislation that might harm the interests of AmCham's corporate membership. In the spring of 1999, for instance, AmCham lobbied strenuously to change EU waste management proposals which prioritised recycling over incineration. It cynically urged the EU to 'move away from a rigid interpretation of the hierarchy' and to recategorise incineration as environmentally-friendly.[14]

AmCham is viewed as one of the most powerful lobby groups in Brussels, and the organisation is proud of the remarkable access and close working relations it has forged with EU institutions. 'I never say "the EU Committee did this and we influenced that and those amendments were ours",' says Russell modestly. 'But if the Commission contacts you or wants to have a meeting with you, or when you contact them and they are more than happy to meet with you, then that is useful.' The EU's regulations on electronic commerce are only some of the many policies on which AmCham fingerprints can be discerned; thanks to energetic lobbying, the group successfully discouraged business-unfriendly taxation and other government regulation. The multinational nature of AmCham facilitates the rigorous comparison of rules and regulations in the various countries in which its member companies operate. Russell explains admiringly that the multinational club of industries can 'bring their expertise, from a global perspective, on what's happening in other areas ... It is almost a benchmarking of what is good in other regimes.'[15]

Pro Globalisation, Pro EU

Economic globalisation explains the phenomenon that AmCham and European corporate groupings like the ERT and UNICE are able to speak in unison to Brussels decision makers. According to Russell, the AmCham constituency 'tends to be those that are in the mainstream of globalisation'. Thus, European TNCs 'tend to be very much our natural allies', whereas those 'parts of European industry that are tied very much to the local economies' are disregarded. Like its European sister groupings, AmCham is an avid fan of European unification. 'We may disagree with the Commission or the Parliament on certain issues,' says

Russell. 'But this strategic direction of where Europe is going – as far as greater integration and companies preferring to deal with Brussels rather than with fifteen member state administrations and political systems – is quite straightforward.'[16]

For US corporations, which generally lack political access in the EU member states, the growing powers of the disconnected European Commission in the 1980s provided a golden opportunity for political influence. Their efforts have primarily been channelled through AmCham,[17] and thus it is not surprising that the lobby group vociferously supports a strong, centralised European Union. According to Russell, AmCham is continuously 'calling for more power to Brussels – even more probably than European industry, because they are tied more to the vested interests of particular member states'.[18]

None the less, representing the interests of US-based corporations, AmCham does face certain limitations in what it can say and how it operates. 'We are extremely careful of the boundaries,' explains Russell. 'There is still the foreign label, there is a sensitivity.'[19] Indeed, high-profile Commission initiatives are more likely launched in collaboration with a representative of the ERT than with an AmCham CEO. Furthermore, membership in high-level working groups like the Competitiveness Advisory Group (see Chapter 3) is not feasible for so-called 'European firms of American parentage'. There is no doubt, however, that in the less visible, day-to-day operations of the Brussels political machine, AmCham is a real heavyweight.

Polishing the EMU:
The Association for the
Monetary Union of Europe

Tonight, I really feel at home among friends. When I became President of the Commission in 1995, the Association was about the only body which supported us in our firm belief that the single currency would become a reality. So it feels like playing a home game.
Jacques Santer in a speech to the AMUE Board of Directors in February 1998

The ERT's Financial Offspring

The Paris-based Association for the Monetary Union of Europe (AMUE) was created in 1987, well before the advent of the Maastricht Treaty and Economic and Monetary Union (EMU). Officially the initiative of former French president Giscard d'Estaing and former German chancellor Helmut Schmidt, in reality the AMUE was founded by five corporations active in the European Roundtable of Industrialists (ERT, see Chapter 3): Fiat, Philips, Rhône-Poulenc, Solvay and Total. Wisse Dekker, then CEO of Philips and ERT chair, and previously one of the key people behind the creation of the Single Market, was the AMUE's first chairman. Currently, seven of the thirty AMUE board members are ERT members or top managers in ERT companies: Viscount Etienne Davignon of Société Générale de Belgique; François-Xavier Ortoli of Total; Fiat's Giovanni Agnelli; Rhône-Poulenc's Jean René Fourtou; André Leysen of Gevaert; Philips' Dudley Eustace and Karl-Hermann Baumann of Siemens. Furthermore, approximately one-third of the companies currently represented in the ERT double as AMUE members.[1] Beyond this sturdy base of Roundtable representatives, the majority of the AMUE's nearly three hundred current members come from the EU's financial and banking sectors.

Despite the obvious overlap, the AMUE does not link itself with the ERT in its publications. However, when asked about the relationship between the two groups, AMUE Secretary-General Bertrand de Maigret explains: 'We decided that the ERT would not work on monetary issues, and that we would. We have friendly links – a kind of division of tasks.'[2] Etienne Davignon, former Industry Commissioner and ERT member and currently president of the AMUE, confirmed the division of tasks, but stressed that 'there is no difference in the findings.'[3]

Minting the Coin

The ERT – obsessed with international competitiveness – was an early and vocal proponent of European Monetary Union. 'Japan has one currency. The US has one currency. How can the Community live with twelve?' it asked in 1991.[4] Thus, AMUE was created as a single-issue task force, to supplement the ERT's own campaign for economic and monetary union in Europe.

The founders of the AMUE decided to limit membership to the corporate and financial services sectors, excluding trade unions, consumer organisations and other interest groups. As AMUE president Davignon put it, 'We don't speak for everybody, we speak for ourselves. It [EMU] could only be effective if it was proposed by the people who were in favour, without the necessity to compromise between themselves.'[5] UNICE, the European employers' confederation, is also a member of the AMUE, and both its current and former presidents, George Jacobs and François Perigot, sit on the Association's board.

Putting EMU on Track

During the first years of its existence, the AMUE had a clearly defined mission: putting EMU squarely on the EU's agenda. For years, many European politicians had dreamt about economic and monetary union between the member states of the European Economic Community. Thus, significant political will for such a project already existed when the AMUE was founded. However, as Commission President Santer gratefully acknowledged in 1998, 'The members of the Association have been a major driving force behind the EMU project. Many of your companies have played a leadership role by clearly advocating the advantages of the single currency for the private sector and society as a whole.'[6] Furthermore, when politicians couldn't agree about whether they should set precise dates for EMU implementation in the Maastricht Treaty, the

AMUE, the ERT and other corporate lobby groups successfully pressed for the inclusion of a well-defined time schedule. According to the AMUE's de Maigret, governments were 'very glad to find the support of industry and the bank community in preparations for the writing of the treaty ... We had discussions on various high levels.'[7]

Davignon also has a rather self-congratulatory perspective on the role of the Association. 'You cannot be vain about this. At the end of the day, a lot of drops make the sea,' he said. 'What is significant is that we were always considered as very useful by the Commission. And also by the various member states, all of which have now set up technical groups dealing with this type of problem. They always ask representatives of the AMUE to be there.'[8] The AMUE can also claim to have increased the support for economic and monetary union within the European business and finance worlds.

Ensuring EMU

Although the Maastricht Treaty had put Economic and Monetary Union firmly on the official political agenda of the European Union, it was only at the 1995 Madrid EU Summit that crucial decisions were made about its practical implementation. The AMUE itself views this meeting as a watershed: 'Before the Madrid Summit, efforts were directed at convincing companies and governments of the benefits of having a single currency ... Efforts after that concentrated on preparing banks and companies for the changeover to the euro.'[9] The AMUE claims to have organised over one thousand conferences and seminars since 1989, more than half of which took place in the period between 1996 and 1998.[10] Often of a technical nature, the meetings involved officials from the Commission and from national states. Efforts were strategically focused on the countries with the strongest EMU phobias: in 1997 and 1998, for example, the Association organised 90 meetings in Germany 'to garner support for the euro from an often sceptical public'.[11] The AMUE claims that almost half of these meetings 'were organised at the request and with the active participation of German Members of Parliament'.[12] In addition to the meetings, the AMUE hired a public relations firm to issue broad-based weekly information bulletins on monetary union to the German and Austrian press.[13]

Yet cooperation between the AMUE and EU institutions goes well beyond joint meetings. In a May 1994 report, for example, the AMUE recommended that the European Commission establish an independent committee to further analyse the changeover to Economic and Monetary Union.[14] In fact, the Commission had already decided to create an 'independent expert committee on the introduction of the euro as the single currency'. What the Commission meant by 'independent' became clear in July 1994 when this committee's composition was announced: three of the twelve experts turned out to be AMUE board members, whereas consumer organisations had only one representative.[15] Based upon this committee's work, the Commission published a Green Paper[16] on the procedures for single currency changeover in May 1995, which was quickly followed by a report from the European Monetary Institute[17] supporting the paper's proposals.[18] The two reports were used to support the European Council decision to launch a speedy introduction of EMU at the December 1995 EU Summit in Madrid.[19]

Besides taking part in official expert groups and helping to formulate the final transition scenario for monetary union, the AMUE has produced academic studies and reports (such as a 1998 report on the stability of EMU)[20] with the aim of countering widespread critique and scepticism. With the financial support of the Commission, the AMUE has written and distributed millions of practical preparation guides.

A further measure of its influence is that the AMUE is often chosen by both the Commission and the European Parliament for public tenders requiring expertise in monetary matters.[21] Indeed, the European Commission frequently consults the group on monetary questions, both formally and informally. 'It is a very confident way of working,' explains AMUE Secretary-General de Maigret. 'They call us, we call them, they see us, we discuss matters. They are quite flexible. I'm not one of those who criticise the Commission administration. They are very open for discussion, at least in the monetary field.'[22] According to Etienne Davignon, governments have always been interested in listening to the AMUE: 'They gladly come to our general assemblies in various countries. Prime ministers usually come to address these, and governors of central banks also attend.'[23]

Unlike other symbiotic processes between businesses and politicians within the EU, groups outside of the business and financial communities have paid no attention to the AMUE/Commission connection. According to Davignon, 'In these issues, industry is much less suspected than in other issues. This is not the lobby for the car industry, or for electronics, or multimedia, or the deregulation of banks or whatever, but the discussion over the improved use of the internal market.'[24]

The Euro is Born

The birth of the euro on 1 January 1999 did not spell the end of the AMUE; on the contrary, the Association seems more ambitious than ever. To ensure that industry and banks are able to reap the predicted benefits of EMU, the AMUE has set up a special benchmarking programme for companies and continues to assist business in its preparations for the euro by organising conferences and distributing information material. Retailers and the tourism industry in particular have been assisted in their transition preparations, and consumers have been smothered in propaganda in order to foster a quick and easy acceptance of the euro. The Association also plans to encourage EMU membership by Denmark, Sweden and the UK, and to inform the Norwegian, Swiss and Central and Eastern European business communities about the promised benefits of the single currency so that companies in those countries can in turn lobby their national governments to join the EMU.

The AMUE's Tentacles Reach Abroad

The Association's latest fascination is with the global dimension of the new currency. It is envisaged that the euro will give Europe a global currency advantage, which will in turn increase European exports. To improve the stability of financial markets, the AMUE has started a dialogue with US and Japanese businesses to prevent excessive fluctuations of euro, dollar and yen exchange rates. At home, the AMUE regards the EMU's birth as a chance to redesign European capital markets. It lobbies for the harmonisation of company law and stock market legislation with the hope of catalysing an enormous growth in European stock markets. In order to translate the economic size of the euro-zone into global political clout, the AMUE wants the EU to speak with one voice in the international arena, and stresses that the euro-zone should have a single representative at G-8 meetings.

The global dreams of the AMUE were reflected in their ninth annual meeting in Frankfurt on 1 July 1998, which featured a razzle-dazzle simultaneous link-up to financial conferences in London, Milan, New York, Paris and Tokyo. Another conference was organised in New York in April 1998, giving several hundred US financiers the opportunity to discuss the euro with EU Economic and Financial Affairs Commissioner Yves-Thibault de Silguy, Alexandre Lamfalussy, the then President of the European Monetary Institute, and US Deputy Secretary of the Treasury Lawrence Summers. But perhaps the crowning example of the AMUE's integration into the global financial world was the timing of its September 1998 meeting in Hong Kong, parallel to the annual meeting of the IMF and the World Bank. From its humble origins as the brainchild of a few corporate CEOs and EU commissioners, the AMUE has quickly risen in the ranks to become a major player in the game of global economic and monetary planning.

Single Market, Single Currency

The AMUE presents economic and monetary union as a logical step towards the completion of the Single Market, which is still not as 'efficient' as industry would like. According to AMUE Secretary-General de Maigret, EMU will bring 'monetary stability and long-term certainty, which will increase productive investment, generate economies of scale and eliminate production costs, which in turn will increase competitiveness, sales, economic growth and employment'.[25] But the AMUE is silent about other euro-zone realities. In fact, the euro is one of the most far-reaching economic experiments of the last decades, and has already caused widespread social and economic upheaval across Europe.

The focus of EMU critique from progressive groups has been the convergence criteria agreed upon in the Maastricht Treaty. These criteria oblige EMU candidate members to bring government debt, inflation rates, budget deficits and long-term interest rates below certain benchmark levels. In most countries, these criteria have been achieved through spectacular budget cuts targeting national social, health and educational programmes, in combination with controls on wages and massive privatisation. Today, European unemployment is significantly higher than it was when the Maastricht Treaty was concluded at the end of 1991. Germany alone has seen over three million new people flocking to the unemployment queues.

The convergence criteria were consolidated and further tightened with the Stability and Growth Pact adopted at the June 1997 EU Council in Amsterdam. Under this agreement, EMU members committed to keeping their national budget deficit below 3 per cent of gross domestic product (GDP). If they are unable to meet these conditions, they face heavy fines. Commissioner de Silguy has gone even further, suggesting an additional decrease in the permitted maximum budget deficit to an average of 1.5 per cent of GDP in 1999.[26] The AMUE remains hopeful despite the social upheaval already caused through these structural adjustments. 'The convergence path to EMU seems to have been a painful purgatory to a better life in EMU. Whether paradise is eternal remains to be seen', it comments in a recent report.[27]

Another point of critique has been the EMU's threat to democracy at the national level. With single monetary policy to be decided by the new European Central Bank (ECB),[28] EU member state governments lose some of their most powerful policy tools for reacting to economic downturn. EMU members may not devalue their currencies, adjust interest rates or temporarily allow budget deficits to revitalise the economy. The EMU will be run from the ECB, an unelected and unaccountable body which will follow the rigid inflation-fighting policies of the German Bundesbank.

The AMUE's response to this democratic gap is not exactly reassuring. The organisation argues that this lack of accountability has been approved by elected heads of state, and that the ECB will need full freedom in order to fulfil its task of guaranteeing price stability.[29] When quizzed on this concern for democratic procedures, Viscount Davignon's response proves unequivocal: 'I find it total rubbish.'[30]

Euro 'Side-effects'

European Monetary Union will give a massive boost to the wave of mergers and acquisitions that has swept Europe in the past years as a result of the single market and increasing economic globalisation. In particular, the banking and insurance sectors have been hard hit by merger mania as companies search for larger markets, cuts in costs, advantages of scale and higher profit margins. Weaker competitors are being bought up or crowded out by the new banking and insurance giants. Recent examples are the take-over of the Belgian bank BBL by the Dutch-based ING Group, and the merger of Zurich and BAT, two large insurance companies. Tens of thousands of jobs are expected to be lost, and analysts predict that up to half of the 166,000 bank branches in the EU will be closed. The impacts will not be limited to the financial services sector: in a conservative estimate, the new wave of mergers and corporate downsizing in the European Union as an effect of the single currency could leave one out of every twenty industrial workers unemployed.[31]

Companies that previously organised their operations on a country-by-country basis increasingly operate on a European level. The euro accelerates this process by removing the last barriers – such as the risk of currency fluctuations – in the Single Market. US corporations have also given a warm welcome to the euro, envisioning golden new opportunities to exploit economies of scale in a newly barrier-free market even larger than their own. As Rob Fried of the US-based electronics/arms producing company Allied Signal explains, operating pan-European provides corporations with huge advantages over smaller companies producing for local markets as it 'eliminates expenses across Europe and leads to economies of scale'.[32]

One striking example is Reebok International, the US-based sportswear producer. In 1995, Reebok had 14 distribution warehouses for its European market; in 1998, only 10 were left. By 1 January 1999, when the euro was born, a single distribution centre remained. Today, the entire continent is provided with Reebok products from this central point in the Netherlands.[33] This trend not only leads to job cuts, but also is responsible for an increase in the ecologically-unsound long-distance transport of goods.

Monetary union is also expected to result in ever-fiercer cross-border competition. The euro will make the instant comparison of prices and productivity within the whole euro-zone possible, increasing the trend of relocations to the most competitive areas. The obvious effect will be to intensify competition between countries and regions to attract investments.[34] To quote a Morgan Stanley economist: 'If you remove currency as a safety valve, governments will be forced to focus on real changes to become more competitive: lower taxes, labour market flexibility, and a more favourable regulatory backdrop for business.'[35]

Over the past decade, almost all EU member states have systematically lowered corporate and other taxes to increase their attractiveness to investors (see Chapter 1). It comes as no surprise that captains of industry welcome this as a highly positive development. 'The market forces unleashed by the euro will be felt not just by corporate managers but also by political leaders,' DaimlerChrysler's Jürgen Schrempp explains. 'Elected officials, facing competition as they try to attract the investments that create jobs, will eventually lower corporate tax rates and streamline regulation.'[36] The competition between euro-zone regions to offer the most favourable investment climate will almost inevitably reduce the chances of progressive policies like a shortened working week, ecological tax reform and other measures which involve the protection of people and the environment.

The EMU is very different from the other large single currency zone it is often compared with: the United States. In the US, geographical mobility is much higher than in the EU, which is characterised by significant differences in languages and cultures. Large-scale intra-EU migration of labour from jobless regions to areas with available jobs is difficult to imagine. And unlike the US federal government, the EU does not have the capacity to provide financial support to states experiencing economic problems and high unemployment. This is a serious flaw, as there is little doubt that the single currency will lead to larger regional disparities within the EU. The fiercer competition between regions over the pool of global investments will have winners and losers, and many observers expect that 'less favoured regions' including parts of Spain, Portugal and Greece will become further marginalised. A more equitable distribution of wealth between EU regions would, however, demand far higher contributions from member states to the EU budget.[37]

The debate in early 1999 on European Central Bank (ECB) policies was perhaps the most disturbing example of how the single currency, in combination with economic deregulation, limits the scope for democratic decision making. Social democratic politicians like former German Finance Minister Oskar Lafontaine argued publicly that the ECB should assist in efforts to create more employment by lowering interest rates. ECB President Wim Duisenberg reacted promptly and with great hostility, stating that the ECB was independent and price stability its main mission. He moreover blamed Lafontaine for the weakening exchange rate of the euro compared with the US dollar, arguing that the finance minister's interference had undermined the confidence of financial markets in the new currency.[38]

Thus not only does the ECB operate beyond democratic control, but even a debate about its policies is taboo due to possible retaliation by the financial markets! Economic analysts rightly compare the single currency to a 'Trojan horse'[39]: a sneaky way to wheel in dramatic structural changes causing painful social impacts with minimum opposition from voters and social movements. The negative effects of the EMU will only be fully recognised when it is too late to stop the havoc it has, and will continue to have wreaked on European societies.

Doing Business in Amsterdam: The ERT, UNICE and the Treaty of Amsterdam

In the cold morning hours of 2 October 1997, a group of demonstrators gathered in front of the Royal Palace in central Amsterdam. They shouted Euro-critical slogans at the EU heads of state who emerged one by one from their limousines and were ushered inside for the ceremonial signing of the new Treaty of the European Union. Demonstrators and limos alike lingered until the afternoon, waiting for the EU leaders to re-emerge from the palace. Few noticed the men who hastily exited through a back door and deposited several sealed aluminum containers into a van. The Brussels-bound vehicle with its precious cargo – the signed originals of the Amsterdam Treaty – was escorted by police through the city. With this discreet operation, the secretive birth of the new treaty was drawn to a close.

Both the European Roundtable of Industrialists (ERT, see Chapter 3) and UNICE, the European employers' confederation (see Chapter 4), worked strenuously to influence the revision of the Maastricht Treaty. During the 15-month period of the Intergovernmental Conference (IGC) process, which culminated in the June 1997 EU Summit in Amsterdam, both lobby groups took full advantage of their privileged access to top decision makers. Their demands were quite similar. First, the power of the EU and in particular the role of the Commission should be strengthened, as should its 'ability to act'. Second, the EU should stick to previously-adopted schedules for Economic and Monetary Union and for enlargement towards Central and Eastern Europe. And finally, the treaty revision should avoid integrating new elements, such as environmental and social clauses, which might damage industrial competitiveness. In fact, the resulting treaty is less aggressively oriented towards unification than was its forerunner, a deliberate attempt to avoid the negative public reactions invoked with the signing of the Maastricht Treaty five years previously. None the less, the Treaty of Amsterdam does not stray from the industry-friendly path set out by its predecessor.

The Intergovernmental Conference

The 1991 Maastricht Treaty foretold its own revision in a 'conference of representatives of the governments of the member states'[1] scheduled to start in 1996. In preparation, the European Council set up a Reflection Group in June 1995 to identify the issues upon which the IGC should focus.[2] The group, chaired by then Spanish Secretary of State for EU Relations Carlos Westendorp, presented its final report to the December 1995 meeting of the European Council. The report defined three main goals for the IGC: 'making Europe more relevant to its citizens', 'enabling the Union to work better and preparing it for enlargement' and 'giving the Union greater capacity for external action'.[3]

Despite the professed aim to 'bring the Union closer to its citizens', the IGC, launched in March 1996, was characterised by a definite lack of transparency. At the Amsterdam Summit in June 1997, over 50,000 people demonstrated against unemployment, poverty and social exclusion, issues that they felt were neglected by the EU in the treaty revision process. The message to political leaders was clear: the 20 million unemployed and more than 50 million EU citizens living in poverty was unacceptable. But EU leaders conducted their meetings in a safe cocoon, insulated by thousands of riot police who swept the streets clean of EU opposition with periodic mass arrests. Symbolically, the final negotiations took place at the fortress-like headquarters of the National Bank of the Netherlands, surrounded by cordons of special security police forces.

The NGOs that had dreamt the IGC would turn the EU into a 'social and ecological Europe' had every reason to be disappointed. After extensive horse-trading during the final hours of the Amsterdam Summit, Dutch Prime Minister Wim Kok spoke of successes and improvements in areas like democracy, employment and environment at the final press conference. But a closer look at the Amsterdam Treaty casts serious doubts on Kok's enthusiastic claims. Under the new treaty, the EU will continue more or less along the lines set out in the Maastricht Treaty. Over the past five years, this regime has proved to be extremely beneficial to the corporate lobby crowd. No less than its predecessor, the new treaty welcomes and facilitates corporate demands for further cuts in public expenditure, deregulation, privatisation, expansion of infrastructure, global trade liberalisation and so forth. And in some areas, the Amsterdam Treaty is even more accommodating to industry, thanks to ambitious lobby campaigns waged during the IGC negotiations by the European Roundtable of Industrialists (ERT) and the European employers' federation UNICE.

The Elite Troops

The ERT ensured that decision makers at both the European and national levels were well aware of its priorities for the IGC. According to former Secretary-General Keith Richardson, the Roundtable's contribution to

Figure 2   50,000 demonstrate against unemployment and social exclusion during the EU Summit in Amsterdam, June 1997. (Photo: Ferd Crone/*Trouw*)

the IGC was 'to meet politicians and government officials, and simply encourage them to move forward'.[4] The ERT has been efficient and methodical in its lobbying: 'We try to see every government that deals with the European presidency,' explained Richardson at the beginning of 1997. 'For example, we met and talked to Wim Kok early on this year because he's got the presidency.' Other governments were also treated to explanations of industry's perspective: 'We've talked to the Spaniards, the Italians, the Irish, the Dutch, and we've talked to the Germans and the French because they are lead players.'[5]

The ERT sowed the seeds for corporate involvement in the treaty revision at an early stage in the IGC process. Well before the start of negotiations, it had already set up a special IGC working group, chaired by Nestlé CEO Helmut Maucher.[6] Maucher succeeded in meeting with Reflection Group chair Carlos Westendorp while the group was still preparing its report to the European Council. In May 1995, an ERT delegation met with then German Chancellor Helmut Kohl to discuss a position paper produced by the IGC working group. 'All kinds of meetings have taken place, quite a lot of them at a very high level,' according to Richardson. 'Part of the ERT success is that all of these people [ERT members] are engaged in discussions independently all the time; they are all meeting their own governments, newspaper editors, industrial federations. I meet a lot of people in Brussels, and I convey these messages in my way. So a lot of communication has taken place on the subject of the IGC.'[7] Keith Richardson explains the reason for this special treatment granted to ERT members: 'What we've got to offer is that if Wim Kok meets the ERT, he meets with five or six company chairmen. And they talk with a certain personal authority.'[8]

A Host of Bureaucrats

With this sort of unfettered access, the ERT has a distinct advantage over the less high-profile UNICE, whose interests are represented by officials from national employers' organisations. None the less, the group's strategies to influence the IGC also reached ears at every level of the European decision-making hierarchy. 'We will make approaches to whoever is presiding over the Intergovernmental Conference,' explained then Secretary-General Zygmunt Tyszkiewicz in early 1997. 'At the moment it's the Dutch. Before that it was the Irish. In the second half of the year it will be the Luxembourg government ... Each of our member federations is talking to its own representative to the Intergovernmental Conference on the basis of the policies that we devise here.'[9]

As usual, UNICE's lobbying strategy also included deluging key IGC figures with letters and position papers. A September 1996 letter from UNICE President François Perigot to then Irish President of the European

Council John Bruton, for example, summed up UNICE's wish list for the treaty revision and requested a meeting before the upcoming extra European Council meeting in Dublin.[10] Copies of this letter were sent to all EU heads of state, the Commission President and MEPs.

Getting the Structure Right

One of the main official goals of the IGC was a thorough revision of voting procedures and national representation in EU institutions in order to prepare for the accession of new member states. Such an institutional reform was also among the demands posed by both UNICE and the ERT, not only to facilitate the enlargement process but as 'a better way of managing Europe'.[11] They lobbied for more efficient institutions (more power for the Commission and qualified majority voting in the Council 'so that essential decisions are not delayed')[12] and simplified procedures for the Parliament, 'especially as regards co-decision'.[13] Industry made no secret of its view that the institutional legacy of Maastricht was an impediment to the competitiveness of Europe as a whole. 'We feel very strongly that Europe cannot move at the pace of the slowest,' stressed Richardson. 'The United States could do nothing if every decision had to be ratified by 52 states.'[14]

In fact, institutional reform was by far the most controversial point during the negotiations, and significantly fewer structural changes in the EU were adopted than had been anticipated. Although the Council of Ministers' mandate to vote by qualified majority was extended in a number of fields,[15] these did not include the areas in which such voting and the corresponding co-decision procedure could have made a substantial difference (for example taxation, including environmental taxes). However, the European Parliament's powers were somewhat strengthened with the expansion of the co-decision procedure to a number of new fields.[16] Industry was particularly pleased with the greater power granted to the president of the Commission, which according to Keith Richardson will 'minimise that lack of coherence within the Commission which makes life so difficult for industry'.[17]

Completing the Single Market

Protecting as well as perfecting the EU internal market has long been an obsession of the business lobby, and both UNICE and the ERT predictably stressed this point during the IGC negotiations. UNICE, for example, proposed a new deadline of 1 January 1999 for the liberalisation of public procurement and the energy, transport and telecommunications markets, as well as for the implementation of Trans-European Networks (see Chapter 8) and the elimination of tax barriers. In a position paper for the IGC, the group stressed that 'all temptations to legalise new trade barriers, *inter alia* for environmental reasons, should be resisted'.[18]

Again, both corporate lobby groups can be content with the outcome. The Amsterdam Summit approved the Single Market Action Plan, which was proposed by the Commission after intensive consultations with industry groups. The Action Plan proposed the opening of a number of new fields – including energy, transport, telecommunications and patent protection for biotechnology products – to full EU-wide competition before 1999. One and a half years later, most of the objectives of the Single Market Action Plan have been attained. A February 1999 Commission press release proudly announced that the percentage of Single Market directives not yet implemented in all member states had been reduced from 35 to 13.9 per cent. Furthermore, directives on the removal of barriers to electronic commerce, the protection of biotechnology inventions, and liberalisation of the gas sector were adopted in the post-Amsterdam period.[19]

Competitiveness, Jobs and the Environment

According to former Secretary-General Richardson, increasing European competitiveness was a prime reason for the ERT's interest in IGC proceedings: 'The way in which Europe is managed is an important issue for business. We have to compete all over the world, and we are tremendously concerned about the competitiveness of Europe. In that sense, the IGC is not just a private game for politicians.'[20] UNICE shared the same concern. 'It is extremely disappointing that up to now, UNICE's principal policy recommendation to include competitiveness among the objectives of the European Union appears to have been ignored,' explained Tyszkiewicz. 'As a result, the balance between economic and social objectives in the Treaty is at risk of being upset.'[21] UNICE even went so far as to propose mandatory impact assessments of the effects of every EU proposal, directive and regulation on the competitiveness of European industry.

From UNICE's perspective, threats to competitiveness include public policies on job creation, social security, environment and workers' rights. Indeed, the inclusion of a chapter on employment in the Treaty made UNICE nervous, and the mention of workers' rights aroused violent reactions: 'UNICE most strongly opposes inclusion of the Social Charter or of a set of basic social rights in the Treaty, as well as the suggestion that the Union should accede to the European Convention on Human Rights and fundamental freedoms.'[22]

The ERT's attitude was more laid back. Richardson was not bothered by the idea of an employment chapter that would be 'a large waste of time ... If politicians feel it is important to get a chapter referring to the desirability of full employment, and if they think that will help with public opinion we don't really object ... It won't help jobs, but it won't do much damage – provided of course that it remains in general terms, related to aspirations.'[23] Such cynicism can be explained by the Roundtable's access to top politicians: 'Enough people in government have now understood that the chapter is relatively meaningless. Several Prime Ministers have commented that writing a chapter in the treaty will not create jobs.'[24] What alarmed the ERT more, however, was a request by the environmental movement that environmental issues be integrated into every chapter of the treaty. 'This is really damaging,' said Richardson. 'If you write environment into every chapter of the treaty, you might as well write everything else into every chapter of the treaty ... I think they are asking for too much.'[25]

In the end, the new Treaty did introduce a chapter on employment, but there was no need for corporate fretting as the concluding statement of the Amsterdam Summit recommends that 'more attention be given to improving European competitiveness as a prerequisite for growth and employment.'[26] Not surprisingly, the Employment Chapter included in the new treaty has been criticised by the large trade unions assembled in the European Trade Union Confederation (ETUC) for being 'too limited in scope' and only paying lip service to tackling unemployment problems.[27]

Instead, the focus in the Employment Chapter is on creating flexible 'McJobs' which offer little security to workers. EU governments agreed to 'work towards developing a coordinated strategy for employment and particularly for promoting a skilled, trained and adaptable workforce and labour markets responsive to economic change'.[28] While the need for competitiveness, completion of the Single Market and economic growth are stressed, no concrete actions for job creation are outlined, nor are sanctions proposed for governments not living up to the commitments of the chapter.

UNICE was quite satisfied with this outcome. As Tyszkiewicz summed up: 'We never wanted an Employment Chapter in the first place, but if we have to have one, then this version is not too bad.'[29] He even went so far to suggest that the new Article 3.2, which states that 'employment shall be taken into consideration in the formulation and implementation of Community policies and activities', could act as 'a brake on initiatives that hurt European competitiveness, such as proposals to increase energy taxes ... if applied properly.'[30]

In its IGC position papers, the ERT used job creation as the carrot in its enticements for competitiveness. The Amsterdam Council faithfully adopted the highly questionable link made by the corporate lobby between the elements of competitiveness (deregulation, liberalisation and growth) and job creation. The member states are instructed to 'promote a skilled and adaptable workforce and flexible labour markets responsive to economic change' so that the EU can 'remain globally competitive'. Moreover, the European Council recommends a 'reduction in the overall tax burden' and 'a restrictive restructuring of public expenditure' to 'encourage investment in human capital, research and development, innovation and the infrastructure essential to competitiveness'. Furthermore, the Council encourages 'training and lifelong learning' in order to improve 'the employability of workers'.[31] All to the benefit of corporate Europe, and to the detriment of the worker seeking job security. The ERT's Richardson was understandably satisfied with the focus of the Amsterdam Summit: 'They talked about employment, the top political issue, with a clear focus on the right policies – competitiveness, innovation, employability and flexible labour markets.'[32]

International competitiveness is therefore more clearly than ever inscribed in the EU's constitution as the key to employment and welfare in Europe. Scant attention is paid to the risk that ever-increasing global competition poses to job security, social protection, environmental legislation and many other crucial areas. The environmental movement's success in having sustainable development included as an official EU objective to be integrated in all policies is consequently undermined.

New Markets in the East

Both the ERT and UNICE lobbied vigorously for the speedy enlargement of the EU towards the East. Western Europe-based corporations regard Central and Eastern European (CEE) countries as an enormous market waiting to be conquered, as well as a reservoir of highly skilled and cheap labour. According to the ERT, enlargement is fundamental: 'It will bring great economic benefits. These countries will bring new people, a lot of skills, technology, education, know-how. They will bring material resources including land and energy, and they will bring markets for our products.'[33] UNICE is no less enthusiastic about the potential for profit. 'In the West we have mature markets,' explains Tyszkiewicz. 'We are already consuming everything that we are able to consume. You cannot drive two cars at the same time. So we have a slow growth economy ... To the East of us, we have around a hundred million people with sophisticated tastes who lack all the items that we are already consuming. They need those items.'[34]

Both lobby groups, however, insist that CEE countries undergo stringent structural adjustment prior to accession. National economic policies must be harmonised with those set by the Union, and markets must be fully opened to Western goods, services and investments. In other words, governments are expected to relinquish control over their economies, a death knell for local businesses.

Although the Amsterdam Treaty didn't accomplish all of the institutional reforms needed for EU expansion eastwards, enlargement was put firmly on the agenda soon after the Amsterdam Summit with the Commission's presentation of the so-called Agenda 2000 proposal to the Council and Parliament. Agenda 2000 was officially adopted by the European Council during a special summit in Berlin in March 1999. Negotiations with the first wave of candidate countries – Poland, Hungary, the Czech Republic, Estonia and Cyprus – had already been set in motion a year earlier. These countries are now busy bringing their legislation in sync with Single Market requirements, thus fulfilling the business groups' main objective: a harmonised market and liberalised investment regime for the whole of the European continent.

Speaking with One Voice

Corporate Europe liked the way the Uruguay Round of the GATT was handled, with the European Commission negotiating on behalf of all 15 member states, and proposed that an increased use of this type of bloc bargaining be mandated in the new treaty. The ERT claimed that 'the IGC should equip the EU with a strong and unified voice on all matters of external economic relations ... The all-important Common Commercial Policy should be extended to ensure unified negotiating positions on all external commercial issues, including trade in services, investment and the protection of intellectual property'.[35] UNICE strongly supported the extension of the scope of Article 133 of the Maastricht Treaty, which gives the EU Commission competence to negotiate on behalf of the member states in matters concerning international trade in goods. This, they felt, would allow industry and the EU to operate more effectively within the trading system set up by the World Trade Organization.

These corporate sentiments were echoed in the draft treaty prepared by the Irish presidency for the Dublin Summit in December 1996. The document proposed that the scope of Article 133 be extended to trade in services, intellectual property and public procurement. Industry lobby groups could also be quite content with the letter that Commission President Jacques Santer sent to heads of state and government just days before the Amsterdam Summit. In that letter, Santer supported the kind of changes to Article 133 that industry had been lobbying for, warning that 'any further weakening would cause it to lose all meaning and would even be counterproductive.'[36]

Yet in the end, the Summit fell short of fulfilling the Article 133 ambitions of both the European Commission and the corporate lobby. Due to national resistance against the proposed changes, notably by French President Jacques Chirac, deals made by the EU in the previously mentioned areas must still be ratified by the Council of Ministers and by all 15 EU countries.[37] The fact that the Council of Ministers is now given the opportunity to transfer national sovereignty over international trade negotiations on services and intellectual property rights to the European Commission without having to undergo a new treaty revision is not enough for the ambitious industry groups. As Keith Richardson explained, 'Europe is poorer and weaker because of this failure.'[38]

Corporate Europe on the Amsterdam Treaty

The Amsterdam Treaty was negotiated at a time when the accomplishment of Economic and Monetary Union (EMU) was an absolute priority for the EU. Many national governments found themselves under significant pressure at home due to the massive cuts in social expenditures required to fulfil EMU criteria. Thus, a new treaty that would provoke public controversy and jeopardise ratification had to be avoided at all costs.[39] Despite gains in several areas, corporate lobby groups were disappointed by the treaty's failure to deliver the desired changes both in institutional reform and in the Commission's powers in external trade matters.

'A mixed result, but generally positive', was UNICE's preliminary conclusion directly following the conclusion of the Amsterdam Summit.[40] However, UNICE Communications Director Christophe de Callatäy was later more sceptical: 'We have to be politically correct. We have to say in a public statement that it is a step in the right direction, but there is still much progress to be made and so on. [We need] diplomatic language which hides the fact that it was not much, nothing new after Maastricht.'[41] Former ERT Secretary-General Keith Richardson welcomed the progress made at the Amsterdam Summit, but noted that the IGC had failed to deliver on 'the real need for reform'. He explained: 'The EU economy is in many ways as strong as the American, but we lose out in Europe because our economic structures are still too fragmented and our political system is slow to take decisions and stubbornly resistant to innovation.'[42]

Since the 1991 Gulf War, the ERT has increased its campaign to strengthen the EU's foreign policy powers and for the creation of joint EU military forces by arguing that the Union should be able to defend the global interests of European business.[43] Richardson was therefore disappointed by the 'little progress towards a unified foreign policy to protect Europe's overseas interest, and none at all towards the integrated defence which we need if we are to preserve competitive defence industries'.[44] Industry is surely looking forward to the next IGC to deal with this unfinished business.

Oiling the Wheels: Lobbying for European Transport Infrastructure

My objective ... is to implement the Trans-European Transport Networks, and their extensions in Central and Eastern Europe, as quickly as possible in order to ensure that we have a European transport system that can properly serve the European Single Market in a sustainable way.

EU Transport Commissioner Neil Kinnock at the 'Bridging Gaps in Financing Infrastructure' conference in Amsterdam, 31 March 1998.

With a total estimated budget of 400 billion euros, the Trans-European Networks (TENs) are the largest transport infrastructure programme in the history of the world. The more than 150 projects planned for construction by the year 2010 include thousands of kilometres of new motorways, high-speed passenger train links, freight railway lines, airport extensions and waterways. To date, the vast majority of these mega-projects have been completed or are under construction.[1]

The European Commission acts as a booster and provides strategic funding for this megalomaniac masterplan. In the last few years, the expansion of the TENs to Central and Eastern Europe (CEE) has become a major priority for the EU. To facilitate the predicted four or fivefold increase in freight transport on international East–West routes, it has reserved some 15 billion euro from various EU funds for the construction of new transport infrastructure in CEE in the period between 2000 and 2006.[2]

TENs construction proceeds despite the current growth of traffic – and particularly road traffic – far beyond ecologically sustainable limits in all countries of the European Union. Between 1985 and 1995, the amount of the greenhouse gas CO_2 generated by road transport grew by nearly one-third. Environmental non-governmental organisations (NGOs) predict that the TENs projects will cause severe environmental damage all over Europe, including the destruction of more than 60 important nature sites. Greenpeace has estimated that the construction of TENs will result in a 15–18 per cent increase in greenhouse gas emissions from the transport sector.[3]

Making the Blueprint

The European Roundtable of Industrialists (ERT, see Chapter 3) was instrumental in putting the expansion of large-scale investments in motorways, high-speed trains and other Europe-wide transport infrastructure on the European Union's political agenda. As early as 1984, its *Missing Links* report criticised the existing 'underdeveloped' crossborder infrastructure network as a 'barrier to European economic and social progress'. A 'Scan-Link' bridge and motorway project linking Germany, Denmark and Sweden, high-speed trans-European rail links and the Channel tunnel were pinpointed as crucial lacunae in European transport infrastructure. In a subsequent document, *Missing Networks*, the ERT stressed the urgency of new roads through the 'Alpine and Pyrenean barrier and to Eastern Europe'.[4]

Many ERT corporations have a direct interest in the continued growth of transport in Europe. The attraction is obvious for oil companies like British Petroleum, Petrofina, Shell and Total; car producers such as DaimlerChrysler, Fiat and Renault; companies producing electronics and other parts for the car industry including Pirelli and Pilkington; high-speed train construction firms including Siemens and ABB; and road-building companies like Titan Cement. Moreover, the construction and improvement of European transport infrastructure enables transnational corporations (TNCs) to restructure their production on a European scale. Faster transport infrastructure, especially motorways, is also a condition for new flexible 'lean production' systems. Favoured by TNCs in the 1980s and 1990s, these systems rely on 'just-in-time' production by specialised subcontractors based on the immediate requirements of the market.

The ERT has been astonishingly successful in building political support for its vision of the development of European transport. In 1985, Volvo CEO Pehr Gyllenhammar boasted to his ERT colleagues that the European transport ministers were 'referring to *Missing Links* as the masterplan for European infrastructure'.[5] Close cooperation between the ERT and the European Commission was instrumental in placing TENs on the political agenda. The Commission funded many ERT activities on transport issues, including the ERT's 1989 study *The Need for Renewing Transport Infrastructure in Europe*. The ERT was also directly involved in the detailed shaping of TENs through its participation in the official

Motorway Working Group, which put together the formidable list of Trans-European Roads Network (TERN) projects.

Terrible TENs

In 1991, the European Commission presented its plans for 12,000 kilometres of new motorways in Europe as part of the overall TENs scheme. Later that year, a commitment to construct the Trans-European Networks (including high-speed trains, waterways and airports) was written into the Maastricht Treaty. The TENs chapter of the Treaty contained no reference to the enormous environmental damage that such a massive expansion of transport infrastructure would necessarily entail.

The guidelines for Trans-European Networks first came up for discussion in the European Parliament only in 1995. Although the environmental movement had lobbied the European Parliament extensively in order to draw attention to the ecological devastation associated with the adoption of the TENs, the few of its demands that were met were heavily watered down. For example, although an overall Strategic Environmental Impact Assessment (SEIA) for the whole TENs scheme was included in the 1996 guidelines, construction of projects can begin long before its completion. Three years down the road, whereas TENs construction is well underway, work on the SEIA has hardly begun.

Although TENs were adopted as an official EU policy objective in the 1991 Maastricht Treaty, the ERT continued to obsess about the relaxed speed at which the plans were implemented. It repeatedly encouraged EU leaders to 'accelerate the construction of Trans-European infrastructure networks – with greater political determination' and 'a commitment to more resources'.[6] As always, when the ERT speaks, governments sit up and take notice. When the Roundtable called for additional funding for TENs in a letter sent to heads of state and government prior to the 1992 EU Summit in Edinburgh, leaders promptly agreed to set up a special investment fund of seven billion euros.

ECIS is Born

After 1993, the ERT transferred most of its activities in the area of transport to its infrastructure institute ECIS, the European Centre for Infrastructure Studies. 'We do not do so much work on infrastructure any more,' explained then ERT Secretary-General Keith Richardson in 1997:

> Everything that we could say, we had said: that Europe needs a better infrastructure. A lot of that is being done. On the whole, we have

transferred our interests to an organization called ECIS ... They do a lot of good work. But a lot of this is now in detail. I think the issue in principle is there. The Channel Tunnel has been built, the high-speed trains are being built, the crossing from Scandinavia to Denmark is being built ...[7]

The idea of setting up a new organisation that could speed up TENs construction was launched at a June 1992 ERT conference in Lisbon. According to ECIS founder Umberto Agnelli of Fiat, 'there was an immediate surge of support from the international audience of decision makers, which included representatives from all twelve EC governments, European transport and research associations, industry and – not least – from several members of the European Commission.'[8] Encouraged by this positive response, Agnelli began to hand-pick the members of this new ERT offshoot in the autumn of 1993. By early 1994, a secretariat had been opened in Rotterdam, the Netherlands.[9] ECIS membership included regional and national governments, municipalities, EU institutions, research institutes, banks and corporations.[10]

ECIS Gets Busy

The remaining barriers to the fulfilment of the ERT's infrastructure ambitions were now mainly financial and technical. For a couple of productive years, the European Commission and ECIS worked in tandem to remove these hurdles. ECIS, for example, prepared studies on behalf of the Commission and organised conferences 'to educate Commission officials' and others.[11] Following the endorsement of the Delors White Paper on Growth, Competitiveness and Employment by heads of state in December 1993, TENs moved into the fast lane. The Commission gave its Christophersen Working Group[12] the mandate to identify a list of priority projects and to find solutions for potential obstacles to speedy construction of the projects.

ECIS was of great assistance in this process. For example, it proposed that a 'single agent' with the authority to raise private capital and press for project implementation be set up for each transborder scheme.[13] The next year, 'encouraged by the European Commission'[14], a semi-official High Level Panel on Private Finance was established. Chaired by ECIS founder Umberto Agnelli and board member Sir Alistair Morton, the Panel's mission was to present proposals to the decisive EU Summit in Essen in December 1994.[15]

Meanwhile, the Christophersen Group had concluded that the 'regulatory framework' of decision making in the EU was 'a major delaying factor'[16] for TENs projects. Subsequently, the Commission asked ECIS to organise a workshop on these decision-making bottlenecks. At this 1994 workshop in Rotterdam, 'representatives from the private sector, member states and EU organizations examined ideas which could accelerate the implementation of TEN projects.'[17] The helping hand of ECIS during this period was not in vain: at the December 1994 Essen Summit, EU leaders allocated substantial new funds for TENs and endorsed the ECIS proposals for public-private partnerships and 'single agents' for crossborder projects. Both principles are used today in the implementation of TENs projects.

Economic Benefits?

The next major success for ECIS, and a classic example of its close rapport with the European Commission, was executed in late 1995. In December of that year, Transport Commissioner Neil Kinnock presented a study on the economic advantages of the PBKAL high-speed train network (which includes the Amsterdam–Paris and Brussels–Cologne lines).[18] Based on the report, he informed the media that these high-speed train links, and indeed the TENs in general, would bring about much higher economic growth than was commonly assumed. The author of this report, *Lost and Found: the Community Component of the Economic Return on the Investment in PBKAL*, was none other than Dr Dana Roy from ECIS.[19] Not one journalist seems to have investigated which 'independent' research institute came to these optimistic conclusions. In November 1996, ECIS published another report, *The Macroeconomic Effects of the PBKAL*. This report was again written upon the request of the Commission, which used it to promote investments in TENs. Both the Commission's special report to the European Parliament on job creation through TENs[20] and its 1996 report on TENs relied heavily upon this ECIS study.

Exit ECIS, Enter the Infrastructure Choir

In 1997, ECIS entered troubled waters, as funding from both the European Commission and industry dried up. At the end of the year, it announced its closure,[21] but the departure of ECIS by no means silenced the European infrastructure choir.

For instance, the European Construction Industry Federation (FIEC) launched an offensive in 1997 to increase investments by EU member states in TENs.[22] FIEC feared that the race to meet EMU criteria would slow down investments in European infrastructure, and its chairman Ioannis Papaioannou warned European politicians that Europe would lose out in global competition if TENs coffers were not replenished. The organisation also pleaded for greater opportunities to be provided for 'private corporations investing in roads, bridges and tunnels'. FIEC clearly lacks the subtlety of ECIS, which used a neutral, scientific style when presenting its infrastructure demands. Whereas a number of ECIS proposals became official EU policy, FIEC's blunt approach has thus far failed to make great inroads on the EU agenda.

Also in 1997, the lobby for speedier construction of the many remaining TENs projects was stepped up with the foundation of the European Construction Forum. This new coalition of European infrastructure companies announced 'a more powerful and coordinated approach' towards European infrastructure projects and was 'warmly welcomed by commissioner Kinnock'.[23] The newest actor on the block is the European Coalition for Sustainable Transport (ECST), an umbrella group led by the aggressive International Road Federation (IRF).[24] Despite its 'green'-sounding name, ECST proclaims that road transport is the most sustainable form of mobility.

In contrast to ECIS and the FIEC, the IRF and its new Brussels branch, the European Road Federation (ERF), lobby only for more motorways. The European Road Federation clearly envies the generous funds that have been allocated to high-speed trains and other rail links. Its first deed was to 'call for pro-road revisions to the Trans-European Network Guidelines' in order to achieve a further 'extension of the trans-European road network'.[25] In an interview with the *European Voice*, IRF Director-General Wim Westerhuis urged the EU and its member states to follow the example of the US government, which recently raised the federal road building budget by 38 per cent. 'There is a profound lesson for European politicians flowing from this US decision,' observed Westerhuis.[26]

In his crusade to raise more funds for the TENs, Transport Commissioner Neil Kinnock actively solicited the assistance of the transport and infrastructure lobby. 'It would help if business organisations – many of which have been very supportive – could make their voices heard more clearly,' Kinnock stated in one of his many complaints about the reluctance of member states to provide additional TENs funding.[27] In 1998, in order to complete the transport network by the 2010 deadline, Kinnock proposed that EU governments double the TENs budget to 5 billion euros between 2000 and 2006.[28] Kinnock also hopes to raise additional money from private sources through the creation of the so-called public-private partnerships originally proposed by ECIS.[29]

TENs: the EU Job Machine?

Both the European Commission and the infrastructure lobby have likely welcomed the signals coming from some of the new social democrat governments within the EU. In 1998, the Italian, German and French governments all called for more government spending on TENs, using the job creation argument. In November of that year, German Finance

Minister Oskar Lafontaine and Italian Prime Minister Massimo D'Alema called for a relaxation of EMU budget criteria, for example recommending the exclusion of public investment spending on transport infrastructure.[30] However, this proposal was instantly rejected by the European Central Bank, Finance Commissioner Yves-Thibault de Silguy and other monetarists.

The European Parliament has also repeatedly called upon member state governments to increase their investments in infrastructure. In October 1998, MEPs called upon governments to devote at least 1.5 per cent of their total budget resources to the TENs. Again, the argument was 'the multiplier effect of such investment for the economy and jobs'.[31]

Since their adoption, TENs have featured prominently in the EU's job creation initiatives, including the 1993 Delors White Paper on Growth, Competitiveness and Employment and Santer's 1996 Confidence Pact for Employment. Apart from the immediate employment generated by pumping billions of euros into the building of infrastructure, the EU claims that the more indirect stimulation of crossborder trade will also create hoards of jobs. In its 1996 Annual Report, the European Commission published estimates of the employment effects of TENs, claiming that the 14 priority projects would generate between 130,000 and 230,000 jobs and that the entire TENs masterplan would create between 594,000 and 1,030,000 new jobs in Europe. However, as these figures were to a large extent based upon ECIS calculations, their objectivity must be seriously questioned.

The environmental movement has challenged the EU's faith in TENs as a job creator as being based on flawed assumptions. The report *Roads and the Economy*, published in 1996 by the European Federation for Transport and Environment (T&E), summarises the academic discussion and concludes that 'the assumption that road building generates long term employment cannot be justified on the basis of available evidence and research'.[32]

This critique was supported by the highly-publicised 1998 report of the UK government's Standing Advisory Committee on Trunk Road Assessment (SACTRA). SACTRA explicitly criticised the European Commission's figures, stating that it was 'unpersuaded' by the claims that the construction of TENs would create many jobs. In particular, SACTRA challenged the claim that TENs would support the economic development of peripheral regions. 'While in certain circumstances transport schemes may bring added economic benefits to an area needing regeneration, in other circumstances the opposite might occur,' SACTRA concluded.[33]

Such critique however did not impress the European Commission. In a report on the implementation of TENs published in late 1998, the Commission repeated its earlier job creation claims for TENs, arguing that the infrastructure networks are 'vital for EU competitiveness'.[34]

Is there any truth to the assertion that a more smoothly functioning Single Market will create new jobs? Does shifting goods from one corner of the continent to the other increase employment? In fact, the connection between increased transport and new jobs is murky at best. For example, the number of lorry kilometres driven in the EU grew by 30 per cent between 1991 and 1996; meanwhile, unemployment increased at the same rate. Infrastructure projects for fast long-distance transport – in particular motorways and high-speed rail links – generally facilitate further centralisation of production. The TENs provide the largest corporations with easy access to markets in every corner of Europe, thereby strengthening their grip over the European economy. The loss of numerous 'local' jobs with 'less efficient' small producers all over Europe is the negative side of this centralisation process.

It should also be pointed out that if the entire TENs budget were made available for investments in local public transport and housing in cities, towns and rural areas, and for work in the fields of health care and education, many more jobs could be created. At the same time, the environment would be spared and local economies would be strengthened. Unfortunately, such a logical and rational solution has not been considered by EU institutions.

The Alpine Barrier

Just how sacred the free movement of goods is for the European Union became clear in the conflict with non-member state Switzerland about lorry transit from EU countries. In a 1994 national referendum on the protection of the Alpine area against transit traffic, the Swiss voted that all freight crossing the country must go by rail beginning in the year 2004. To achieve this goal, the government planned to impose high levies on freight lorries wishing to pass through Switzerland. These policies were supported by the outcome of another referendum in the autumn of 1998.

The EU strongly objected to these restrictions upon freight transit. It put the Swiss government under heavy pressure to review its policies, for example by threatening to block six trade agreements between the EU and Switzerland that were then under negotiation. Dutch Transport Minister Annemarie Jorritsma even threatened to withhold landing rights for SwissAir if the country stuck to its position. In December 1998, the Swiss government finally caved in, increasing the number of heavy lorries from EU countries allowed to cross the country (from 250,000 in 2000 to 400,000 by 2003), granting unlimited access for lighter lorries beginning in 2001, and charging a maximum toll of 200 euros per trip, far below the planned 350 euros.

However, Swiss environmental groups strongly objected to this deal, and the final agreement may still be rejected by the Swiss population in a new referendum. A recent European Commission study predicts that freight transport across the Alps will increase by 75 per cent between 1992 and 2010. Public resentment and anger is also growing within EU member states located in the ecologically vulnerable Alpine region with the upsurge in lorries passing through narrow valleys and the building of new infrastructure to accommodate the traffic. In June 1998, protesters peacefully blocked the Brenner motorway through the Austrian Tirol region. A month later, the Mont Blanc tunnel in Chamonix, France was blocked by local groups.[35]

The Auto-Oil Programme

Instead of addressing the relentless growth in transport volumes, the EU has set its hopes on repairing some of the damage with technological improvements. The Auto-Oil Programme, for instance, aims to reduce air pollution by setting tougher standards for automobiles and fuels. In fact, the programme was created in collaboration with industry, and attempts to make it more stringent were in part repelled by massive industry lobbying.

Work on the Auto-Oil Programme began in 1993 with three years of consultation between the European Commission and the auto and oil industries to agree on 'the most cost-effective' measures of pollution reduction. Member state governments and NGOs criticised this approach as well as the resulting proposal of June 1996, which was clearly biased towards the interests of the oil industry in particular. NGOs pointed out that the calculations of 'cost-effectiveness' were not reliable, as the cost estimates were supplied by the oil and car industries themselves. According to the Commission proposal, substantial levels of sulphur, benzene and other pollutants would still be allowed in petrol and diesel until 2005, and reductions would begin only in 2010.

Both the Council of Ministers and the European Parliament rejected the Commission's proposal as too weak, much to the surprise of the oil industry which immediately started a massive lobbying offensive to prevent the tightening of the minimum standards for fuel. The assault was led by EUROPIA, a lobby group representing 29 oil companies operating in Europe, and its dramatic warnings that the proposed standards would mean the end of oil refining in Europe had an impact on several national governments.[36]

In the first half of 1998, the Commission presented a revised version of the Auto-Oil Programme to the Council and Parliament. This time, the UK government, which at that time held the presidency of the EU, received special attention from EUROPIA. The oil industry claimed that the revised proposal would be far too expensive, and threatened to close all refineries in the UK. Although these threats were later shown to have been invented solely for the purpose of manipulation, they did incite Labour MPs from constituencies with refineries (for instance the area surrounding the Elf refinery in South Wales) to lobby the Blair government to accept the original Commission proposal.[37] In the end, the Council accepted a weak, industry-friendly Auto-Oil Programme.

The European Parliament, which had veto power on this issue,[38] was less impressed by EUROPIA's lobbying campaign. In a report drawn up by Finnish MEP Heidi Hautala, the Parliament accused the oil industry of greatly exaggerating the costs of introducing cleaner technology. The Parliament's calls for much tougher standards led to a conflict with the Council of Ministers, and a compromise was reached only after a three-month conciliation procedure. The 2005 deadline for improved fuel standards was made obligatory rather than merely indicative, but the Parliament ultimately accepted the less stringent standards proposed by the Council of Ministers.[39] The Auto-Oil Programme, which also bans leaded petrol in most EU countries beginning in 2000, could in the most optimistic scenario halve automobile air pollution per kilometre. But if nothing is done to prevent the anticipated doubling of traffic volumes within the next 15 to 20 years, air quality will still be a dire problem in the next century.

Dealing with CO_2

The Auto-Oil Programme includes no standards for CO_2 emissions from cars. Instead, in the summer of 1998, the European Commission made a voluntary agreement with European car industry representatives gathered under the umbrella of ACEA (the European Automobile Manufacturers Association) to reduce average CO_2 emissions for new cars. Whereas Commissioner for Environment Ritt Bjerregaard claimed to be 'very pleased with this agreement',[40] environmental NGOs called it 'a setback for efforts to combat global warming'.[41] Critics pointed out that pressure from the car industry had forced the Commission to lower the CO_2 emissions reduction target, and that the agreement between the Commission and ACEA was not binding for the individual car-producing companies. The watery agreement means that there will be no new legislation in this field until 2008, even if the car industry fails to live up to the agreed targets.

The deal with ACEA is a major pillar in the Commission's promise to halve the expected growth of CO_2 emissions from transport by 2010. Other elements are the promotion of intermodal transport systems and 'fair and efficient pricing', which sounds like ecological taxes but will likely entail the funding of future infrastructure expansion through road tolls.[42] Finally, reducing CO_2 emissions by increasing freight transport by rail[43] is used by the Commission as an argument for the further privatisation of railway companies and the introduction of Europe-wide competition – 'completing the internal market in rail transport' – a policy which has met with opposition in many EU member states.[44]

With the Amsterdam Treaty, the EU committed to integrating environmental concerns into all Union policies. It remains to be seen whether EU transport ministers dare to break the taboo of curbing the growth in transport volumes. Instead, they may simply continue to facilitate the transport boom, only partially compensating for the growing damage through cleaner technology. Unfortunately, recent history shows that the influence of vested corporate interests upon both the Commission and the Council of Ministers makes a revolution in EU transport policies highly unlikely.

Forcefeeding Europe: The Biotech Lobby

Despite the opposition of a majority of Europeans, biotechnology corporations have been permitted to inundate the EU market with an alarming number of genetically modified (GM) products over recent years. The pro-biotechnology position of the European Commission, without doubt influenced by its friendly rapport with corporate coalitions like EuropaBio, has been a key factor in this process. In 1998, following a corporate lobby effort that broke financial records, the biotech industry achieved its biggest victory to date with the European Parliament's approval of a directive allowing the patenting of life forms. The tide, however, may now be turning. The Life Patents Directive has been challenged in the European Court of Justice; persistent consumer resistance has forced several EU countries to ban GM products, and there is increasing pressure for an EU-wide moratorium on Genetically-Modified Organisms (GMOs).

Biotechnology is arguably one of the most contentious issues in Europe today. Its proponents contend that it is the beginning of a 'biological revolution' that will vastly improve our way of life as the industrial revolution did at the turn of the century. Critics, on the other hand, believe that the perceived benefits of biotechnology are outweighed by the potential risks posed to people and the environment through genetic modification and the ownership of life through patenting. One thing is clear: the vast majority of Europeans are deeply distrustful of this technology, and support a tight legislative regime for biotechnology. In a 1998 survey published by the European Commission, 61 per cent of those polled believed that biotechnology posed risks and could result in dangerous new diseases. According to the surveyors, these fears were not necessarily based on ignorance about the issues: 'It is rather the case that those who are the most ignorant on the subject tend to be less concerned. Being more informed does not necessarily mean being less worried.'[1] A recent Eurobarometer poll showed that only 5 per cent of the population has full confidence in the biotech industry.[2]

The self-termed 'life sciences' industry, however, sees things differently and is pushing hard on many fronts to establish a foothold in the European economy. Biotech zealots reject public concern as baseless, claiming that it is grounded in incomprehension and emotions rather than upon 'sound science'. Despite mass protests, court battles, parliamentary debates and even the physical removal of GM crops by activist groups across Europe, the European biotech industry has blithely forged ahead with its mission.

Sustained by one of the most ambitious and successful lobby networks in Europe, policies promoting the spread of biotechnology have been at the centre of the EU's growth strategies since the early 1990s and were featured in the Delors 1993 White Paper on Growth, Competitiveness and Employment and Santer's 1996 Confidence Pact for Employment. Rather than addressing public concerns through legislative protection, the European Commission claims that biotechnology is for the good of Europe and has implemented policies designed to nurture and maintain the global competitiveness of the industry. Furthermore, new funding lines for research and development, tax incentives for small start-up companies and rapid approvals of mergers help biotech firms to flourish. All of this has been made possible through some very strategic lobbying by Europe's powerhouse bioindustry coalitions.

EuropaBio: Boosting the Bioindustry

Virtually the entire European biotechnology industry is united in EuropaBio, which was created in the autumn of 1996 through the merger of the Senior Advisory Group on Biotechnology (SAGB, a working group of the chemical industry federation CEFIC) and the European Secretariat for National Bioindustry Associations (ESNBA).[3] Then EuropaBio Chairman Jürgen Drews (also president of International Research at Hoffman-La Roche) announced the merger at a Brussels conference[4] with the greatest confidence: 'From now on, we will speak with one strong voice when discussing with the EU and national politicians and legislators the need for a regulatory environment in which European industry can grow and expand.'[5] EuropaBio is made up of some 600 companies, ranging from the largest bioindustry companies in Europe (including the European offices of US companies like Monsanto) to national biotech federations representing small and medium-sized enterprises. Member companies include all of the major European multinationals interested in biotechnology, for example Bayer, the Danone Group, Novartis, Monsanto Europe, Nestlé, Novo Nordisk, Rhône-Poulenc, Solvay and Unilever.[6]

Beginning in the late 1980s, EuropaBio's predecessor SAGB campaigned for a stronger role for biotechnology in the European Union's economic development policies, in particular arguing for the deregulation of rules for genetic manipulation. Numerous glossy SAGB reports[7] were accompanied by a succession of high-level meetings between the lobby group and EU institutions. Examples include a November 1992 meeting in which senior SAGB delegates visited European Commissioner for Industrial Affairs Martin Bangemann, Commission Secretary-General David Williamson and other top Commission officials and agreed on 'the vital contribution of biotechnology to future European competitiveness'.[8]

More recently, in collaboration with the European Roundtable of Industrialists (ERT, see Chapter 3), the SAGB urged European commissioners to prevent member states from imposing bans on controversial biotech products such as genetically modified maize.[9] In the EU's decision-making process, the Commission has the final word in approving products to be marketed within the Single Market. In the case of the Novartis maize, an overwhelming majority of EU governments were opposed to giving the product the green light. None the less, the Commission decided to go ahead, thereby forcing all EU countries to accept the controversial food.

The probable breakthrough for biotechnology as a major element in EU economic strategies was provided by the 1993 Delors White Paper on Growth, Competitiveness and Employment. In this policy document, then Commission President Jacques Delors extolled biotechnology as 'one of the most promising and crucial technologies for sustainable development in the next century'.[10] The White Paper trumpeted biotechnology as a major engine for economic growth and employment in the next century, and public concerns were written off as 'unfavourable factors' due to 'technology hostility and social inertia' which 'have been more pronounced in the Community in general than in the US or Japan'.[11] The central position of biotechnology in the EU's overall economic strategy was later confirmed in the Confidence Pact for Employment in Europe, presented by Commission President Jacques Santer and adopted by the European Council Summit in June 1996.

EuropaBio's PR Strategy

However rosy the situation may have seemed for the European biotech industry over the past years, it remained unclear whether or not consumers would accept GM products due to feared health or environmental risks. In fact, storms of protest broke out in several countries when the first biotech products hit shop shelves. This resistance posed a life-threatening risk to the biotech industry, which needs to sell its GM products in order to earn back the huge investments sunk into developing or acquiring the technologies.

Enter the world's largest PR firm, Burson-Marsteller, which bills itself as a specialist in 'perception management' (see Chapter 2). Just a week after the conclusion of the June 1997 EU Summit, Amsterdam hosted the first European Bioindustry Congress, EuropaBio '97. A few days before the conference, Burson-Marsteller's PR proposal for EuropaBio was leaked to Greenpeace.[12] Biotech critics were shocked to discover the PR firm's cynical strategy for soothing public fears and outrage and ensuring widespread acceptance of the new biotechnologies.

According to Burson-Marsteller, EuropaBio has 'firmly established [itself] as the primary representative of European bioindustrial interests within the political and regulatory structures of Europe', and the organ-isation has an 'indispensable direct role in the policy-making process'. However, to deal with the outbreak of unfavourable public opinion, Burson-Marsteller recommended a 'sustained communications strategy and programme able to generate favourable perceptions and opinions beyond the policy world'. The PR firm explained that 'public issues of environmental and human health risk are communications killing fields for bioindustries in Europe'. Moreover, 'all the research evidence confirms that the perception of the profit motive fatally undermines industry's credibility on these questions'. Therefore, Burson-Marsteller advised industry to refrain from partaking in any public debate on these issues, leaving it to 'those charged with public trust in this area – politicians and regulators – to assure the public that biotech products are safe'. Apart from staying off the 'killing fields', Burson-Marsteller recommended the creation of 'positive perceptions' around products made possible through genetic engineering without emphasising the controversial technology itself.[13]

According to Burson-Marsteller's analysis, the 'public outrage and resentment over the introduction of genetically modified food' originates in 'a sense of powerlessness in the face of what are perceived to be malevolent (and foreign) forces threatening facets of life held dear'. Therefore, the proposed PR campaign attempted to create the general perception that food-producing companies, retailers and consumers could freely choose whether or not to use, sell or buy genetically modified products. This, claimed the Burson-Marsteller spin doctors, would 'largely defuse' the sense of powerlessness.[14]

The leaked paper also contained a detailed PR plan for the EuropaBio conference in Amsterdam. Burson-Marsteller's basic advice was to keep the media away from the event as its presence would 'automatically draw protesting environmental groups to the Amsterdam venue ... EuropaBio will have set the table and Greenpeace will have eaten the lunch.' Instead, the perception managers advised EuropaBio to feed the media with the pre-cooked, positive stories which 'we really want running back home'.[15]

Yet however well conceived, a multi-million pound PR campaign can easily be spoiled. In Amsterdam, conference attendees arriving at the stylish former stock exchange building were welcomed by activists loudly voicing their concerns about the risks of biotechnology. The next morning, Greenpeace dumped a truckload of soybeans in front of the congress centre entrance. As conference PR manager Peter Linton commented to reporters: 'Greenpeace came early on purpose, before the conference had started and people from industry could argue against them. Now TV stations all over Europe show pictures of a load of beans outside the industry conference. We missed a chance there.'[16]

Whereas the biotech industry's PR campaigns have not been able to sway public opinion in favour of biotechnology, they have been very successful in legislative arenas, with industry-proposed policy initiatives agreeably taken on board by the EU. Such was the case with the recent European Life Patents Directive.

Industry and the EU Life Patents Directive: A Case Study

> Our eurocrats, stimulated by omnipresent multinationals, are about to prepare a particularly nasty meal for us. They want to approve a directive that, believe it or not, allows industry to patent living organisms or parts of them, created by that apprentice sorcerer's technique that is genetic manipulation.
> *Dario Fo, Nobel Laureate*[17]

Industry lobby groups marvelled at their own success in achieving a complete turnaround in European Parliament opinion on the Directive on the Legal Protection of Biotechnological Inventions, which was adopted by an overwhelming majority in 1998. The Directive will extend current European patent law to permit the patenting and thus ownership of life itself. In 1995, the same parliament had rejected a virtually identical directive.[18] During the final phase of this major biotech battle, which raged throughout 1997 and 1998, various 'safeguards' proposed by the European Parliament were drastically weakened or removed entirely following pressure from the Commission, member states and industry. To win this profitable battle, biotech companies manipulated the concerns of interest groups made up of patients, cleverly disguising the fact that the pro-directive lobby was effectively an industry campaign.

Commonly referred to as the Life Patents Directive, this controversial piece of legislation will allow for the patenting of genes, cells, plants, animals, human body parts and genetically modified or cloned human embryos. Why did the Parliament, the only directly elected governing body in the EU, not vote according to the wishes of the majority of Europeans who are sceptical about or opposed to biotechnologies and the ownership of life?[19] What transformed the opinion of a Parliament that initially vetoed the proposed directive in 1995? According to geneticist Ricarda Steinbrecher of the Women's Environmental Network, MEPs 'sold out to the pharmaceutical and biotech industry'[20] when they approved legislation declaring that genes can be 'inventions'.

EuropaBio Whispering Sweet Nothings

As intellectual property and life patents are relatively new frontiers, industry laboured to ensure that the development of legal and legislative frameworks on these issues are in their best interest. Teamed with the European Commission in an effort to nurture the European biotech industry, EuropaBio and other lobby groups have been able to exert a strong influence on this process. The Commission and corporate groupings have been hurriedly pushing relevant legislation through the system, arguing that the European biotech industry cannot afford to wait to establish itself as a contender in the global marketplace.

During its aggressive lobbying for the Life Patents Directive, the biotech industry whispered some key words into the ears of decision makers: 'jobs', 'growth' and 'competitiveness'. Their argument that life patents will help European companies to help Europe's economy and its citizens was largely effective in swaying the Parliament's vote in favour of the directive. EuropaBio, for instance, focused primarily on convincing decision makers that a globally competitive European biotech industry would create more jobs. In its 1997 report *Benchmarking the Competitiveness of Biotechnology in Europe*, EuropaBio highlighted the relatively relaxed regulatory environment for the biotech sector in the United States, and suggested that the same formula would benefit Europe.[21] With no substantial evidence, the report claimed that biotechnology would create three million jobs by the year 2005. Given the current high unemployment rates in the EU, this argument won some converts.

Other Corporate Groupings

In 1997, EuropaBio joined the Forum for European Bioindustry Coordination (FEBC), a lobby platform consisting of an impressive collection of sectoral industry groups set up specifically to press for the Life Patents Directive.[22] During the run-up to the vote, the Forum issued a flood of lobby papers, including briefing papers on specific scientific and legal principles raised in the directive. Considering the complexity of the issues and the limited information held by MEPs, these briefings played a significant role in shaping their decisions. Many of them offered misleading interpretations of the directive text, suggesting that all of the Parliament's original concerns leading to their historic 1995 veto were now properly addressed in the Commission's revised draft. The Forum warned that 'any weakening of the draft would put Europe at a further disadvantage and will shift the emphasis of research in biotechnology further towards the USA and Japan.' Furthermore, it claimed, that 'without patents there could be fewer or no new treatments, cures, food products or environmental solutions generated in and adapted to Europe.'[23]

Other major industry groupings that put their energies behind the Life Patents Directive were the International Chamber of Commerce (ICC, see Chapter 18) and the European chemical industry association CEFIC. The ICC, for instance, issued a statement in October 1997 while the Council of Ministers was preparing to take a decision on the directive. The statement went into great detail concerning the directive, commenting on specific articles and clauses and even going so far as to suggest entire passages of text to be included.

The chemical industry federation CEFIC, meanwhile, issued a number of position papers on patenting and the directive, also referring to the more simplified laws in the US as a strategic advantage for US corporate domination of the world market in chemicals. They threatened that if the EU's patenting system did not become more business-friendly, the European chemical industry would be unable to compete with US corporations[24] and would be forced to fire a significant number of its claimed two million employees.

SmithKline Beecham: Manufacturing Consensus

'Genes are the currency of the future!'
George Poste, Research Director, SmithKline Beecham

The pharmaceutical giant SmithKline Beecham was one of the most aggressive campaigners for the directive, launching its own lobby campaign even before EuropaBio existed. According to SmithKline Beecham lobbyist Simon Gentry, the company allocated £20 million towards its pro-directive campaign.[25] The company also actively manipulated and instrumentalised patient interest groups, knowing very well that these groups could influence decision makers in a way which industry could not. Its tactics included the direct support of patient charities and organisations. Having witnessed the efficacy of the environment lobby prior to the initial Parliament vote in 1995, SmithKline Beecham hired the former assistant to the chair of the

European Parliament's Environment Committee as its Director for European Policy Affairs. Not only did this facilitate the company's access to the Parliament, but it provided insight into the tactics and strategies of the environmental movement.

Patient Interest Groups

The most influential lobbyists for the directive were clearly the patients themselves, who swayed the votes of many MEPs in what was described as 'the largest lobby campaign in the history of the EU'. On the day of the July 1997 vote, a number of people in wheelchairs from patient interest groups demonstrated outside the Parliament building in Strasbourg, chanting the pharmaceutical industry's slogan 'No Patents, No Cures' in an emotional appeal to MEPs to vote for the directive.

Perceiving a strong and unified position in favour of gene patenting from the patient interest groups, MEPs voted accordingly. Further investigation, however, has revealed that the views of most patient interest groups were not expressed by these demonstrators, and that the vocal exceptions were largely co-opted and financed by pharmaceutical companies such as SmithKline Beecham. Biotech companies had persuaded these groups that they were actively seeking cures for their maladies, highlighting the need for supportive legislation which would encourage the development of the much needed medicines. By painting a picture in which 'patents on life' correlates directly with 'cures for all known diseases', industry sought to make an emotional appeal to the Parliament that was difficult to refuse.

GIG and EAGS

The Genetic Interest Group (GIG), a UK umbrella organisation, and the European Alliance of Genetic Support Groups (EAGS), have both been very active in lobbying for the directive. This was not always the case. Up until the initial 1995 vote, the main spokesperson for both groups, Alastair Kent, publicised their opposition to the patenting of genes. Kent changed his tune however when SmithKline Beecham began making donations to the GIG. He soon began lobbying aggressively for the directive, still in the name of both organisations.

SmithKline Beecham's support for Kent also included the hiring of professional consultancy GPC Market Access to help with the lobby campaign. It was during this time that the slogan 'Patents for Life' became the title of a series of lobby documents issued in the name of EAGS. With the assistance of GPC Market Access, a massive disinformation campaign was launched which tried to inflate the emotions of decision makers with rhetoric about saving lives, ending hunger and creating jobs. Another consultancy group, Adamson Associates, was also recruited by the biotech industry to work on the directive, and was engaged in similar activities. Adamson organised an information event on human gene patenting in January 1997 which was presented as an event organised by patient groups.[26]

After the 1997 vote in which the efforts of Kent and his well-oiled lobbying machine helped to sway the decision, some patient interest groups became aware of the fact that his activities in the name of GIG and EAGS were in fact contrary to their own views on the directive. After this information emerged, the chair of GIG issued a letter restating the views of the group, which is firmly against gene patenting.[27] Patients have now woken up to the fact that they were manipulated by industry and its lobbyists, and have since clarified their positions on the patenting of genes. The shift, however, came too late to change the Parliament's opinion.

Can Europe Resist?

Critics of the Life Patents Directive, including scientists, farmers' organisations, activists for indigenous peoples' rights, environmental organisations, church groups, and many others argue that the legislation will assist corporations in acquiring monopoly control over life itself. They question whether it is right that corporations should own the 'biological underpinnings of life'. They point to the activities of 'bio-prospectors', who have been deceiving indigenous people in order to steal their collective knowledge and patent their medicinal plants and even their own genetic materials, that is, their DNA.

The patentability of life opens up a whole new arena for TNC profits and a virgin market over which to establish control. Companies are racing to patent genetic material, even if they have no clear application in mind. As the world's food supply and health services are concentrated more and more into a corporate oligopoly in which a few TNCs make decisions about what crops to plant, what drugs to develop, what prices to charge and so forth, people are increasingly losing control of their basic survival needs. In 1996, the top 10 agrochemical corporations accounted for 82 per cent of global agrochemical sales, the top 10 seed corporations controlled over 40 per cent of the global commercial seed market, and the top 20 pharmaceutical companies controlled approximately 57 per cent of the world market for drugs.[28] This process of corporate concentration will only accelerate as long as the rules of the economy are shaped in the interest of industrial giants.

By strategically forcing biotechnological products into the world's food supply, companies such as Monsanto argue that biotechnology and patents on life are inevitable and resistance is futile. 'Our genes are incorporated into approximately 19 million acres around the world – covering an area larger than Switzerland and the Netherlands combined,' says Tom McDermott, head of Monsanto's European Public Affairs division. 'Can Europe at this point really resist?'[29] In fact, the resistance is heating up: in 1998–99, Europe has witnessed an enormous biotech backlash. Activist groups in the UK have taken up 'non-violent civil responsibility' campaigns to uproot GM crops growing in 'test field' sites. The European media has been uncovering scandal after scandal in the biotech industry. Connections between industry and politicians have come under close scrutiny, as have PR campaigns such as Monsanto's £1 million advertising blitz which was condemned by the British Advertising Standards Authority as making 'wrong, unproven, misleading and confusing' claims.[30]

Meanwhile, a number of European countries – including Greece, France, Luxembourg and Austria – have taken action, independent of EU law, to restrict the import and cultivation of various GM foods. Public pressure for a moratorium on approving new GM products may soon bear results in several countries. A few months after the final European Parliament vote, the Dutch government initiated a legal challenge against the directive in the European Court of Justice. Italy later joined the challenge. All of this comes at a time when public mistrust of biotechnology is very high. The future of biotechnology in Europe is clearly on shaky ground. It remains to be seen how the industry lobby will overcome the burgeoning mass opposition, as well as the criticism of its role in what are supposedly democratic decision-making processes.

Part II

Going Global

Globalisation: Corporate-led, EU-fed

In concert with its creation of a unified European market over the past decade, the EU also began to embrace economic globalisation. Today, the Union is simultaneously reshaping European societies to become 'internationally competitive' and actively promoting transatlantic and global trade deregulation. Whereas the EU's recipe for competitiveness at home – which contains the socially distasteful ingredients of deregulation, privatisation, flexible labour markets and public budget cuts – has provoked substantial debate and protest, its crusade for further international liberalisation and the deregulation of markets was until recently shrouded in silence.

Despite a generous layer of 'feel good' pro-globalisation rhetoric, the goals of the EU's international trade and investment policies are brutally inflexible. Its policies are propelled by a craving for unfettered market access for European-based TNCs and the dismantling of local regulations in order to create a so-called global 'level playing field'. A similar logic rules the policies adopted by other major global powers, and the predominant political blocs have joined forces within the World Trade Organization to dismantle barriers to trade and investment in the less industrialised nations. As Josh Karliner observes in *The Corporate Planet*: 'To a large degree, the triad of Japan, EU and US can be seen as three large corporate states, at times cooperating, at times competing with one another to promote the interests of their rival transnationals across the globe.'[1]

This section will present three important case studies of how the EU, led by the European Commission, is aggressively campaigning for international trade and investment deregulation. In the process, it works very closely with large European corporations and their lobby groups. As was evident in the process of creating a European internal market, the Commission and European corporations share nearly identical visions, not just for within Europe but for the role of the EU in the world.

TEPtoeing Across the Atlantic

The Transatlantic Business Dialogue (TABD) provides a striking example of corporate-political synergy. Largely unknown to the public on either side of the Atlantic, the EU and the United States have been engaged in the systematic removal of barriers to transatlantic trade and investment since 1995. From the beginning, the TABD – which brings together over a hundred captains of industry from the EU and the US – has played a central role in the process. The TABD helpfully identifies what it considers barriers to trade, and governments generally commit to dismantling the nuisances. In both Washington, DC and Brussels, the TABD's access to the political process is remarkably institutionalised.

The TABD hopes to remove so-called 'non-tariff barriers' to trade, including the European eco-labelling system and restrictions on the marketing of genetically modified products, and in the US, public spending provisions to support local economies. In 1998, this largely informal process of mutual deregulation was rebaptised and further streamlined in the official Transatlantic Economic Partnership (TEP). By adopting a stealthy step-by-step approach, the TEP strategically avoids any mention of a transatlantic free trade zone, although this is clearly the end goal of the process.

Sinking the MAI

While the TEP has not yet been the target of concerted campaigning by environmental and other activist groups, the Multilateral Agreement on Investment (MAI) did not escape this fate. This controversial investment treaty was negotiated in the Organization for Economic Cooperation and Development (OECD) between 1995 and the end of 1998, at which point public outrage brought about its demise. Negotiated in secret with input only from international business, the MAI would have banned a wide range of policies for regulating corporate investments and protecting local economies, labour rights and the environment. Furthermore, it would have granted transnational corporations (TNCs) access to an unaccountable international dispute settlement court to pursue financial compensation for government policies perceived as 'discriminatory'. The victorious campaign against the MAI can be seen as a possible turning-point in the flood of global trade and investment deregulation in the 1990s.

The European Commission remained firmly behind the MAI, pushing for its completion before public opposition spiralled out of control even while one government after another abandoned the sinking negotiations. The battle was led by powerful EU Trade Commissioner Sir Leon Brittan, who takes a hardline neoliberal political stance. According to World

Trade Organization boss Renato Ruggiero, Brittan is 'one of the most important free trade advocates of this decade'.[2]

Trading the World

In 1998, the European Commission launched its campaign for a sweeping new round of trade and investment liberalisation in the World Trade Organization (WTO), the so-called Millennium Round. In preparation, the Commission has freshened up its connections with European industry and encouraged corporate networks to provide input towards EU negotiating positions. This political-corporate relationship, which was solidified during negotiations on the WTO Financial Services Agreement in 1997, has been complemented with an opportunistic parallel process of 'dialogues' with civil society.

In the first four years of its existence, the WTO has built up a dark environmental and social record. Large corporations have been the satisfied beneficiaries of its treaties, while communities and small farmers around the world have suffered. Additionally, the organisation's model of economic development is increasingly identified as being incompatible with ecological sustainability. In its rulings in trade disputes on bananas, beef hormones and numerous other products, the WTO has put trade above all else, overruling environmental, social, consumer and health considerations. Yet despite the accelerating backlash against the WTO and its treaties, the European Commission hopes to further expand the scope of the body's mandate as well as its power.

Democratic Gap

Decision making on international trade and investment policies is arguably one of the areas in which the EU's democratic gap is most pronounced. Member states have delegated most of their powers upwards, giving the European Commission an agenda-setting role. The Commission negotiates for its member states in bodies like the WTO, and has the exclusive right to undertake new trade initiatives. The bulk of the EU's decisions on trade and investment are made in the powerful '133 Committee',[3] which consists of trade officials from member states and Commission representatives. Only major or controversial issues are brought before the EU foreign trade ministers.

'The Commission is like a dog on a very long leash,' observed MEP Michael Hindley, and this description is particularly applicable to free trade zealot Commissioner Brittan.[4] Although the European Parliament is informed, it lacks decision-making power on external trade policies. National parliaments fail to exert effective control over their EU trade ministers due to a combination of lack of information and limited awareness about the importance of international trade and investment decisions. These critical issues have been treated as mere technical matters for far too long. Happily, thanks to the public uproar about the MAI and the devastating global financial crisis, the EU's policies are increasingly coming under scrutiny.

The financial crisis of the late 1990s has demonstrated the alarming instability of the deregulated global economy. Unprecedented suffering has been inflicted upon millions of ordinary people in the hardest-hit countries. The United Nations International Labour Organisation (ILO) estimates that 20 million workers became unemployed between July 1997 and September 1998 alone; this was even before Russia and Brazil were heavily impacted by the crisis.[5] In June 1999, the World Bank estimated that up to 200 million people had been thrown into 'abject poverty' due to the financial meltdown. This raised the number of people living in poverty to over 1.5 billion worldwide.[6]

The EU, however, refuses to reconsider the current model of economic globalisation. It has callously blamed the governments of the affected countries for catalysing the crisis through poor financial management, and vehemently denies any link with trade and investment liberalisation. Clearly, the EU hopes to avoid a debate about the pitfalls of the high-speed deregulation of recent years, given its lofty ambitions for the strengthening of such policies within the WTO. Its continued promotion of international trade and investment liberalisation despite increasing social misery and environmental destruction is indefensible.

Contrary to the promised 'trickle-down effect' of economic growth based on international trade, the global gap between rich and poor continues to widen. UNCTAD's *1997 Trade and Development Report* concludes that globalisation in its current form is responsible for a dramatic increase in global inequality. In 1965, the average personal income in G-7 countries was 20 times that in the seven poorest countries in the world. In 1995, the difference was 39 times greater. Income inequalities and polarisation are also growing within countries: the share of wealth pocketed by the top 20 per cent of the population has increased in most nations since the early 1980s.

UNCTAD blames the liberalisation of market forces for these develop-ments, and considers the current situation inevitable until the economy is refitted with regulations. The EU, on the other hand, argues that further liberalisation and expanded trade is the solution, despite the fact that more than one-quarter of global production is currently exported in comparison with only seven per cent in 1950.[7] Many smaller countries in the South already depend upon international trade for up to 40 per cent of their gross domestic product, placing them in extremely vulnerable positions. Growing inequalities are becoming strikingly prominent even within affluent Northern economies, which generally profit most from corporate-led globalisation. Although EU studies admit that the turbulent present is 'the time when unskilled workers will be at risk of losing their jobs', the EU continues to reiterate its increasingly hollow claim that economic globalisation can ultimately only benefit European societies.[8]

Who Profits?

The obvious beneficiaries of EU trade and investment policies are those European-based TNCs that have evolved into global players. Although corporations like Nestlé, Shell and Unilever have profited from transnational gianthood for decades with an established presence in over a hundred countries around the world, they are being joined on a global scale by other ERT companies like Ericsson, Saint-Gobain and Pirelli. Large TNCs based in the US, the EU and Japan dominate the emerging global economy; the top 500 companies in particular control over two-thirds of world trade and more than one-third of the world's total productive assets. Almost every sector of the global economy is under the grip of a handful of TNCs, the most recent being the services, automobile and pharmaceutical sectors.

This economic tyranny will only intensify in coming years. TNCs will continue to benefit from economies of scale and technological advantages, with their positions firmly buttressed by the policies and rules set by international institutions like the WTO and the International Monetary Fund (IMF). While the world economy increases by between two and three per cent each year, large corporations typically grow by eight to ten per cent annually.[9] Perpetual mergers and acquisitions, which make up 80 per cent of all foreign investments, further fuel TNC growth.[10] In 1997, transborder mergers and acquisitions reached the unprecedented level of US$342 billion, and the trend is expected to accelerate.[11] Foreign direct investment (FDI) has more than doubled since 1990, and has multiplied no fewer than seven times since 1980 to reach a new record of US$430 billion in 1998.[12]

The financial crisis has only increased the EU- and US-based TNCs' hunger for companies in the 'emerging markets' of East Asia and Latin America. Recent IMF 'recovery packages' for the shattered economies of South Korea, Thailand, Indonesia and Brazil included a number of provisions that could have been taken straight from the text of the MAI, forcing these countries to remove virtually all remaining obstacles to foreign investment.[13] With these economies more exposed, TNCs are buying out local companies at bargain prices, and at the same time gaining new market territory for themselves.[14]

Although TNCs present themselves as creators of wealth and employment, the figures reveal otherwise. In fact, one of the main characteristics of a competitive and profitable corporation is the 'shedding' of jobs. Between 1993 and 1995, global turnover of the top 100 TNCs increased by more than 25 per cent, but during this same period these companies cut 4 per cent of their global workforce of 5.8 million – over 225,000 people.[15] TNC tendencies towards mergers, relocations, automatisation and centralisation of production and distribution are recipes for job losses. Some part of the obsolete workforce may be employed by subcontractors which TNCs increasingly make use of as a 'flexible' source of labour. Subcontractors are often skilfully played off against each other, resulting in lower prices for the corporations as well as reduced wages and declining working conditions. FDI also unfortunately leads to the buying up and restructuring of local companies by TNCs so that they can produce more with fewer employees.

A survey carried out in 1996 among affiliates of TUAC (the OECD's Trade Union Advisory Council) showed that TNCs are 'increasingly using the threat of delocalisation to influence the outcome of collective bargaining, withholding information from unions and in some cases blatantly derecognising them, while undermining environmental and health and safety standards'.[16] The threat is based on the disturbing global trend of TNCs relocating parts of their production to countries with lower wages and weaker environmental standards and enforcement. A recent review of the production patterns of 22 computer companies based in industrialised countries showed that they had moved half of their manufacturing and assembly operations, which involve highly toxic materials, to the South.[17]

Economic globalisation and deregulation have created a vicious cycle in which dependency upon investment forces workers, communities and governments into increasingly harsh competition on wages, taxes, environmental protection and other factors that might influence investment conditions. International competitiveness is becoming the single most important indicator of a society's health. This will inevitably lead to a downward spiral in social and environmental standards, delaying or freezing desperately needed progress in these areas. When the accelerated exploitation of natural resources (for example, through large-scale agriculture, mining, fisheries and forestry) and the massive amounts of energy used to shift goods around the world are factored in, the conclusion that corporate-led globalisation is inherently unsustainable becomes indisputable.

The unpleasant truth about TNCs is that the increased growth, investment, monopolisation and concentration upon which they rely – as well as the resulting job losses and environmental degradation – are a major structural deficiency of the current neoliberal economic model. Fortunately, however, those calling for a halt to this endless pursuit of deregulation are gaining in mass and volume both within the European Union and elsewhere in the world.

The Transatlantic Connection

In November 1998, the EU Ministers of Foreign Affairs gave the green light for the European Commission to launch negotiations with the United States on a Transatlantic Economic Partnership (TEP), a programme to remove barriers to transatlantic trade. The TEP is a reworked version of the European Commission's controversial New Transatlantic Marketplace (NTM) proposal, a plan for the creation of a EU–US free trade zone by the year 2010 which was blocked by the French government in early 1998.

Although less ambitious than the NTM and replete with soothing language, the TEP none the less poses serious threats to democracy as well as to environmental, safety and health regulations on both sides of the Atlantic. And by adopting and building upon what the Transatlantic Business Dialogue (TABD) has accomplished since 1995, the TEP condones a central role for this unaccountable corporate-state structure in determining EU and US trade and other policies.

Killing the NTM?

The February 1998 New Transatlantic Marketplace (NTM), another of EU commissioner Sir Leon Brittan's free trade babies, proposed the dismantling of all remaining barriers to trade in services as well as all tariffs on goods by 2010.[1] Technical and non-tariff barriers to trade were to have been scrapped through harmonisation and mutual recognition of standards and regulations. Government procurement, intellectual property and investment would have been fully liberalised. A separate transatlantic dispute settlement mechanism would enforce the deregulation.

Several EU governments, led by France, felt that Brittan had gone much too far with his NTM idea. French Foreign Affairs Minister Hubert Vedrine expressed his 'deep disagreement on the substance of the initiative'.[2] The French government feared, among other things, that the

US would use negotiations with the Commission as an excuse to prise open the European audiovisual and agricultural sectors. Moreover, the French were peeved that they had not been properly consulted by Brittan, who began discussing the NTM with the US government even before receiving a mandate from the EU member states. At the Council of EU Foreign Affairs Ministers in April 1998, the French blocked the start of negotiations on the NTM.[3] However, Brittan did not seem particularly discouraged, pointing out that his proposal was a 'beginning, not an end'. It soon became clear what he meant.

In the two weeks between the April meeting and the EU–US Summit in May, intense negotiations took place first within the Senior High Level Group (which brings together senior trade and economic officials from both sides of the Atlantic) and the Committee of EU Permanent Representatives (COREPER, see Appendix 1), and later between the British (then holding the EU presidency) and the US governments. At a joint press conference after the EU–US Summit, US President Clinton, EU Commission President Santer and UK Prime Minister Blair announced the birth of the New Transatlantic Economic Partnership, soon after rebaptised as the Transatlantic Economic Partnership.[4] The TEP was billed as a comprehensive new trade initiative in which the EU and the US 'will work to dismantle trade barriers, both bilateral and multilateral ... in about a dozen areas in all', according to President Clinton.[5]

What's in the TEP?

Under the Transatlantic Economic Partnership, the EU and the US will begin negotiations on the 'reduction and elimination' of barriers to trade as well as increased regulatory cooperation in a large number of areas with the aim of achieving 'substantial results by the year 2000'. Attention will be paid to services, industrial tariffs, intellectual property rights, investment, government procurement and the agricultural sector. The emphasis is on 'those barriers that really matter', or in other words, 'those ... that hinder market opportunities, both for goods and for services'[6] beginning with what is achievable within the first two years. The first details were outlined in the TEP Action Plan of September 1998.[7]

Whereas the NTM was too politically controversial to be adopted, the TEP is far less likely to encounter significant public opposition. Despite nearly identical aims, the TEP approach of step-by-step removal of barriers to trade and investment efficiently moves the process away from the political and into the technical sphere. Controversial words such as 'harmonisation', not to mention 'common market' and 'free trade area', are carefully shunned and soothing words on health and the environment added. Yet although the process of creating joint regulation is disguised, the end result of the TEP is nothing short of harmonisation. The aim, according to the TEP Action Plan, is 'removing or substantially lowering remaining barriers resulting from any additional or different regulatory requirements to be met by imported products coming from the other party, while maintaining our high level of protection for consumers, human, animal, and plant health, safety and the environment'.[8]

The EU and US administrations undoubtedly learned lessons from their experience with the Multilateral Agreement on Investment (MAI, see Chapter 12), a typical 'big bang' treaty committing the signatory countries to the ultimate accomplishment of full-scale investment liberalisation. The MAI ran into unprecedented opposition from a wide-ranging global coalition of social movements, and was ultimately defeated in its proposed form. The proposed NTM was similarly vulnerable due to its threatening language and ambitious timeline. The strategically-packaged TEP, which incorporates various dialogues with trade unions and civil society and less stringent deadlines, was deliberately fashioned to make as few ripples as possible among members of civil society.

EU–US: Global Partners

The TEP does more than simply construct a common EU–US market. The second pillar of the agreement is an equally ambitious agenda for 'multilateral action', in which the EU and the US reaffirm their 'determination to maintain open markets, resist protectionism and sustain the momentum of liberalisation'. The EU and the US 'will give priority to pursuing their objectives together with other trading partners through the World Trade Organization (WTO)'.[9] The TEP Action Plan officially established a regular and structural dialogue between the EU and the US to achieve common goals within the WTO.[10]

The commitment to work in tandem with the WTO will in fact formalise and accelerate a process which has existed since the early 1990s. Joint positions on WTO issues have been negotiated for years within the so-called Quad, which includes the EU, US, Japan and Canada, and at previous EU–US summits. When the world's largest economies have reached consensus on their common interests, it has in most cases proven impossible for trade-hungry Third World governments to resist their demands. This is in part why WTO agreements are so biased towards the interests of Northern governments and their transnational corporations.

Public Procurement and Biotechnology

Among the first in the queue of bilateral trade issues to be tackled within the TEP are public procurement and biotechnology. Within what will in effect be a EU–US single market for public procurement, governments on the national, regional and local levels will be obliged to offer contracts to the EU or US company with the best bid, regardless of its place of origin. This granting of 'national treatment' to any EU- or US-based corporation will mean the end of 'buy local' and other provisions for strengthening local economies that have survived previous liberalisation waves.[11]

Concerning biotechnology, the TEP Action Plan proposes 'the setting in place of an early warning system to help to minimise disputes in areas such as food safety and genetically modified crops'.[12] The US government explains that the TEP will 'facilitate exports and reduce trade friction in our $15 billion two-way agricultural trade, with soybeans, corn, consumer foods and animal feed among the top US agricultural crops'.[13] According to the US Trade Representative, the TEP will 'improve the efficiency and effectiveness of regulatory procedures with regard to food safety and the approval of biotechnology products'. Although all of this may sound benign, a look at what US industry and government biotech crusaders hope to achieve from the TEP unveils a disturbing scenario.

US Government and Industry Ambitions

A congressional hearing in July 1998, for instance, verified that US industry welcomes the TEP because of the possibilities it offers for undermining 'cumbersome' European regulations. TEP advocate Mary Sophos from the Grocery Manufacturers of America (GMA) made no secret of the fact that she views the agreement as an opportunity to reduce government intervention in the agro-food sector.[14] On behalf of the GMA – the world's largest association of food, beverage and consumer product companies with annual US sales of more than $430 billion – Sophos launched an attack on EU regulations governing market access for genetically modified products. Arguing for harmonisation between the two trade partners, she proposed that the TEP start with 'making the relevant US and EU regulatory processes transparent, predictable and compatible'.[15]

David Aaron, the US Under-Secretary of Commerce, offered an even more explicit testimony. 'Unfortunately,' he explained, 'the European Union, which is a major market for US foods, feed ingredients, and other agricultural products, has a slow and unpredictable process for approving new US agricultural products developed through advanced biotechnology.'[16] Aaron described the hurdles to obtaining market access for specific bio-engineered products including Monsanto's Roundup Ready soybean and Novartis' Bt maize, and concluded that 'the EU approval process for the products of biotechnology is non-transparent and overly political. We need to work closely with the EU to finalise approval, and develop for future biotech crops a workable, timely, and transparent approval process.'[17]

Aaron was optimistic, as 'the European Commission appears to understand our frustration with the EU approval process and is trying to make up for lost sales as we speak by opening up more corn tenders this year.' As an illustration of how such transatlantic cooperation works, Aaron pointed to the thorny issue of the labelling of genetically modified organisms (GMOs), demanded by many European consumers and resisted by industry. 'US negotiators are meeting with the Europeans this week to help clear guidelines on when products must be labelled,' he explained. 'GMO labelling and the EU approval process for GMOs will also be taken up in the Biotech Group of the Transatlantic Economic Partnership.'[18]

As the point of increased EU–US regulatory cooperation in the field of biotechnology and food safety is the removal of barriers to the flow of food products, there is every reason for concern. The TEP aims to put an end to the conflicts which have raged over recent years on market access for products such as hormone-laden beef and milk products and genetically manipulated foodstuffs. Although the TEP agreement stresses that 'high standards of safety and protection for health, consumers and the environment will be maintained', environmental groups are already critical of existing EU procedures for the approval of biotechnological products as undemocratic and biased towards corporate interests. Creating procedures for harmonising regulations between the EU and the US will likely only aggravate these problems.

Furthermore, US industry and government ambitions for European deregulation also jeopardise ordinary environmental and consumer protection laws. Sophos, speaking on behalf of the Grocery Manufacturers of America, pinpointed European eco-labelling schemes as ripe targets for dissolution under the TEP. Eco-labels 'generally reflect local cultural values and environmental concerns and discriminate against international competition,' she pointed out.[19] She also attacked the EU Packaging Directive and particularly the German recycling system as constituting barriers to trade, and instead advocated 'shared responsibility' and 'voluntary cooperative programmes'.[20] Nutritional labelling information and the EU's 'very restrictive' food additive laws were also singled out for deregulation in Sophos' testimony.

Approved Once, Accepted Everywhere

Mutual Recognition Agreements (MRAs) are another central element of the Transatlantic Economic Partnership, beginning with the 'mutual recognition of testing and approval procedures, of equivalence of technical and other requirements'. Through 'progressive alignment', the

ultimate goal is 'the adoption of the same standards, regulatory requirements and procedures'.[21] Few people are aware of the fact that the first
basket of MRAs, covering six broad sectors, was already signed at the
May 1998 EU–US Summit. The six sectors covered by these MRAs are
telecommunications, medical devices, electromagnetic compatibility,
electrical safety, recreational craft and pharmaceuticals.

This first basket of MRAs deals principally with testing procedures.
Mutually recognised tests mean that an EU-based exporter can use US
testing procedures in the EU for the products it wants to export to the
United States. Such simplifications are obviously advantageous to international business, which appreciates minimal bureaucratic red tape in its
export ventures. Although the EU stresses that the importing country
still has the ability to set its own standards, ambitions for future MRAs are
much higher. One US NGO, the Community Nutrition Institute (CNI),
has expressed 'deep reservations' regarding these agreements due to their
'potential to lower health, safety, and environmental standards in both
the US and the EU'.[22] MRAs, according to CNI, 'will make it increasingly
difficult for regulatory authorities to uphold their statutory obligations to
ensure the health and safety of people in the US'.[23]

This is not surprising. The primary goal of MRAs is to increase trade
flows through the removal of barriers, and they are initiated in order to
ensure market access rather than high environmental, safety and health
standards. The starting point for MRA negotiations is usually the lowest
common denominator (in other words, the lowest existing standards),
meaning that one party will by default be forced to accept standards
lower than its own democratically-instituted ones. The fact that MRAs
are agreed upon as package deals further undermines the transparency
of the process. MRAs, not coincidentally, were also a major instrument
in the construction of the European Single Market in the 1980s when
EU governments were hesitant to fully harmonise their legislations.[24]

TABD Connections

The high priority given to MRAs in the TEP Action Plan is just one
example of the key role played by the Transatlantic Business Dialogue
(TABD) in this latest step in transatlantic trade liberalisation. After
having been in the pipeline since 1995, MRAs were singled out in 1997
as 'top priority' by the TABD's Joint EU–US Working Group on Standards
and Regulatory Policy when government foot-dragging became
apparent.[25] According to the TABD: 'In the era of the transnational
corporation and rapid global economic integration, the nation-based
regulatory regime is no longer rational nor efficient. National regulatory
regimes can act as *de facto* trade barriers, denying foreign access to a
national economy.'[26]

Next on the TABD's wish list is an EU–US MRA on chemicals. The Business Dialogue also dreams of mutual recognition of genetically modified products, and has helpfully identified 'barriers to trade' in the use of biotechnology within the agri-foods sector. At its 1997 conference in Rome, for example, the TABD urged governments to agree on 'compatible regulatory requirements leading to full consensus on and mutual recognition of safety assessments'.[27] To hasten progress in this lucrative field, the TABD is pushing for the creation of a joint EU–US industry and government body. The TABD's biotech initiative, led by Unilever and Monsanto, brings together EU and US gene technology companies 'to identify potential causes for trade difficulties and propose ways to eliminate them'.[28] Its ultimate goal is to develop MRAs that include 'third countries' so as to 'develop a worldwide network of bilateral agreements with identical conformity procedures'.[29]

Old Friends Reunited

The Transatlantic Business Dialogue (TABD) – consisting of the largest EU- and US-based transnational corporations – was established in 1995 as a joint initiative of the European Commission (led by Commission Vice-President and Commissioner for Trade Sir Leon Brittan and Commissioner for Industrial Affairs Martin Bangemann) and the US Department of Commerce. The press reported that the European Roundtable of Industrialists (ERT, see Chapter 3) was also a driving force behind the initiative. Sir Leon Brittan explained the necessity of such a dialogue:

> As companies and financial institutions become bigger players, they must also be aware of their political responsibilities. We should continue to examine new ways of involving leaders of the private sector in discussions about international economic policy priorities. One forum in which we are beginning successfully to put this principle into practice is the Transatlantic Business Dialogue.[30]

The TABD has attracted a familiar crowd of industrial champions. Jan Timmer, chairman of Philips, was European co-chair in 1997. He was followed in 1998 by DaimlerChrysler's Jürgen Schrempp and by Jérôme Monod of Suez Lyonnaise des Eaux in 1999. Active European corporations, all of which are current or former ERT members as well, include Asea Brown Boveri, Bayer, Bertelsmann, Ericsson, ICI, Olivetti, Pirelli, Philips, Siemens, Solvay and Unilever. Some of the influential TABD companies on the other side of the ocean are Boeing, Enron, Federal Express, Ford, IBM, Motorola, Nokia, Pfizer, Procter & Gamble, Time Warner, Westinghouse and Xerox.[31]

The TABD's inaugural conference was held in Seville, Spain in November 1995. Since then, annual TABD conferences have been held in Chicago, Rome and Charlotte, North Carolina. The conferences typically bring together over one hundred corporate CEOs as well as government ministers, commissioners and other high-level officials. After Seville, Jan Timmer of Philips (then a leading member of the ERT) reported that 'there was absolute agreement that there are far too many rules now, and that they are great and unnecessary impediments to trade.' The follow-up gathering in Chicago was 'an innovative and exciting occasion', according to Sir Leon Brittan:

> We and the American government had asked businessmen from both sides of the Atlantic to get together and see if they could reach agreement on what needed to be done next. If they could, governments would be hard put to explain why it couldn't be done. The result was dramatic. European and American business leaders united in demanding more and faster trade liberalisation. And that had an immediate impact ...[32]

Tackling Barriers

The goal of this hybrid animal is 'the realisation of a true transatlantic marketplace through developing an action plan for the removal of obstacles to trade and investment flows across the Atlantic'.[33] To identify these barriers, TABD members have opted to conduct their dialogue in numerous separate issue groups, which focus on specific themes such as standards, certification and regulatory policy in various sectors (including the biotech, pharmaceutical and chemical sectors); multilateral trade issues in the World Trade Organization and other trade agreements; investment; intellectual property rights, and so forth.

An impressively large number of the TABD's recommendations – up to 80 per cent according to US officials[34] – are taken up by the EU and US governments and turned into official policy. As Sir Leon explains, 'It is incumbent upon us to seek to implement their recommendations – or at the very least to sit down with them and explain why we cannot and try to work out another approach.'[35]

Although the TABD would have liked the NTM to have proceeded as planned, it is also a strong proponent of the TEP. TABD EU Director Stephen Johnston explains:

> Just before our big conference in Charlotte, the governments were still arguing about the TEP Action Plan and couldn't agree. Because of the conference, and because Al Gore was going ... they didn't want to embarrass the vice president [so] they managed to agree on the Action

Plan just before the conference. So this was an example of the power of the TABD high-profile conference actually pushing through an agreement in due time.[36]

The TABD has no formal, juridical existence, and also keeps its organisational structure to a minimum by relying on its corporate leaders for direction. As Johnston explains: 'The TABD is just comprised of the businesses that get involved. There's no real core fabric. This office could disappear in a matter of minutes; it is not permanent, nor should it be.'[37] According to Johnston, the CEO founders of the TABD made a conscious decision not to set up a new organisation: 'They wanted something that was focused and punchy and wasn't going to be a waste of money or time. So that's why they set up this little office.' Running costs of the Brussels office and its staff are paid by the company holding the European co-chair of the TABD.[38]

'Participation' in the TEP

Another difference between the NTM and its successor, the TEP, is that the participation of civil society has been given a somewhat higher profile in the latter. The basis for the third pillar of the TEP, joining bilateral trade and investment liberalisation and closer EU–US cooperation in setting the WTO's agenda, is that 'interested non-governmental organisations [are invited] to participate and extend this dialogue on consumer protection, scientific, safety and environmental issues relevant to international trade as a constructive contribution to policy making.'[39] At a London press conference following the May 1998 EU–US Summit, President Clinton announced that the EU and the US 'will make an effort to give all the stakeholders in our economic lives – environmental stakeholders, labour stakeholders, other elements of civil society – a chance to be heard in these negotiations'.[40]

There are good reasons to harbour suspicions about the motives behind the TEP's invitation for NGOs to 'participate'. In the first place, this overture came very late in the game, after the TABD had been operational for three years and the TEP had been shaped in full detail. It also came at a time when the EU and US governments were facing unprecedented opposition to their agendas for trade and investment liberalisation, as was evidenced with the OECD's Multilateral Agreement on Investment and the refusal of the US Congress to grant fast-track trade negotiating powers for US trade policy to President Clinton. Seen in this light, the invitation to 'participate' smells like a classic cooptation strategy adopted in order to minimise opposition to the transatlantic liberalisation agenda.

Transatlantic Dialogues: 'Greenwashing' the TEP?

Governments initiated a Transatlantic Dialogue for Sustainable Development back in 1997, and a Transatlantic Labour Dialogue, a Transatlantic Consumer Dialogue and a Transatlantic Environment Dialogue followed over the next year. Although most NGOs seemed pleased with the invitations, there are striking differences between the different 'dialogues'.

The labour dialogue, coordinated by the AFL-CIO in the US and the European Trade Union Confederation (ETUC) in Europe, met for the first time in April 1998. This dialogue hopes to be able to address upcoming EU–US summits, a right enjoyed by the Transatlantic Business Dialogue since 1995.[41] The dialogue on sustainable development, which began in June 1997 with a conference in Portugal, consists of representatives of governments, NGOs and business. European Partners for the Environment, which was set up by the European Environment Bureau and Dow Chemical in 1993 to increase dialogue between environmental NGOs and industry, is the European coordinator of this dialogue. Among the active corporations – and funders – of the sustainable development dialogue are Monsanto and Du Pont.[42]

The Transatlantic Consumer Dialogue, which first met in September 1998, is coordinated by the Consumers Federation of America and Consumers International for Europe. This dialogue intends to present a list of important issues to government leaders at biannual EU–US summits.[43] The NGOs currently involved in launching the Transatlantic Environmental Dialogue (TAED) hope to obtain the same privilege. The European Environment Bureau and the National Wildlife Fund were respectively appointed by the European Commission and the US government to set up the TAED.[44] Involved NGOs do seem cognisant of the risk of legitimising an agenda that is not theirs, and plan to use the process to attack fundamental elements of the TEP, for instance, the downward harmonisation associated with MRAs.

All of the dialoguing NGOs are taking a gamble by entering a pre-designed framework with an end goal that lacks a democratic mandate, that of transatlantic 'free' trade. NGO participation in the TEP risks legitimising the agreement and further undermining effective democratic control. It is virtually impossible for the 'participation' offered to NGOs to correct existing imbalances in the agreement. Certainly NGOs have not been offered the same level of 'participation' enjoyed by the business sector within the TABD since 1995, which involves their identification of barriers and subsequent government commitments for the removal of these inconveniences.

A Closer Look at the TABD

Commenting on the recently-established transatlantic dialogues on labour, consumers, sustainable development and environmental issues, TABD EU Director Stephen Johnston claims that business will lose interest in the process 'if they have to sit down and spend half an afternoon arguing with environmentalists'.[45] On the other hand, the TABD does not expect that 'the Commission and the US government are going to be totally beholden to the other dialogues'. At any rate, the TABD has little fear that its extremely advantageous position will suffer from competition from the other dialogues. 'We are more organised and more efficient in putting the message across,' says Johnston.[46]

For several years, TABD co-chairs have attended the biannual EU–US summits to present the organisation's mid-year reports and current desires. On the first morning of the May 1997 summit in The Hague, two TABD representatives, Jan Timmer (TABD EU chair, former ERT member and CEO of Philips Electronics) and Lodewijk de Vink (TABD US chair and CEO of Warner-Lambert), presented the 1997 TABD Priorities Paper to US President Bill Clinton, EU Commission President Jacques Santer and Dutch Prime Minister Wim Kok. Their message did not fall on deaf ears: Mr Kok remarked that 'the paper provides ... useful building blocks and inspiration to explore further possibilities of liberalising trade and investment flows'.[47] The following year, DaimlerChrysler's Jürgen Schrempp personally handed over the TABD's 1998 wish list to Tony Blair and Bill Clinton. Over the past few years, the TABD has presented its demands in the form of a 'scorecard', setting 'priorities' for governments to focus on, and even going as far as to set 'deadlines' for completion. The audacity of this 'scorecard' approach reflects the cosy relationship the TABD enjoys with governments, and its conviction that its recommendations will be carried out.

Apart from these high-level encounters during annual TABD conferences and EU–US summits, 'there is much more frequent contact, almost daily contact' with Commission officials according to Johnston. The TABD's contacts with the Commission are with none but the top players. 'Last year we had two or three meetings on the European side, Schrempp with Brittan and Bangemann,' says Johnston.[48] The Commission 'has published a list of contacts, mimicking the TABD issue groups, so every TABD issue group has a Commission contact point. The two work together and show each other the papers and start to develop a relationship,' he explains. 'It's ongoing. They have a good flow of information and proposals, and it is a positive, structured dialogue. The Commission is cooperative, helping business by giving them the information that they need. But eventually it's business that makes its recommendations.'[49]

Reclaiming Democracy

With the Transatlantic Economic Partnership (TEP) *de facto* legitimising the continuous move towards the creation of a single EU–US market, and the unprecedented agenda-setting role they have been granted through the TABD, transnational corporations have every reason to celebrate. The deregulation process – which actually boils down to re-regulation in the interests of large TNCs – will further accelerate the process of corporate mega-mergers and economic power concentration. The social and environmental 'side-effects' – from job losses to increased transport flows and intensified competition on rules – are predictable.

The threat to democracy is no less acute. A far-reaching corporate–state alliance has been allowed to evolve on the transatlantic level with virtually no public debate. Reining in the completely inappropriate powers which have been granted to corporate leaders through this process may be one of the most essential struggles for reclaiming democracy in the coming years.

MAIgalomania: The Global Corporate Investment Agenda and the Citizens' Movement Opposing It[1]

On a late October morning in 1998, more than a hundred opponents of the Multilateral Agreement on Investment (MAI) swarmed into the elegant Paris headquarters of the International Chamber of Commerce (ICC). The activists, representing more than twenty countries, peacefully occupied the offices for the morning to protest against the ICC's influence in the ongoing MAI negotiations. Canadian anti-MAI campaigner Tony Clarke told the ICC staff: 'We did not elect you to set the rules, so stop manipulating our governments! We call upon our governments to follow the example of France and get the hell out of the OECD's MAI negotiations.'[2]

Secrecy, haste and intrigue characterised the negotiations around the MAI. This treaty was the masterplan of proponents of economic globalisation for the dismantling of the remaining barriers to investment all over the world in the quest for a more open world economy. After a smooth first 18 months, the negotiations entered a far rockier phase in early 1997. Anti-MAI campaigns emerged in the Organization for Economic Cooperation and Development (OECD), and governments demanded an increasing number of national exceptions to the proposed MAI rules.

Following a six-month suspension of the negotiations, the French government was the first country to withdraw from the MAI talks in October 1998; it was soon followed by Canada, Australia and the UK. In December 1998, the OECD's MAI negotiations finally ground to a halt. The demise of the MAI was rightfully celebrated by campaign groups all over the world as a historic victory, and as a possible turning point in the wave of economic liberalisation that has swept the world over the past two decades. Most OECD governments, however, continue to support MAI-like investment principles, and the pressure is increasing for the adoption of similar rules in other international fora, primarily the World Trade Organization (WTO, see Chapter 13).

The 1994 completion of the Uruguay Round of the General Agreement on Tariffs and Trade (GATT) and the subsequent creation of the WTO were great victories for transnational corporations (TNCs), which had both lobbied their governments and cooperated with them in removing barriers to trade in goods and services. The next logical corporate challenge was the creation of a treaty which, by dismantling barriers to investment, would provide investors with a so-called 'level playing field' across the globe. Such was the ultimate goal of the proposed Multilateral Agreement on Investment. It would have granted TNCs extensive new powers, while at the same time making it more difficult for governments to control foreign direct investment in their countries. The MAI negotiators seemed oblivious to the fact that the rules and regulations which hinder 'free' foreign investment and which would be dismantled under the MAI are often those that protect workers and jobs, public services, domestic businesses, the environment and cultures.

Why the MAI?

The MAI was a child of the Paris-based OECD, an intergovernmental body consisting of 29 of the world's richest industrialised countries. Although only OECD states partook in the negotiation process, the MAI was intended to be a 'freestanding' international treaty. Later, non-OECD countries would have been invited to sign the agreement on a 'take-it-or-leave-it' basis, with only certain time-limited reservations permitted. The MAI was also designed as a benchmark for negotiations on global investment rules in other international fora, notably the WTO.

Over the past decade, the European Union has followed a two-tier strategy to attain global rules on investment: working within the OECD, and simultaneously pushing for negotiations on a treaty in the WTO. As European Commission Vice-President Sir Leon Brittan explained in 1995: 'We need to tear down existing obstacles to investment and stop new hurdles being thrown up in its way. Nothing short of a comprehensive set of binding international rules will create the level playing field which is so vital for the European economy.'[3]

Amidst the euphoria caused by the signing of the GATT, the EU launched a first offensive for the initiation of investment liberalisation negotiations within the WTO. But fierce Third World resistance to this so-called MIA (Multilateral Investment Agreement) resulted in a compromise at the WTO's first Ministerial Conference in Singapore in December 1996. Only a WTO working group on investment was formed, with the mandate to study and discuss the relationship between trade and investment. Three years later, the countries that had initially opposed the MIA proposals – including India, Malaysia and Pakistan – still rejected negotiations on a WTO investment treaty. The Uruguay Round of the GATT taught these countries that enormous pressure to conclude far-reaching treaties is generated once negotiations are initiated.

In negotiating the MAI without the participation of Third World countries, the OECD governments – notably the US, Canada, Japan and the EU – aimed to ensure the 'highest standards' of protection and rights for corporate investors. A total of 477 of the world's 500 largest TNCs are based in OECD countries, and most of these are organised in groupings like the International Chamber of Commerce (ICC), the US Council for International Business (USCIB) and the European Roundtable of Industrialists (ERT). All of these corporate lobby groups have been directly or indirectly involved in the shaping of the MAI.

The reason for these lobby groups' interest in a global investment treaty, intended as much for Third World countries as for the OECD states negotiating the agreement, is revealed in the increasing percentage of corporate investment flowing Southward. The total value of foreign direct investment by TNCs in Southern countries rose from US$34 billion in 1990 to over US$150 billion in 1997.[4] Yet Southern countries still apply many protective regulations to foreign investment. As the International Chamber of Commerce (ICC) put it: 'The preponderance of restrictions on foreign investment lie outside the OECD area ... Business needs the benefits of an international regime to include the fast-growing countries of Asia, Central and Eastern Europe and Latin America.'[5]

Since 1995, governments all over the world have been modifying national investment legislation, mostly in the direction of greater liberalisation. The MAI would have augmented and institutionalised this trend. As William Witherell, a high-level OECD official, explained: 'Although investment regimes have become much more open and welcoming in recent past, there is no assurance that they will remain so in the years to come.'[6] EU commissioner Sir Leon Brittan agreed upon the need to harness and intensify investment trends in the MAI:

Investment is a desirable and desired thing ... Nonetheless, governments still sometimes find it threatening, because free direct investment limits administrations' ability to control and shape their countries' economic destiny. This is a small price to pay for allowing private sector decision-makers to generate economic benefits worldwide. But it is a price that some governments in some sectors still find difficult to pay. That is a tragedy.[7]

At their May 1995 Ministerial Conference, OECD countries decided to initiate negotiations on a Multilateral Agreement on Investment, aiming to finalise an agreement within two years. A negotiating group chaired by Dutchman Frans Engering, with representatives of all OECD states as well as the European Commission,[8] kicked off the negotiations in September 1995. The main thrust of the agreement had in fact already been laid out in a four-year feasibility study carried out by the OECD. Shortly after the start of negotiations, the OECD began to solicit other countries to join the future agreement. Several non-OECD countries expressed interest in joining the MAI from the outset, including Argentina, Brazil, Chile, Colombia, Hong Kong, Egypt and the three Baltic states: Estonia, Latvia and Lithuania.

Informal Encounters

Corporate lobby groups had been consulted during the important preparatory phase of the feasibility study, and they remained in close touch with negotiators throughout the duration of the discussions. The Business and Industry Advisory Council (BIAC), which unites numerous business associations and has formal consultative status with the OECD, was wholly involved at an early stage. Aside from the formal consultations carried out by the negotiating group with BIAC and the OECD's Trade Union Advisory Council (TUAC), a 'group of BIAC experts' met with and advised OECD negotiators prior to each negotiation session.[9] Other corporate lobby groups, such as the International Chamber of Commerce, jumped at the opportunity to be part of this groundbreaking process. The negotiators made extensive use of the ICC's 'expertise', for instance, in the shaping of the agreement's dispute settlement mechanism. In fact, the draft MAI proposed the ICC's own court of arbitration as one of the three possible bodies to be used by corporations to resolve disputes.

No less important than these direct infusions into the OECD process was the lobbying done by industry on the national level. The US Council for International Business (USCIB), for example, had 'regular meetings with US negotiators immediately before and after each MAI negotiating session'.[10] Similar close cooperation between industrialists and national negotiators took place in many other OECD countries, including Japan, Canada and the Netherlands. Corporate lobby groups like the ICC made good use of their political access at the highest levels, using globally important summits like the annual G-7 meeting to stress the need for a speedy completion of an agreement unencumbered by labour and environmental demands. Overall, there appears to have been almost complete consensus between MAI negotiators and the business lobby. In fact, almost all of the proposals in the ICC's April 1996 *Multilateral Rules for Investment* report can be found in the first MAI draft, completed nine months later.

Generally, countries were represented by their economic or trade ministry officials in the MAI negotiations. In the Netherlands, the traditionally close connections between industry and economic and trade ministries were exploited to their full potential. The Dutch negotiators sided with industry in their mutual aim to get 'as many obstacles as possible to foreign investment removed'.[11] Astonishingly, in many countries, the MAI went largely unnoticed by other ministries – for instance those of environment, social affairs and culture – until a very advanced stage in the negotiations.

What was in the MAI?[12]

In short, the MAI would have required countries to open all sectors of their economies, and would have given TNCs the right to file complaints about national government policies in non-transparent international dispute settlement panels. In effect, the agreement would have subjected national and local priorities to the needs and wishes of foreign investors. The impacts would have been most devastating in less developed countries, where policies to encourage balanced economies or to break dependency upon commodity exports and resource extraction by TNCs would have been impeded. The MAI would have banned most of the tools traditionally used by Southern countries to ensure that local communities benefit from investments, or to protect local producers in strategic sectors such as agriculture, media, health, education and banking.

The main elements of the MAI were as follows:

1. *A very broad definition of investment*, encompassing not only direct corporate investment, but also stocks, bonds, loans, debt shares, intellectual property rights, leases, mortgages and concessions on land and natural resources.

2. *National treatment and most favoured nation status for foreign investors.* In plain language, this would have required governments to treat foreign investors as well as or better than domestic investors, and thus would have automatically favoured transnationals over smaller, domestic companies. National restrictions on foreign investment in sensitive sectors – for example, the audiovisual sector or natural resources – would have been prohibited. Limits to foreign ownership of land would have been outlawed, and non-domestic investors would have had equal bids upon any public services being privatised.

National treatment under the MAI would have applied not simply to the text or intention of domestic laws and regulations (*de jure*), but also to their impact (*de facto*). This could have had far-reaching consequences. For example, a country banning the construction of large shopping malls outside of urban areas in order to support local businesses in inner cities and reduce car traffic could have been challenged by an international retail chain arguing that this restriction constitutes *de facto* discrimination in favour of domestic retailers. In fact, the Finnish government concluded that a large part of the country's environmental and spatial planning legislation could have been challenged under the MAI as discriminating *de facto* against foreign investors.

3. *A ban on so-called 'performance requirements'*, which are measures specifically designed to protect workers and communities. Government requirements for a minimum number of local employees in a foreign firm, for (re-)investing a minimum amount in the local economy, for the use of a certain percentage of domestic products and for technology transfer would have become illegal under the MAI.

4. *No restrictions on capital flows in and out of countries.* This MAI rule would have facilitated speculative short-term investments of the type that caused the 1994 Mexican peso crisis and more recent stock market crashes in South-east Asia and Latin America. 'Speed bumps' for capital, such as those that exist in Chile and Malaysia, would have been banned.

5. *Strong and binding dispute settlement, including investor-to-state dispute settlement.* Unlike other multilateral treaties, the MAI included a dispute settlement mechanism allowing investors to sue national and local governments not only for breaches of national treatment, but also for 'expropriation' and 'measures having an equivalent effect'. This would have granted TNCs the power to challenge local and national legislation established by democratic political processes. The implications of such a mechanism for national environmental, health and safety regulations are enormous, as is demonstrated by the growing number of cases under the North American Free Trade Agreement (NAFTA). In one very controversial case, the US-based Ethyl company sued the Canadian government for US$250 million, claiming a loss in profits and reputation due to the banning of a toxic gasoline additive. An out-of-court settlement was reached in the autumn of 1998 with the result that the Canadian government was forced to pay Cdn$20 million to Ethyl!

6. *Locking-in of investment liberalisation measures.* Through the principle of 'standstill', the MAI forbade signatory states to introduce laws or

policies reversing a once-established level of investment liberalisation. Through the mechanism of 'roll-back', countries would have been forced to gradually open up sectors and laws temporarily exempted from the general MAI rules. During the MAI negotiations, OECD countries tabled more than a thousand pages of such exemptions, ranging from public broadcasting legislation in the Netherlands to all state laws in the US. A cycle of negotiating rounds, similar to that in the WTO, would have been initiated to ensure the dismantling of all non-MAI compliant legislation and policies in signatory states.

7. *A lock-in period of 20 years.* MAI signatory countries could only withdraw from the agreement after five years, and all foreign investment by other MAI signatory states would have remained covered under MAI provisions for an additional 15 years.

Finally, the provisions in the MAI contradicted several international agreements, including the Climate Convention and its Kyoto Protocol, the Basel Convention on Hazardous Waste, and the Convention on Biological Diversity. The Convention on Biological Diversity, for example, allows countries to control access to genetic resources, thereby ensuring that the local population benefits from them. Under the MAI, such investment regulations would have been considered 'discriminatory'. The MAI would also have contradicted the 1974 UN Charter of Economic Rights and Duties of States, which explicitly grants governments the authority to regulate foreign investment and the operations of transnational corporations within their territories.

Safeguarding Environment and Labour?

At a very late stage in the game, negotiators tried to decorate the fledgling MAI agreement with wording on social and environmental standards. This was a hopeful attempt to neutralise the scathing critique of the labour and environmental movements and to improve the chances of getting the agreement through national parliaments. The belated ornamentation of the MAI was never very convincing to critics of the agreement, also because it remained unclear whether these tacked-on clauses would be binding. OECD members Korea, Australia and Mexico strongly opposed any obligatory language on environment and labour, as did the major corporate lobby groups. The US delegation was in favour of adding additional language on environment and labour, proposing to use the provisions in NAFTA. The European Union countries preferred an environmental 'exception' similar to Article XX of the GATT. Both the NAFTA and the GATT clauses, however, have already proven completely inadequate in preventing environmental regulations from being challenged as barriers to the free flow of trade and investment.

Internal European Commission documents strongly suggest that the environmental wording discussed in the OECD was indeed not much more than window dressing.[13] During the February 1998 negotiating session, a Commission representative stated: 'Taken together, this is a package which will allow us to defend the thesis before our Parliaments and public opinion that the MAI cares for environmental protection and labour standards while at the same time remains an investment agreement, attractive for business and appealing for non-member countries to adhere to.'[14] The Commission opposed binding environmental and social clauses: 'Although these might please certain of our constituencies, they will erode business support and the interest of potential accessions to the MAI. In addition, such language is not without risk in case of a dispute settlement procedure.'[15]

More fundamentally, even a watertight clause on environmental standards would not have diminished the threat emerging from the MAI's aim to grant TNCs unlimited 'equal access' to markets and natural resources all over the world. For instance, the MAI would have granted TNCs 'equal access' to oil and mineral reserves, fish stocks and primary forests. Even without a MAI, corporate logging activities are already jeopardising the world's last primary forests in countries like Brazil, Suriname, Papua New Guinea, Congo and Cambodia. The MAI would have further facilitated and institutionalised such access: if local companies had logging rights, TNCs would by extension enjoy the same, and governments would be in no position to intervene. Overall, the current rapid extraction of natural resources and destruction of biological diversity would have been accelerated by the MAI.

Troubled Waters

The first draft of the MAI saw the light of day in early 1997. Until then, the agreement had been sailing along quite smoothly, with the general public and even most elected public officials oblivious to its very existence. But both the complicated reservation process and the discovery of the MAI process by the NGO community served to slow down, and eventually fundamentally disrupt, the charted course of the planned agreement.

Governments submitted their 'reservations' to the MAI in February 1997. In addition to specific national exceptions, they had also decided to exempt some core, open-ended areas of the agreement which would not need to be 'rolled back'. In some countries, the exemption process probably involved governmental actors who had previously been uninformed about the MAI, and who were now reacting with cold feet to its far-reaching provisions. The US demanded an exemption for all sub-federal law, which would grant states and localities immunity from the MAI, and the EU wanted to retain the right for regional economic areas to treat investments originating inside the region preferentially. In this way, the EU tried to ensure that the MAI would not prevent candidate EU member states from changing their laws to match EU legislation. Another broad carve-out was proposed by France and Canada for their cultural sectors.

To add insult to injury, country-specific exemptions to the MAI grew to the hefty total of a thousand pages, with some governments exempting several key sectors of their economies. The daunting volume of specific exemptions and their sometimes far-reaching implications served to unsettle the previously trouble-free MAI negotiations. A decision to postpone the deadline for the negotiations until May 1998 was taken at the May 1997 OECD Ministerial Conference, with ministers arguing that a 'high-standard' MAI required more time.

Public Explosion

The second, and simultaneous, spanner in the MAI's works was the explosive reaction of the international NGO community after a draft text of the MAI was leaked at the beginning of 1997. Canadian and US NGOs, indignant at the OECD's secrecy around the negotiations, were quick to post the draft text on their web sites. Campaigning spread like wildfire to other parts of the world. Still, more than six months after the publication of the draft by NGOs, the OECD continued to state publicly that the MAI text was not available for public perusal.[16]

NGO strategies have included public education, lobbying of government officials and parliamentarians (many of whom first heard about the MAI from the NGO community), demonstrations, actions and street theatre. In October 1997, the first global NGO strategy meeting on the MAI was organised in Paris prior to an informal consultation with the OECD. The consultation/strategy session brought together representatives of development, environmental and consumer groups from over seventy countries, and resulted in a call for a fundamental overhaul of the agreement that was ultimately signed by over six hundred organisations from all over the world. The NGO coalition organised a successful International Week of Action against the MAI in the middle of February 1998, just before the OECD's High-Level Negotiation Session. Simultaneously, local 'MAI-Free Zones' began to emerge in many parts of the world. The city council of Berkeley, California was the first to declare its city a MAI-Free Zone; it was soon followed by numerous other cities in the US, Japan, Canada, Belgium and the UK.

With NGOs and trade unions breathing down their necks, MAI negotiators felt obliged to deal with the issue of integrating labour and environmental standards into the agreement. All of these developments were a source of great vexation to industry, and the OECD's Business and Industry Advisory Council (BIAC) launched a counter-offensive in the early months of 1998. At an official consultation between BIAC and the OECD MAI negotiating group in January, industrialists expressed their concerns about the direction the discussions were taking. 'We now hear of disturbing signs that many of the elements we were hoping for may not be possible. What then, we are beginning to ask ourselves, is in the MAI for us?' complained Herman van Karnebeek, chairman of BIAC's Committee on Multinational Enterprises.[17] OECD negotiators tried to calm BIAC's fears by asserting that liberalisation remained at the top of the agenda, but that compromises were necessary in order to complete the MAI by April 1998. 'Remember, this is only the first step – like the GATT in 1947,' BIAC was consoled by an OECD official. 'We are entering a process of historic dimensions.'[18]

In March 1998, the beleaguered MAI received yet another blow when a massive majority in the European Parliament approved a resolution criticising both the process and contents of the negotiations. The resolution demanded a thorough analysis of the MAI's effects on EU legislation, fully accessible to the public, and ended with a call to 'the parliaments and the governments of the member states not to accept the MAI as it stands'. Although the European Commission and member governments were under no legal obligation to fulfil this request, the resolution further undermined the legitimacy of the agreement.

The NGO plot to kill the MAI has been termed the 'Dracula strategy': simply bringing public attention to a treaty that cannot survive the light of day. Campaigns against the MAI increased in strength day by day and in country after country, with the media finally starting to take notice in some countries. The fact that the MAI became front-page news in France in the spring of 1998 had a major impact on the French government, whereas the conflicts over reservations and the heated public debate made completing the treaty by the April 1998 deadline increasingly unattractive to the US and Canadian governments.

After the High Level Negotiation Session in February, only the EU and the OECD secretariat still hoped to meet the April 1998 deadline. The European Commission had issued a strong warning against further delay at the February negotiations: 'Buying more time will make things more difficult, not easier, as special interest groups everywhere discover the questionable value found in denouncing the MAI for their own purposes which have nothing to do with investment.'[19] The Commission stressed that a failure of the MAI negotiations would also jeopardise the ultimate goal of an investment agreement in the WTO: 'It would be bad for the globalised economy in general. The world would be further away from global investment rules than ever, and this for a long time, if we in the OECD cannot agree on the first cornerstone'.[20] The US, on the other hand, indicated to the other negotiators that it was 'not ready to make a deal',[21] and instead favoured 'a reflection period and intensified bilateral contacts as the best way to make progress'.

In late March, the OECD announced that it was seeking a new mandate for another year of negotiations. But much to the organisation's chagrin, the ministerial meeting at the end of April decided upon a six-month suspension of the negotiations. According to the official statement of the ministerial conference, these six months were intended to be 'a period of assessment and further consultation between the negotiating parties and with interested parties of their societies'.[22]

EU Business Leaves the Sinking MAI

Like the other major corporate lobby groups behind the MAI – UNICE, USCIB and its Japanese counterpart Keidanren – the ICC was quite disappointed about the miscarriage of the April 1998 deadline and the six-month suspension of negotiations. The organisation launched a new offensive in support of the MAI, with ICC President Helmut Maucher publicly complaining about the delay and urging governments to 'move on MAI'.[23] Perhaps in anticipation of the impending failure of the OECD's MAI, the ICC now stressed the completion of a global treaty for investment liberalisation in the WTO as the ultimate goal. This message was also brought to the G-8 Summit in Birmingham in May 1998.

Just a few months later, European business appeared to have made a total strategic U-turn. During the ICC's Geneva Business Dialogue in September 1998 (see Chapter 18), industry displayed a remarkable lack of support for the MAI. The conference declaration stressed the need for 'a truly global framework of rules for cross border investment ... especially in view of the lack of progress so far at the OECD'. Commenting on the crisis in the MAI negotiations, ICC president Helmut Maucher remarked that his enthusiasm for the MAI had waned 'because they added social wording at the very last moment'. He claimed that Southern countries would oppose 'protective' social and environmental clauses, and advocated a 'more cautious approach'.[24] These were the first signs that the ICC had lost faith in a Multilateral Agreement on Investment within the OECD, and would instead concentrate on getting the rules it wanted in the WTO.

During the six-month 'period of assessment and consultation', the international coalition of anti-MAI groups stepped up its campaign. Through informal bilateral and multilateral negotiations, governments tried to find a way out of the crisis, but these efforts proved largely unproductive. A handful of OECD countries – Belgium, Canada, the Netherlands and the UK – carried out formal consultations with civil society groups, but rather than truly seeking 'participation', the goal was primarily to soften up the opposition to the MAI. In most countries, little or nothing was done to fulfil the promises for public involvement contained in the OECD's Ministerial Declaration.[25]

Only in France was a fundamental assessment of the MAI carried out. A task force headed by European Parliamentarian Catherine Lalumière interviewed both proponents and critics of the MAI, and came to the conclusion that the treaty was indeed fundamentally flawed.[26] The report confirmed the main points of the NGO community's critique, and recommended either a radical modification of the contents of the MAI or a complete withdrawal from the negotiations. After having approved these conclusions, the French government announced that it would not attend the planned resumption of the negotiations in October 1998.

Although some governments insisted on ploughing ahead without France, in the end the remaining negotiators met for a single day instead of the planned two, and no negotiations took place. Meanwhile, elsewhere in Paris, hundreds of representatives of the international opposition to the MAI gathered at the International Citizens' Summit Against the MAI and celebrated the breakdown of the negotiations. In the following weeks, the UK, Canada and Australia also pulled out of the negotiations. In early December, the OECD secretariat finally had to acknowledge that negotiations on the MAI had been defeated.

The Turning Tide

With the termination of the MAI negotiations in the OECD, campaign groups could celebrate a major international victory against a treaty that was an essential element in the political masterplan for economic globalisation. Clearly, the struggle against the economic and political philosophy underpinning the MAI has only just begun. The push for MAI-style rules continues within other international economic fora, but there is still good reason to celebrate what has been accomplished. The sinking of the MAI has demonstrated the enormous potential of global grassroots mobilisation on complex but far-reaching issues like trade and investment liberalisation.

The anti-MAI campaign was characterised by the sharing of information and strategies among an increasingly strong international network of citizens, NGOs, workers, environmental groups, international solidarity organisations, women's movements and church-based groups. Newspaper commentators have emphasised the importance of the use of the Internet by the MAI opposition, terming the phenomenon

'Network Guerilla'.[27] The Lalumière report to the French government more precisely noted that

> ... the development of the Internet has shaken up the environment of the negotiations. It allows the instant diffusion of the texts under discussion, whose confidentiality becomes more and more theoretical. It permits the sharing of knowledge and expertise beyond national boundaries. On a subject which is highly technical, the representatives of civil society seemed to us perfectly well informed, and their criticisms well argued on a legal level.

In a less appreciative tone, Abraham Katz of the US Council for International Business also stressed the role of 'labour and environmental activists mobilising through the Internet' in defeating the MAI.[28] Mr Katz, who was personally involved in the shaping of the MAI, warned that 'the enemies of an open market system have marshalled a serious counterattack on further liberalisation of trade and investment and on multinational companies as the main agents of globalisation.'[29] In fact, although the Internet was indeed used efficiently by anti-MAI campaigners, the strength of the coalition was its basis of national campaigns, rooted in work on the grassroots level.

Alternatives to the MAI

Since early 1998, the movements campaigning against the MAI have initiated a very important process of formulating alternatives to the failed investment treaty. A wide range of documents has been produced by anti-MAI groups in various parts of the world. Some advocate internationally binding codes of conduct for TNCs within the framework of the UN, while others propose various policy options to reduce the economic dominance of large corporations and increase the economic diversity and prosperity of local communities. Proposed policy measures include community reinvestment rules, limits on company size to avoid unfair competition, subsidies for local production for local use, efficient taxation of corporate profits to ensure benefits for the local economy, regulation of capital flows and more. There exists a broad consensus within the anti-MAI movement on the need for democratic regulation of investment in order to ensure that it contributes to social and environmental goals.[30]

Aided by an increasingly clear common analysis of the dangers of corporate-led globalisation, progressive groups all over the world are becoming better prepared to defend democracy, the environment and social justice. This is no easy task, as the MAI is not the only attempt to deregulate national and local investment rules. In fact, the political forces behind economic globalisation will try to reach their goal of global investment deregulation through other international fora, like the International Monetary Fund, the UN Conference on Trade and Development, the Transatlantic Economic Partnership (TEP), and, above all, the World Trade Organization. The MAI was stopped in the OECD in the nick of time, but the anti-MAI movement should be on guard for new battles in other arenas.

The WTO Millennium Bug: Corporate Control over Global Trade Politics

Governments should interfere in the conduct of trade as little as possible.
Peter Sutherland, former Director General of GATT[1]

Social movements in both North and South are increasingly turning against the World Trade Organization (WTO) due to its abysmal social and environmental record. The WTO system accelerates the concentration of economic power in the hands of transnational corporations; this is hardly surprising, as corporate lobby groups have been closely involved in the shaping of many of the WTO agreements.

Since early 1998, the European Union, led by the European Commission, has been on a crusade for a new round of negotiations on trade and investment liberalisation within the WTO – a so-called 'Millennium Round'. Not content with the existing mandate of scheduled reviews for agreements on services, agriculture and intellectual property rights, the EU is pushing hard for an expansion of the WTO's agenda to include controversial new issues such as investment, public procurement and competition policy. And, despite its newly-adopted rhetoric to win over NGOs, the EU continues to fashion its international trade policies around the economic interests of European-based corporations.

The WTO is Born

With the conclusion of the Uruguay Round of the GATT negotiations on 15 December 1993, crucial decision-making powers with the potential to impact billions of people were bestowed upon the World Trade Organization. Today, with a membership of over 130 countries, the body's mandate is greatly expanded from that of its predecessor, the General Agreement on Tariffs and Trade (GATT). Moving beyond its historic role of setting tariffs and quotas, the WTO now deals with non-tariff barriers to trade (such as health and environmental standards) as well as every imaginable regulation that might somehow 'distort' or 'obstruct' the free flow of goods and services.

Despite its outwardly democratic appearance due to its policies of equal participation by all member states in consensus-based decision making, the WTO is extremely undemocratic and opaque. Although they represent the majority of the world's nations and peoples, Southern countries have very little say in the negotiation process. Lack of financial and human resources, discussions behind closed doors between the most powerful countries, and most importantly, very strong pressure from the US and the EU, often force Southern countries into accepting deals very much against their interests. The EU and the US prepare their common positions bilaterally within the Transatlantic Economic Partnership (TEP) and within the so-called 'Quad' (comprising the US, the EU, Japan and Canada).

Within this non-transparent system, it is nearly impossible to hold negotiators accountable, with the upshot being agreements strongly biased towards corporate interests in Northern countries. The most powerful countries thus shape the world economy almost exclusively to suit the interests of transnational corporations (TNCs) from industrialised countries, often after close consultation with corporate lobby groups.

The WTO Shows its Teeth

As the millennium draws to a close, a number of high-profile trade disputes between the EU and the US have placed the WTO's unique implementation powers in the spotlight. The WTO's sharpest teeth are its dispute settlement body and its cross-retaliation provisions, both of which enable it to force nations to comply with WTO rules. The increasing number of controversial rulings in which the WTO dispute settlement body has upheld corporate interests over those of people and the environment has severely tarnished the WTO's image.

Within the WTO system, any member state can complain to the dispute settlement body about any other member's policies or laws that are perceived to restrict the free flow of trade. If the panel – composed of unelected bureaucrats – finds a government guilty of non-compliance with WTO agreements, the offending country must change its legislation or face retaliatory trade sanctions by the complaining party, even in sectors unrelated to the dispute. The offending country may also face heavy financial penalties.

During the first four years of the WTO's existence, the dispute settlement mechanism has been invoked predominantly for disputes between the EU and the US. Its first decisions provide a disturbing picture of what can be expected in the future. There have been a total of 177 cases in which a country challenged a law or practice of another country by invoking WTO rules during this first four-year period. The majority of these cases could be settled without interference by the WTO's dispute settlement body. Eighteen of the 177 disputes were settled by a binding panel decision, and another 18 are currently being examined by the WTO panels.[2]

The following two case studies, covering the EU's ban on beef hormones and a selective purchasing law in the US state of Massachusetts that targets companies active in Burma, are examples of how business groupings use the WTO system to pursue their interests at the expense of democratic decision-making processes and citizens' agendas on the national and subnational levels.

Industry's Beef with Consumers

In early May 1997, a three-person WTO dispute settlement panel ruled that a nine-year ban imposed by the European Union on hormone-treated beef was illegal under WTO rules. The ruling, which overturned an important consumer health law, caused outrage throughout Europe.

Over the past decade, Monsanto, a US-based TNC which formerly produced chemicals, has restyled itself into a 'life science' corporation, leaning heavily on the manipulation of genetic material. One of its products is a recombinant bovine growth hormone (rBGH), used by large-scale dairy farmers in the US to increase the milk production of their cows. Other 'natural' hormones such as oestradiol and testosterone are also commonly used by US cattle farmers. In 1995, 90 per cent of US cattle were treated with some type of growth hormone.

In January 1989, the European Union, applying the 'precautionary principle', deemed safety claims by US industry unconvincing and imposed a ban on the import of hormone-treated beef and milk. The ban also applied to producers within the European Union. In response to strong lobbying by Monsanto, the US National Cattlemen's Association, the US Dairy Export Council, the National Milk Producers Federation and other interest groups, then US Trade Representative Mickey Kantor initiated action in the WTO against the EU ban on beef hormones.[3]

On the EU side, industry groups such as FEDESA, the primary lobby organisation for the European animal 'health' products industry, and the European Federation of Pharmaceutical Industry Associations (EFPIA), both members of EuropaBio (see Chapter 9), pressured the Commission to lift the ban, which was affecting European companies as well. In chorus with their US counterparts, they argued that there is always some risk involved with food involving genetic modification or hormone treatment. Pressure from consumer protection organisations and other NGOs made the Commission realise that the lifting of its ban on hormone-treated beef and milk was a political hot potato. Supported by a growing body of evidence suggesting that certain natural and synthetic hormones are linked to rising incidences of cancer, the Commission decided not to lift its ban, despite the WTO ruling.

The preliminary decision in the dispute over hormone beef is the first ruling thus far based on a three-year-old WTO agreement known as the Sanitary and Phytosanitary Agreement. This agreement requires that restrictions based on food health and safety be based on scientific evidence, and accepts internationally agreed standards, such as those decided within the UN system, as a justification for taking protective trade measures. Since the UN Food and Agriculture Organization (FAO) deemed the hormones to be safe, the WTO panel ruled that the EU's ban was unjustified and should be lifted.

This ruling sets a dangerous precedent for national consumer health and safety protection laws. Many experts believe that various EU measures, such as those regulating other animal products, may now also be challenged by the US and other nations, for example, Brazil's recent challenge of the EU's regulatory regime on poultry imports. The process of whittling away consumer protection laws and regulations in Europe and elsewhere for the sake of industry will thus continue unabated unless steps are taken to reverse this trend.

Massachusetts–Burma: Human Rights Objectives Overruled

In the United States, individual states and communities have long expressed their political leanings through the enactment of 'selective purchasing' laws. These laws pressure transnational corporations to cease doing business with repressive regimes by imposing 'pricing penalties' on their goods and services. Since 1996, for example, Massachusetts has imposed a 10 per cent penalty on goods and services provided by companies with financial interests in Myanmar. Formerly known as Burma, Myanmar is infamous for the brutal human rights abuses imposed upon citizens by its illegitimate military government. To date, Siemens, Unilever and several Japanese companies are among those that have been penalised by the Massachusetts legislation, and the law was cited as one of the main reasons for Apple Computers' withdrawal from Myanmar.[4]

The Massachusetts–Burma law has come under attack both on the US domestic front and internationally, particularly in the EU and Japan. The National Foreign Trade Council (NFTC), a coalition of some 600 US-based manufacturers and financial institutions, has taken the state of Massachusetts to court over the law.[5] Oil companies such as Texaco and Mobil have expressed their concern about the impact of such laws on their activities in Burma and other dictatorial regimes.

Seeking to distance itself from charges that the NFTC places economic interests above human rights in Burma, a front group called USA Engage was set up with the assistance of Anne L. Wexler,[6] head of the Washington-based consultancy Wexler Group.[7] USA Engage was officially introduced at an April 1997 press conference where it portrayed itself as a 'broad-based coalition representing Americans from all regions, sectors, and segments of our society'.[8] The group promptly began an intensive lobbying campaign in Washington, DC against selective purchasing laws and other economic sanctions placed on corporations based on social and environmental objectives.

In Europe, European Roundtable of Industrialists (ERT, see Chapter 3) companies including Ericsson, Unilever and Siemens also viewed the Massachusetts law as a dangerous precedent to be quickly crushed. Industry mobilised its forces to pressure the European Commission to challenge the US government to drop the Massachusetts law. Failing that strategy, corporations urged the initiation of action in the WTO. Japanese heavyweights such as Mitsubishi, Sony and Nissan, some of the biggest losers in the Massachusetts law, applied the same pressure to the Japanese government.

It thus came as no surprise when the European Union and Japan requested the creation of a WTO dispute panel in October 1998, arguing that the Massachusetts law was discriminatory and in violation of WTO rules on government procurement.[9] Although the EU suspended the WTO panel in February 1999 (perhaps as a conciliatory move in its bitter banana war with the US government), it has threatened to revive the case if the US federal government does not take action against Massachusetts.

The Massachusetts–Burma case brings up many critical questions about national and local sovereignty and the precedence of trade over social and environmental objectives. It also highlights some of the inequities in the current balance of power within the EU. In September 1998, the European Parliament passed a resolution calling upon the Commission to put an end to all trade, tourism and investment by EU-based companies in Myanmar. The resolution also criticised the Commission decision to call for a WTO dispute panel on the Massachusetts law. The Commission has also been criticised by the European Trade Union Confederation and the International Confederation of Free Trade Unions for ignoring human rights abuses in Burma. Yet according to an EU spokesman, 'Breaking WTO rules doesn't help anyone. The key thing in this case is the United States' failure to honour its international commitments.'[10]

Corporate Involvement in WTO Negotiations

Large corporations have thus far been the main beneficiaries of WTO agreements. This is hardly surprising, as in many cases they have directly influenced the positions of the most powerful WTO members during the negotiation of these agreements. This was certainly the case during the Uruguay Round of GATT negotiations, when the bulk of the WTO agreements were shaped. In addition to bringing Southern countries under the GATT and its discipline and putting new issues on the trade agenda, the Uruguay Round granted Northern TNCs expanded access to Southern country markets. The seven-year round, which began in 1986, helped developed countries and their corporations to achieve further liberalisation in sectors where they had an advantage, such as services, and also introduced intellectual property rights and other protections for TNC activities.

The most strenuous lobbying took place in the US. Not only did individual companies vie for general trade liberalisation and the opening-up of markets, but industry coalitions were also created to push for the inclusion of certain issues under the GATT regime. For example, the Coalition of Service Industries lobbied for a new trade regime for services[11] and the Intellectual Property Committee worked to get the TRIPs (Trade-Related Aspects of Intellectual Property Rights) agreement on the agenda. Industry influence was also evident in the composition of the US delegation: the vast majority of members were from the corporate world.

During the first years of the Uruguay Round, European business lobby groups were not intensively involved in negotiations. EU industry launched a serious lobbying effort only when negotiations came to a deadlock over the agreement on agriculture. According to former ERT Secretary-General Keith Richardson:

> What we tried to say to governments is: whatever the difficulties are, the most important thing is to get the overall deal, because that will bring benefits to the whole of European business. And the total picture is more important than the individual difficulties. It's quite a difficult message, and the only way you really do it is with face-to-face meetings.[12]

While the ERT focused on national governments, UNICE, the European employers' confederation (see Chapter 4), worked closely with the European Commission to bring the negotiations to a close. UNICE analysts chewed over all of the proposals carefully before spitting industry's positions back to the Commission.

The following two case studies, on the TRIPs and the Financial Services agreements, show in more detail how transnational corporations have worked to shape WTO agreements to their own preferences.

Power TRIPs

Industry has identified a major problem in international trade. It crafted a solution, reduced it to a concrete proposal and sold it to our own and other governments ... The industries and traders of world commerce have simultaneously played the role of patients, the diagnosticians and the physicians.
James Enyart, Monsanto[13]

TRIPs (Trade-Related Aspects of Intellectual Property Rights) grant corporations the right to protect their 'intellectual property' in all WTO countries. This forces WTO member states to apply minimum standards in seven areas of intellectual property, including copyright and trademark protection, patents and industrial designs. The TRIPs agreement is the brainchild of an industry coalition with members from the US, the EU and Japan. The first initiative was taken by the Intellectual Property Committee (IPC), which brings together 13 major US corporations including Bristol Myers Squibb, Du Pont, Monsanto, and General Motors. The IPC was created with the explicit goal of putting TRIPs firmly on the GATT agenda.[14]

According to a former Monsanto employee, one of the IPC's first tasks was 'missionary work' in Europe and Japan in order to gather the support of corporate heavyweights for the TRIPs campaign.[15] UNICE and the Japanese business organisation Keidanren were easy converts. According to former Pfizer CEO Edmund T. Pratt, who attended numerous GATT negotiations in the capacity of official adviser to the US Trade Representative, 'Our combined strength enabled us to establish a global private sector government network which laid the groundwork for what became TRIPs.'[16] In 1988, an industry paper on the 'Basic Framework for GATT Provisions on Intellectual Property' made it into the Uruguay Round negotiations, following a lobby campaign both in Geneva and on the national level. Not surprisingly, the position put forth by the influential US delegation was strikingly similar to industry's proposal.

The fundamental imbalance in the TRIPs agreement is that Southern countries possess very little intellectual property, and they furthermore do not have the resources to develop this sector in the near future. They do, however, contain most of the world's biodiversity, from which many pharmaceutical and agricultural patents are derived. Calculations show that up to 80 per cent of patents for technology and products in Southern countries are held by TNCs.[17] This imbalance, coupled with concern about the ethical implications of the private ownership of life, prompted some Southern countries to fiercely oppose all forms of life-form patenting during the TRIPs negotiations. The industry-dominated US delegation, with 96 out of the 111 members from the corporate sector,[18] called for everything to be patentable, including plants and animals.

The compromise result was a so-called 'biodiversity provision' in the TRIPs agreement, which allows countries to exclude plants and animals from patentability under the condition that they develop a similar system of protection (the so-called *sui generis* system). The biodiversity provision is slated for review in 1999 as part of a set of negotiations on a wider range of issues, which has kept the lobby machines working at full speed. The US, now supported by the EU, Canada and Japan, is pressing hard for the expansion of what can be covered under intellectual property rights in the agreement. Southern countries, however, appear determined to stand firm against US and industry pressure, proposing among other things to definitively exclude biodiversity from TRIPs.

Genuinely concerned about the firm stance taken by Southern countries, civil society and some international bodies such as the UN Convention on Biodiversity,[19] industry is joining forces to resist any weakening of their rights under the TRIPs agreement and lobbying their governments not to cave in. If industry has its way, the revised biodiversity article will make it impossible to exclude life-forms from patent law, and Southern countries' control over their biological resources will be further weakened. Ethical, socio-economic, cultural and environmental considerations will also be ignored, reducing the patenting of life merely to a matter of commercial interests.

The Financial Services Agreement: Servicing the North

> This agreement is like taking back the neighbourhood. We need a policeman on the block. We can't have governments behaving in thuggish ways.
> *Gordon Cloney of the US-based International Insurance Council*[20]

In 1997, three new agreements were signed within the framework of the WTO. One agreement dismantled tariffs on trade in information technology products, and another did the same for the telecommunications sector. In December 1997, a third agreement was signed, on the liberalisation of the financial services sectors, including banking and insurance. All three of these 'jewels in the WTO crown', as EU Trade Commissioner Sir Leon Brittan termed them, were the result of systematic pressure on Southern governments by the EU and the US.

According to Brittan, 'Europe was already a force for liberalisation in the Uruguay Round negotiations, but in the sectoral achievements that followed, Europe has unquestionably taken the lead in pushing for greater and faster liberalisation of world markets than any of our partners.'[21] The three sectoral agreements were shaped in very close cooperation with European and US corporations. This can clearly be seen in the case of the financial services agreement, highlighted by Brittan as a model for business involvement in future trade negotiations.

This agreement, which entered into force on 1 March 1999, will remove many obstacles for financial services corporations wanting to enter 'emerging markets', which until recently had policies in place to protect the domestic banking and insurance sectors. It has been signed by 70 WTO member countries, and it is predicted that it will liberalise over 90 per cent of the world market in insurance, banking and brokerage services.[22] The economic interests are obviously enormous. Total global bank assets are estimated at more than US$41 trillion, while the insurance sector brings in over $2.1 trillion in premiums and trade in shares is worth over $15 trillion per year.[23] The Financial Services Agreement does not oblige countries to fully open their markets from the start; countries may file specific reservations. However, the agreement does 'lock-in' liberalisation and market access, banning new protective measures.

The financial services negotiations were an unsolved leftover from Uruguay Round negotiations on services (GATS). In 1995, negotiations on this sector failed once again when the US withdrew, displeased with the reluctance of Asian and Latin American countries to open their markets to US financial services corporations. Some sixty other countries signed an interim agreement, and negotiations were relaunched in April 1997. The European Commission now took the lead, aware that EU countries had removed almost all internal barriers to foreign trade and investment in the financial services sector over the previous years. As Asian countries were loath to further liberalise their financial services sectors, senior trade officials from the European Commission and the US embarked upon a campaign to make them change their minds. They travelled to Asian capitals and presented financial services liberalisation as the cure for sluggish economies, as it would attract new foreign capital flows.

The third partner in this team effort was, according to the Dutch Ministry of Economic Affairs, 'the international financial industry, particularly from the US and the EU, united in the Financial Leaders Group (FLG)'.[24] The FLG's role was to 'identify the barriers to trade in other countries'; the EU and US delegations would then put these obstacles on the negotiating agenda. The group – headed by the largest banks and insurance companies in the world, including Barclays PLC, Chase Manhattan, ING Group, Ford Financial Services Group, the Bank of Tokyo-Mitsubishi, Goldman Sachs and the Royal Bank of Canada – strives for the liberalisation of the financial services sector on a global scale. FLG co-chairmen are Andrew Buxton, head of UK-based Barclays PLC, and

Dean O'Hare of the US Chubb Corporation. Other members include the American International Group, British Invisibles, Bank of America, Aegon Insurance Group, Dresdner Bank AG, Citigroup, ROBECO Group, UBS and over fifty other bank, investment and insurance companies.

EU commissioner Brittan stressed that 'the close links established between EC and US industry ... were an essential factor in obtaining the final deal.'[25] In fact, he found the cooperation with the Financial Leaders Group to be so inspiring that he planned to use it as a prototype for the future. 'Within the EU, we are now considering a private sector involvement in the process of building up our priorities,' he said some months after the deal was finished. 'The example of the EU-US Financial Leaders Group – involving a group of business leaders to provide high-level momentum to the negotiations – has been the model for the creation of a new mechanism for Europe. A similar deal will be needed for the next round of services liberalisation negotiations.'[26] The FLG can certainly count on the full support of the Trade Commissioner in its preparations for the upcoming WTO negotiations on services (including financial services) scheduled to begin in the year 2000.

While banking, securities and insurance corporations based in the EU, US and Japan were jubilant about the signing of the agreement, negotiators from countries referred to as 'emerging markets' were far less enthusiastic. In practice, the benefits are reserved for the Northern corporations which can now enter new markets in Asia, Latin America, Africa and Central and Eastern Europe. The prospect of services companies from the South competing in Northern markets is illusory. When Southern countries signed on to the agreement, it was in the hope of attracting foreign direct investment and financing. The EU, the US and their financial services corporations argued that the market openings will make the banking and insurance industries in 'emerging markets' more efficient by increasing competition. But it is very likely that many jobs will be lost as local banks are swallowed up by Northern financial services corporations with far greater resources. An already unequitable financial cycle will thus be solidified, with profits flowing back to share-holders in the EU, the US and Japan.

The Millennium Round Offensive

> Let us not forget that those who are in difficulty today are also those who most dramatically benefited from globalisation yesterday, and may again tomorrow.
> *EU Foreign Trade Commissioner Sir Leon Brittan.*[27]

The European Commission, spurred on by a very vocal Sir Leon Brittan, vigorously promotes the launching of a broad new round of WTO negotiations covering a wide range of issues following the November 1999 Ministerial Conference in Seattle. Apart from the issues in the WTO's 'built-in agenda' – agriculture, intellectual property rights and services – the Commission has also proposed the initiation of negotiations for agreements on investment, public procurement, competition policy and other areas. The Commission has slowly but surely gained the support of Canada and Japan, and the US, which had initially favoured separate negotiations on a smaller number of issues, is finally warming up to the idea of a grand new round. Southern governments, however, have not given Brittan's initiative an overly warm reception. In fact, their resistance to negotiations on new issues – and particularly on investment – dates back to 1995 when an earlier EU offensive took place.

When the negotiations for a multilateral investment treaty (MAI, see Chapter 12) officially began within the OECD in 1995, the involved Northern countries had a two-track strategy, pushing simultaneously for a Multilateral Investment Agreement (MIA) within the WTO. In fact, the European Union hoped to launch talks on a MIA at the December 1996 WTO Ministerial Conference in Singapore. Southern governments revolted against the MIA from the beginning, afraid that it would impact 'the ability of national governments to regulate FDI flows so as to support national development objectives and priorities'.[28] Instead, they demanded that the investment issue be discussed within the framework of the UN Conference on Trade and Development (UNCTAD).

Despite fierce opposition by Third World governments, a WTO working group was set up to study the relations between trade and investment. This followed an utterly undemocratic procedure involving only an informal group of 30 countries. The cold war between OECD countries and MAI/MIA opponents continued throughout the meetings of the working group in 1997 and 1998. Fearing that the EU would succeed in rallying support for the preparation of negotiations, the groups that opposed the MAI in the OECD insisted that it should not be revitalised within the WTO. In this politically tense climate, the investment working group announced the decision in their December 1998 final report not to bring out any recommendation, but rather to continue discussions.[29] The European Commission's position has not been affected, and it remains a staunch proponent of investment negotiations in the WTO.

Many Third World governments, NGOs and peoples' movements oppose the introduction of not only investment into the WTO, but of other proposed new issues as well. Martin Khor, director of the Third World Network, has pointed out that the EU's motive for a WTO agreement on competition policy is not to limit corporate concentration on a global scale. On the contrary, it hopes to dismantle barriers faced by Northern TNCs in 'emerging markets', such as various laws or policies that favour local firms. These might include policies that give importing or distribution rights to local companies, for example.

On the issue of government procurement, the EU hopes to prevent Southern governments from giving preference to local citizens or firms when distributing public sector contracts (such as for building or equipping hospitals, schools, infrastructure, etc.). Bringing government procurement under the WTO regime with its 'national treatment' principle would mean that foreign corporations must be given the same (or better) opportunities to win contracts as locals. If they feel discriminated against, non-national companies would have access, through their governments, to the WTO's dispute settlement mechanism in order to challenge the offending country and claim compensatory and retaliatory measures. TNCs are drooling over the potential markets for government procurement contracts, which in many Southern countries cover 20 to 30 per cent of total GDP.

In most Southern countries, government procurement contracts remain one of the only ways in which Southern companies can compete against larger Northern corporations. As is the case with the proposed rules for investment, WTO rules for competition policy and government procurement are presented as necessary for the creation of a 'level playing field'. In reality, however, equal competition between giant global corporations and smaller local producers will lead to the extinction of the latter on a massive scale.

The Commission's Many Faces

Sir Leon Brittan has used every conceivable argument to gather support for 'his' Millennium Round. While critics argue that the financial crisis and the accumulating evidence that economic globalisation causes widespread social and environmental damage demand a reconsideration of continued trade and investment liberalisation, Sir Leon has not wavered. On the contrary, the financial crisis, which Brittan claims was caused by 'the mismanagement of the market economy', makes him 'feel strongly that the introduction into the WTO of global rules governing investment is one of the highest priorities in the new round of global trade negotiations'.[30]

In order to ensure that investment negotiations would occur, the Commission – claiming to have learned from the opposition to the MAI in the OECD – began to outreach to NGOs. 'Wide consultation and open debate will be crucial for the success of the Millennium Round. Governments need to keep their electorates fully informed,' Brittan reassured an NGO delegation at one of the 'dialogue meetings' on the proposed Millennium Round organised by the Commission for 'civil society' representatives since September 1998.[31] Business representatives, who also fit the Commission's definition of civil society, were also present at these dialogues. The Commission also promised transparency and participation in decision making in the proposed new negotiations, the publication of information on the EU's web site, and a 'sustainable development impact assessment' of the Millennium Round.

The sense that the Commission had embarked on a charm offensive with questionable substance grew stronger over the following months. During a dialogue meeting in January 1999, the Commission distributed a rather vague paper outlining its ideas for a WTO investment agreement which lacked many of the controversial elements of the MAI.[32] The previous week, however, the NGOs present had received a leaked version of the official Commission proposals. That version, which included nearly all of the elements that had provoked major opposition to the MAI, had already been discussed with the Council of Ministers' 133 Committee (for external trade) the month before.[33] Asked about the status of these two papers, the Commission's only response was that 'especially on investment, the ideas are moving very fast.'[34]

Another blow to the Commission's credibility came in March 1999 when it turned out that it had been pursuing a parallel, and qualitatively different, process of 'consultation and partnership with European business interests over investment issues' with the so-called Investment Network (IN).[35] The IN, representing Fiat, ICI, Daimler-Benz, Carlsberg, British Petroleum, Rhône-Poulenc and some fifty other corporations, was set up to identify the priorities of large European corporations for a WTO investment agreement. The Commission also surveyed more than two thousand European businesspeople in order 'to give a clear picture of the way international liberalisation and international rule-making on investment are perceived by the business community'.[36]

The IN is clearly an outgrowth of the Commission's experience during the Financial Services Agreement negotiations, in which it worked closely with the Financial Leaders Group. Recently, the Commission has also encouraged European corporations in the services sector to set up a European Services Network (ESN), which will 'advise European Union negotiators on the key barriers and countries on which they should focus in these negotiations'.[37] In his speech at the first meeting of the ESN, Sir Leon Brittan was frank about the central role he envisages it playing: 'You are the driving force of the consultation system which we have established; my door is open for any matters of concern. And I expect that whenever the overall ESN comes to some conclusions, these will represent the views of the industry, although I will also be ready to listen to the problems of individual companies.'[38]

The ESN is closely related to the European Service Leaders Group (ESLG), which consists of over forty chairmen and CEOs from various sectors ranging from banking to energy services. The ESLG is supposed to 'give the political impetus and a high public profile' to the new GATS negotiations starting in the year 2000. The active encouragement of the creation of new business structures by the Commission to build support for the Millennium Round and to deliver input into the negotiations will surely strengthen its position *vis-à-vis* the EU member states. As US academic Maria Green Cowles points out, 'By working closely together, the companies and Commission present the member states with a negotiating strategy 'pre-approved' by European industry.'[39]

Business Attack for the Millennium Round

> We want neither to be the secret girlfriend of the WTO nor should the ICC have to enter the World Trade Organization through the servants entrance.
> *Helmut Maucher, International Chamber of Commerce*[40]

A number of highly influential business groupings are concocting their own campaigns in support of the Millennium Round. A common feature of these strategies, following upon the lessons of the failed MAI negotiations, is that industry refrains from opposing social and environmental clauses in the WTO. Industry obviously hopes that this tactic will encourage NGO support for further liberalisation. The European employers' organisation UNICE, for example, is an active participant in the Commission's dialogues with civil society on the Millennium Round.

EU Commissioner Brittan has also become increasingly vocal about the 'mainstreaming' of environment in the new round. Although still claiming that trade and investment liberalisation is entirely consistent with sustainable development, he has come some way in adopting green NGO demands on strengthening the position of multilateral environmental agreements (MEAs) as well as the relevance of judging products on the process and production methods applied, allowing the use of eco-labelling and the precautionary principle. Many of these demands, however, have been rejected by Southern governments. They fear that such provisions would be used to intensify the application of trade instruments to protect Northern interests, thereby shifting the environmental burden to Third World countries. Many Northern NGOs also distrust the Commission's promises, and insist upon a moratorium on further trade and investment liberalisation until the WTO system has been fundamentally reformed.

The European Roundtable of Industrialists (ERT) has a long history of pushing for investment liberalisation, its main objective being an agreement within the WTO. As early as 1993, the ERT stressed the need for 'a GATT for investment' to 'lock in the process of liberalisation'.[41] This wish has been repeated in the five reports on investment produced by the ERT's North–South working group since 1993. The failure of the MAI negotiations in the OECD came as a nasty surprise to the Roundtable, but as Secretary-General Wim Philippa explained, the ERT soon afterwards 'indicated to the Commission that we would very much like to work along with the Commission and with the WTO if that eventually will become the partner, to try to speed up an acceptable MAI'.[42] The ERT has established a separate working group on foreign economic relations, chaired by Peter Sutherland, currently chairman of both BP and Goldman Sachs International.[43] Philippa clearly regards Sutherland, the former GATT Director-General, as the ERT's secret weapon. He explains that 'his knowledge, his experience, his contacts, his channels' will make the ERT 'more proactive' and give it 'a possibility to speed up matters'.[44]

The more than one hundred corporate leaders involved in the Transatlantic Business Dialogue (TABD, see Chapter 11) have a formal role, advising the EU and US administrations on their positions in WTO negotiations. As the crisis in the OECD MAI negotiations deepened, the TABD was increasingly split along Atlantic lines. At the November 1998 TABD summit in Charlotte, North Carolina, EU industry lobbied hard to convince its US counterparts, which had not yet abandoned the OECD dream, to join their offensive for an investment treaty in the WTO. According to European TABD spokesperson Stephen Johnston, 'We have decided to work in the WTO. The TABD has regrouped.'[45] The TABD expects that it will be able to have an impact on the WTO Ministerial Conference in November 1999. As Johnston explains, 'Once you have a powerful agreement, even if it is the day before, that will make a difference for what the people say.'[46]

The International Chamber of Commerce (ICC), one of the most heavyweight corporate players behind the MAI, is also the international business grouping with the closest links to the WTO Secretariat. Stefano Bertasi, head of the ICC Working Group on Trade and Investment, explains:

We've always had, throughout the years, a very close working relationship with the WTO, because obviously they deal with issues which are central to business interests. The ICC has always been a vector for business input into WTO work, since its creation, [and] since the creation of the WTO and the beginning of the multilateral trade negotiations.[47]

The ICC's strategy to influence the process, Bertasi explains, 'is done in two ways: directly through the intergovernmental organisations, and through the member governments of those organisations through our national committees'.[48] The ICC has national committees in over sixty countries.

The ICC has a long tradition of massive lobby offensives to influence WTO negotiations, including a six-month campaign in the run-up to the first Ministerial Conference in Singapore in December 1996. Decisions taken there to remove tariffs on information technology products and to establish new working groups on investment and competition 'met the business agenda for further trade liberalisation as spelled out by the ICC'.[49] In the second half of 1998, the ICC began to gear up for the proposed Millennium Round. 'We have already had several informal contacts with the WTO on the new issues that they are looking at,' says Bertasi.[50] Part of the explanation for these handy connections is the fact that the ICC working group on International Trade and Investment Policy is headed by Arthur Dunkel, Director-General of the GATT during the Uruguay Round.[51] Dunkel is also a registered WTO dispute panelist and a board member of Nestlé. The 'revolving door' between the WTO, EU institutions and industry ensures that key individuals such as Dunkel and Sutherland are able to maintain tight links among this powerful triad (see figure 3).

Figure 3   Then WTO Director-General Renato Ruggiero meets with Arthur Dunkel, head of the ICC's trade and investment committee (and former GATT Director) at the September 1998 Geneva Business Dialogue. (Photo: K. Hedinger)

Time Will Tell

With an increasing number of high-profile trade disputes between the EU and the US, much attention has recently been focused on the WTO. In Southern countries, public awareness about the trade body is growing, and peoples' movements are mobilising against the free trade agenda. This is evident in countries like India, where hundreds of thousands of people have joined public demonstrations against the WTO. Some Southern countries, including India, Pakistan and Egypt, have been very vocal about their opposition to the new round, preferring to stick with the built-in agenda and to make existing agreements more development-friendly. After a few years of experience within the WTO system, many Southern countries are more confident about their positions, and may not back down to US and EU pressure as easily as they have done in the past.

Only time will tell how successful the Commission's attempt to seduce 'civil society' has been. A March 1999 statement signed by hundreds of groups from all over the world rejects the idea of a Millennium Round. The NGOs demanded 'a moratorium on any new issues or further negotiations that expand the scope and power of the WTO'.[52] Instead they stressed the need to 'change course and develop an alternative, humane and sustainable international system of trade and investment relations'.

Part III

Planet Inc.

Landing on Planet Inc.

The upswing of corporate political power on the national level and in regional fora like the European Union has been closely followed in the 1990s by an alarming emergence of synchronised corporate campaigning on the global level. International institutions are increasingly under siege by business lobby organisations, with the presumably idealistic United Nations being the latest victim. This section will introduce some of the major global corporate groupings and present examples of their burgeoning influence.

The phenomenon is not entirely new: a number of international elite fora and think-tanks have laid the groundwork for global corporate lobbying over the past several decades. Structures like the Bilderberg Group, the Trilateral Commission and the World Economic Forum, although not exclusively industry-based, have been critical catalysts for the adoption of the prevailing agenda of economic globalisation by most governments around the world. In the last decade, these established fora have been supplemented by the emergence of new global players. These worldly upstarts, distinguished by modern and flexible structures, are often as influential as their counterparts on the national and regional levels.

A prime example is the World Business Council for Sustainable Development (WBCSD), a global business coalition which poses as the leading voice of industry working for an environmentally sustainable future. Its corporate membership, however, differs little from that of other major lobby groups which make no claims to sustainability. Masquerading behind its carefully-cultivated image as a 'green' industry coalition, the WBCSD has been tremendously successful in promoting global market liberalisation and self-regulation instead of government intervention as the key to sustainable development. It has forged close ties with various international institutions and United Nations bodies, and has left its forceful, decidedly unsustainable mark on both the 1992 Rio Earth Summit and the 1997 Kyoto Climate Convention.

The WBCSD is only one among many corporate groupings campaigning to influence the ongoing UN climate negotiations. A closer look at the results of the UN climate summits in Kyoto and Buenos Aires reveals a history riddled with corporate lobbying efforts, and an agreement predictably full of loopholes which undermine the efficacy of targets that are in themselves insufficient. In particular, industry in North America, Europe, Japan and Australia have invested immense resources and have used a wide range of tactics to protect their commercial interests in the face of greenhouse gas emission regulations. Among the principal actors are several special structures created expressly to channel corporate pressure on the issue of climate change. Generally, business coalitions are pushing for the same 'solution' – namely voluntary action by industry as opposed to government regulation, and market-led initiatives to avoid reduction commitments. Other binding measures are denounced as a threat to competitiveness, the cause of large-scale unemployment, and even economic collapse.

The most effective global business organisation – and the most ambitious – is without doubt the International Chamber of Commerce (ICC). The ICC, which also calls itself the 'world business organisation', was modernised and relaunched in the mid-1990s under the presidency of Nestlé boss Helmut Maucher. It has succeeded in reproducing the privileged position established by corporate lobby groups within the EU, the United States and Japan on a global level. The ICC's significant role within the WTO system was described in Part II; its current designs, however, lie in the penetration of the UN system. The United Nations itself is undergoing an ideological transformation, steered by Secretary-General Kofi Annan, and appears to be eagerly embracing corporate groupings like the ICC. It recently entered into a partnership with the ICC, resulting in several joint projects between business and various UN agencies. Specifically, the UN Conference on Trade and Development (UNCTAD) and the UN Development Programme (UNDP) have embarked upon highly controversial projects with the ICC and individual corporations.

The increasing corporate cooptation of the United Nations is a troublesome development. Historically, the UN system has been a relatively democratic forum which has provided Southern governments and civil society organisations with greater access and influence than in other international bodies. Corporate control over the UN constitutes a serious threat to those groups and interests losing out in the globalisation process, whether they be workers, communities, indigenous peoples, women or the environment. The corporate charm offensive towards the UN is also very much a proactive move to ensure that any regulation of the global economy will be tailored to the interests of international business. If successful, this effort would further undermine opportunities to use the UN to pursue the priorities of civil society organisations throughout the world.

Global Elite Meetings: The Bilderberg Group, the Trilateral Commission and the World Economic Forum

The Bilderberg Group

The Bilderberg Group is one of the oldest and most impenetrable international groupings in which major corporations play a significant agenda-setting role. An attempt to smooth over and solidify post-war transatlantic relations between the US and western Europe, the first Bilderberg gathering of politicians, military strategists, bankers, business leaders, academics, media, trade unionists and other opinion shapers took place in 1954 in the Bilderberg Hotel in Oosterbeek, the Netherlands.[1] This initial meeting covered issues ranging from the 'Communist threat' to Third World development and European integration and economic policy,[2] and was paid for by Dutch TNC Unilever and the US Central Intelligence Agency (CIA).[3] According to political scientist Stephen Gill, 'The purpose of these meetings was to promote open and confidential dialogue and an airing of differences, whilst simultaneously encouraging an ever-growing density of economic, political, military and cultural links between the Atlantic nations.'[4] Additionally, the Bilderberg meetings have provided an unmistakable impetus towards European unification.

Today, approximately 120 global elite from North America and western Europe meet annually under the aegis of the Bilderberg group. There is no fixed membership, but a number of large corporations have taken part over the years, including British-American Tobacco, British Petroleum, Exxon, Ford, General Motors, IBM, Rio Tinto, Shell and Unilever.[5] In 1997, Bilderberg steering committee members included Etienne Davignon, former European Commission vice-chair, current chair of ERT member company Société Générale de Belgique and president of the Association for the Monetary Union of Europe (see Chapter 6); Peter Sutherland, former GATT chief, former European commissioner, and current Goldman Sachs International Partner and British Petroleum CEO; Renato Ruggiero, former WTO director and current Fiat board member, and Percy Barnevik, CEO of ERT member company Investor AB. Henry Kissinger and World Bank President James Wolfensohn are also members of the steering committee.

Striving for Consensus

The Bilderberg agenda remains fixed upon current issues within the neoliberal, free market discourse. It is widely believed that the consensus reached within this forum is a basis for international policy developments. According to a former delegate:

> Bilderberg is part of a global conversation that takes place each year at a string of conferences, and it does form the backdrop to policies that emerge later. There's the World Economic Forum at Davos in February, the Bilderberg and G-8 meetings in April/May, and the IMF/World Bank annual conference in September. A kind of international consensus emerges and is carried over from one meeting to the next. But no one's really leading it. This consensus becomes the background for G-8 economic communiqués; it becomes what informs the IMF when it imposes an adjustment programme on Indonesia; and it becomes what the president proposes to Congress.[6]

The May 1998 Bilderberg meeting in Scotland, for example, covered current hot topics including NATO, the Asian financial crisis, European Monetary Union and the transatlantic marketplace proposal (see Chapter 11). Details of the discussions are extremely difficult to come by. The notorious secrecy of the Bilderberg gatherings is enforced by high-level security guards who literally surround the premises at each meeting. At the 1998 meeting, for instance, a *Scottish Daily Mail* reporter was arrested, handcuffed and detained for eight hours merely for entering the meeting premises.[7]

The 47th Bilderberg Conference took place on 3–6 June 1999 in the Portuguese resort Sintra under the Chairmanship of Etienne Davignon.[8] Apart from the usual corporate suspects, the list of invitees included political heavyweights like Portuguese President Jorge Sampaio, German opposition leader Rudolf Scharping, World Bank President James D. Wolfensohn and New Labour spin doctor Peter Mandelson. Veteran green activist Jonathan Porritt was also invited.[9] The topic of the conference was the 'Atlantic Relationship in a Time of Change'. According to an official press release, the meeting was to discuss NATO, Genetics, Emerging Markets, The New Economy, European Politics, US Politics, International Financial Architecture, and Russia.[10]

The Trilateral Commission

In 1973, members of the Bilderberg group set up the Trilateral Commission, which describes itself as '335 distinguished individuals' from Europe, North America and Japan.[11] In addition to including members of the Japanese political and economic elite, the Trilateral Commission was an attempt to create a more formal, efficient structure than the nebulous Bilderberg. The Trilateral Commission is less shrouded in mystery than its originator, but it promotes the same so-called 'Washington Consensus' – the belief that an unrestricted global free market economy is the only viable model for every nation in the world.

In fact, many of the same elite businesspeople, politicians and bankers who were active in Bilderberg also dominate this and similar fora. Powerful US banker and businessman David Rockefeller was the driving force behind the establishment of the Trilateral Commission, and was its chair during the 1980s. During that same period, Rockefeller also chaired the Council on Foreign Relations, an influential US think-tank of several thousand members 'whose membership controls more than half the wealth of the United States'.[12] Other important Trilateral participants in the first decade included Giovanni Agnelli of the Italian car dynasty Fiat, John Loudon of Royal Dutch Petroleum (later Shell), and former European commissioner Etienne Davignon. Wolfgang Hager, formerly of the European University Institute and more recently the head of the ERT's transport spin-off ECIS (see Chapter 8) was the first European Secretary of the Trilateral Commission in the 1970s. Former US presidents Jimmy Carter and George Bush, along with Bill Clinton, were all Trilateral members, as were other current influential members of the US government such as Secretary of State Warren Christopher and Federal Reserve Chairman Alan Greenspan.

Current Trilateral Executive Committee elites include former UNICE Vice-President and Member of European Parliament Stelios Argyros, European Single Market Commissioner Mario Monti, and ERT company heads Oscar Fanjul of Repsol, Paolo Fresco of Fiat, Baron Daniel Janssen of Solvay and Björn Svedberg of Ericsson.[13] The three-day annual meetings of the Trilateral Commission generally take up the most urgent concerns of the moment. The March 1999 gathering, for example, chewed over the banana conflict raging between the US and European Union inside the World Trade Organization.

Within the Trilateral Commission, there is widespread agreement that the United States is far more adept at playing the globalisation game than are the other two Trilateral regions. 'Crony capitalism' (rather than, for example, irresponsible investments and currency speculation) is blamed for many of the current woes in Asian countries, and Europe's social safety nets are considered as a heavy drag on competitiveness. Thus, the 1999 Annual Meeting of the Trilateral Commission recommended that

'Europe must become more competitive by deregulating labour markets and streamlining burdensome welfare systems.'[14]

According to political scientist Stephen Gill, the economic forces represented in the Trilateral Commission determine the direction of national and international economic policy adopted by its political membership. 'The economic interests represented are predominantly those of internationally mobile forms of capital,' he notes. 'The corporate membership is easily definable, and comprises the heads or deputy heads of giant transnational firms and banks, as well as agribusiness and trading companies.'[15] Small-scale, more nationally oriented enterprises are excluded, and organised labour under-represented. Member companies

> ... have privileged access to the massive growth in the Eurocurrency markets, and borrow funds at cheaper rates of interest than weaker competitors ... The vast majority of their investments during the 1970s and 1980s was geared towards increasing capital-intensity or technology-intensity. Thus their expansion has not tended to generate substantial rises in employment.[16]

In short, these corporations are easily recognisable as the same type working within industry lobby groups like the European Roundtable of Industrialists to further their goal of economic liberalisation.

The World Economic Forum

A third major forum for elite consensus building and strategising is the World Economic Forum (WEF), which holds its annual meeting in Davos, Switzerland. According to the Forum itself, each year '1,000 top business leaders, 250 political leaders, 250 foremost academic experts in every domain and some 250 media leaders come together to shape the global agenda.'[17] A 'unique atmosphere' is created which facilitates 'literally thousands of private discussions' and enables sharing 'information for pursuing business opportunities, progressing on international relations, scoring breakthroughs in major socio-political processes, and forging global partnerships and alliances'.[18] The World Economic Forum claims to play a leading role in economic globalisation and the liberalisation of financial services, and takes credit for the launching of the Uruguay Round of the GATT which culminated in the World Trade Organization.[19] As Trilateral Commission member and political scientist Samuel P. Huntington puts it, 'Davos people control virtually all international institutions, many of the world's governments and the bulk of the world's economic and military capabilities'.[20]

A glance at the heady topics and heavyweight speakers at 1998 Davos meeting sessions is illuminating. European Competition Commissioner Karel Van Miert joined former GATT chief Peter Sutherland, Nestlé chair Helmut Maucher, and Shoichiro Toyoda, head of Toyota, for a discussion on competition policy. Commission Vice-President Sir Leon Brittan hooked up with international financier George Soros, AFL-CIO President John Sweeney and Brazilian President Fernando Henrique Cardoso for a discussion on 'A Social Complement to the Market Economy'. Other well-known figures, such as WTO Director-General Ruggiero, UN Secretary-General Kofi Annan, and prominent businesspeople such as Anova's Stephan Schmidheiny, Monsanto's Robert Shapiro and Shell's Cor Herkströter were omnipresent in the discussions. No matter what the subject, the discussions were peppered with neoliberal platitudes such as Sir Leon Brittan's remark that: 'Competitiveness is the best way to guarantee the European way of doing things', and Shapiro's assertion that in general what people want is 'more stuff'.[21]

Despite the proximity of the ski slopes, the atmosphere at the 1999 annual meeting of the World Economic Forum was more sombre than in preceding years. The global financial crisis has rocked governments and investors, and several politicians and other speakers recommended previously unheard-of measures such as new financial architecture and socially responsible investing, under the new WEF slogan of 'Responsible Globality'. According to WEF founder and president Klaus Schwab, 'this meeting may have been a kind of landmark in reintroducing the notion of social responsibility to the corporate sector.'[22] This change of tune was certainly catalysed by the threatening backlash against economic globalisation. The growing discontent with the economic model promoted by the WEF has been made tangible by the presence of increasing numbers of anti-globalisation protestors in Davos over recent years, and the 1999 meeting was insulated by Swiss riot police wielding plastic shields.

Exploiting Sustainability: The World Business Council for Sustainable Development

While the International Chamber of Commerce (ICC) appears to have recently consolidated its hold on the United Nations' activities in the economic realm (see Chapter 18), another global lobby coalition has long been an active partner in the UN's work on environment and development. The World Business Council for Sustainable Development (WBCSD), which describes itself as 'the pre-eminent business voice on sustainable development'[1] was the first corporate lobby group to forge an institutionalised partnership with the United Nations. A wolf in sheep's clothing, the WBCSD consists of some of the world's most polluting companies, and can be held partly responsible for the lack of global progress in the areas of environment and development since its creation.

Schmidheiny and Strong, Inc.

The Business Council for Sustainable Development (BCSD) was created in 1990 by Swiss industrialist Stephan Schmidheiny upon the request of his friend Maurice Strong, Secretary-General of the United Nations Conference on Environment and Development (UNCED, or the Rio Earth Summit) which was then just beginning its preparatory work. Schmidheiny and Strong were old buddies from the Davos World Economic Forum (see Chapter 15), of which Strong was once chair. Strong, a well-connected industrialist himself, encouraged Schmidheiny, whose wealth came primarily from his Swatch company specialising in colourful watches and major investments in the asbestos industry,[2] to bring together prominent business leaders from around the world in order to form the BCSD.

Many NGOs felt that the 1992 Earth Summit in Rio was ultimately 'hijacked' by the industry lobby, organised primarily within the vocal BCSD. Not only did the Business Council manage to slither out of proposals for regulations on industry, but it ultimately succeeded in having industry heralded as the new partner of the UN in its quest for sustainable development. According to Pratap Chatterjee and Matthias Finger in *Earth Brokers*, 'UNCED set up a process through which TNCs were transformed from lobbyists at a national level to legitimate global agents, i.e. partners of governments. UNCED gave them a platform from where they could frame the new global issues in their own terms.'[3] Indeed, NGO attempts to force some regulation on free-wheeling multinationals failed completely: the only reference to industry in Agenda 21, the Summit's main outcome, was to acknowledge their involvement in sustainable development.

Back to Business as Usual

In 1995, the BCSD merged with the World Industry Council for the Environment (WICE) and became the World Business Council for Sustainable Development (WBCSD). WICE had been initiated by the International Chamber of Commerce in 1992 with the goal of involving industry in Earth Summit follow-up. Its top man, Rodney Chase, a managing director of British Petroleum, became the chair of WBCSD, and former Asea Brown Boveri top man Björn Stigson became executive director.[4] Members, who must be CEOs or the equivalent, currently number around 125 and represent companies including Asea Brown Boveri (ABB), AT&T, Bayer, BP Amoco, Cargill, Dow Chemical, Du Pont, Fiat, General Motors, Glaxo Wellcome, Heineken, Hoechst, ICI, Mitsubishi, Monsanto, Nestlé, Norsk Hydro, Novartis, Procter & Gamble, Rio Tinto, Shell, Sony, Statoil, Toyota, Unilever, Unocal and the Western Mining Corporation. Club membership does not come cheap at US$50,000 per individual; however, the green prestige which companies can claim when associated with the WBCSD is no doubt a valuable commodity.

Today, the Geneva-based WBCSD continues to promote environmental protection through economic growth, self-regulation and unencumbered markets. Its solution to all environmental woes is eco-efficiency, a concept which it claims to have developed in its 1992 report *Changing Course*.[5] Eco-efficiency, which involves waste and energy use reduction during the production phase, is an attractive concept for industry as it can increase competitiveness without reducing public consumption levels or overall sales.

Five Years Later ...

Executive Director Stigson, while admitting that WBCSD member companies themselves are not necessarily models of environmentalism, stresses that the body helps them to highlight their specific green activities.[6] For example, when world leaders gathered in New York to evaluate progress on environmental commitments and sustainable development in the five years that had passed since the Rio Earth Summit, the WBCSD was there to showcase its accomplishments. A closer look at the WBCSD's glossy report released at Earth Summit II reveals a collection of carefully-chosen minor environmental success stories from selected member companies in areas including eco-efficiency, life-cycle analysis and environmental accounting. Shell, for example, had 'introduced a Shell management system for health, safety and environment which is used all around the globe'. Dow Chemical 'has learned from experience that voluntary projects are often more cost-effective long term than projects required by regulations and legislation.'[7]

The WBCSD was also busy behind the scenes at Earth Summit II. On 24 June 1997, Ambassador Razali Ismail, President of the UN General Assembly, and the WBCSD's Stigson hosted a luncheon for corporate representatives, three heads of state, the UN Secretary-General and several senior government officials[8] 'to chart a formalisation of corporate involvement in the affairs of the United Nations'.[9] At the meeting, UN Secretary-General Kofi Annan called on governments to stimulate corporate foreign investment in Southern countries. According to economist and author David Korten[10] who attended the meeting as one of the three NGO/academic representatives, Annan is 'firmly committed to using UN and other public funds to subsidise the corporate buy-out of Third World economies'.[11] Korten found the event 'a shattering experience, for it revealed a seamless alliance between the public and private sectors aligned behind the consolidation of corporate rule over the global economy.'[12]

Indeed, the WBCSD has gradually been solidifying relationships with various UN bodies as well as the Bretton Woods institutions. Its cooperation with the UN Environment Programme (UNEP) is well established, and the fruits of that union include regular joint reports, projects and programmes. It has closely followed the negotiations spawned by the Rio process leading to a climate convention, and has successfully lobbied for the adoption of several business-friendly 'solutions' to global warming including joint implementation and tradable emissions permits (see Chapter 17). In this vein, the WBCSD 'closely cooperates with the UNCTAD (UN Conference on Trade and Development) in their task of developing a mechanism for trading certified tradable offsets' and advises the World Bank in its planned carbon investment fund.[13]

These developments are distressing in that they lump the United Nations, which many have viewed as a bastion of hope for global equity and peace, together with more undemocratic and neoliberal global institutions including the multilateral development banks and the World Trade Organization (WTO). Indeed, the WBCSD is a regular guest in the halls of the WTO. According to Stigson, 'We participate in an informal, advisory capacity. We've produced reports about trade and environment that were well-received, and we are often contacted.'[14] The WBCSD also closely monitored the process of the OECD's failed attempt at a Multilateral Agreement on Investment.[15] In a letter dated 9 January 1998, WBCSD president Björn Stigson expressed his concern to OECD official Donald Johnston about the inclusion of binding language on environmental standards in the MAI, and took the opportunity in the same letter to promote the WBCSD's gospel of self-regulation by industry.

Greener is Better?

Image, of course, is key for large corporations in the current climate of increasing public suspicion about the economic and political power wielded by TNCs. In keeping with demands from civil society, the WBCSD has set up a working group on corporate social responsibility. It is hard, however, for the critical observer to put much faith into this group, however, which is chaired by Rio Tinto and Shell, each the focus of long-standing campaigns by local communities and international civil society groups around the world. The WBCSD has also set up stakeholder dialogues bringing together a mixture of 'senior business people' and a 'range of environment, development and intergovernmental groups'.[16] Tony Juniper of Friends of the Earth England, Wales and Northern Ireland, an observer at one of these dialogues, feels that the dialogues miss the point:

> The corporate representatives present at these meetings are sincere enough, but won't achieve very much until they change the system. Their firms will not contribute to a sustainable economy until they adopt better regulatory frameworks, new economic indicators and ecological taxes to shape new business practices that deliver on more than just financial aims. Instead, they still parrot the tired rhetoric of free markets and voluntary action.[17]

Most WBCSD companies are also members of other industry lobby groups that use significantly less environmental rhetoric, such as the European Roundtable of Industrialists (ERT, see Chapter 3). In fact, founder Stephan Schmidheiny himself was an ERT member until 1994, and the ERT publication *Reshaping Europe* commends the 'powerful idea' of the

BCSD, which 'can replace entirely the piecemeal approach of many existing programmes that seek to control polluters through punitive measures'.[18] However, Stigson attempts to create distance between the two groups: 'Their focus is on competitiveness,' he said about the ERT, but then continued, 'That is important, of course. We think profit is important too.'[19]

The WBCSD specialises in greening the reputations of some of the most aggressive, destructive companies in the world, as well as trying to portray the corporate world in general as caring and sensitive: 'Negatively viewed, business is swashbuckling around the globe largely uncontrolled by weakening governments. A more positive view holds that business, through freer trade, is spreading the technology, skills, and processes required for development and, given the right global frameworks, for more sustainable development.'[20] Thus, some of the most reprehensible companies in the world are portrayed not only as the bearers of sustainable development, but also as the spreaders of wealth and 'equity of opportunity' with their global investments.[21]

Under the earthy hype, however, the WBCSD's message is virtually indistinguishable from that of any other business lobby group looking for new markets. Privileged access to decision makers, close relationships with other leading industries, and the same basic goals of competitiveness and profit – all coated with a heavy layer of green paint – ensure that the WBCSD will continue to be a leading influence on global environment and development policies.

The Weather Gods: Corporations Profit from Climate Change

The verdict is in: the globe is getting hotter. Public, scientific and growing political consensus has been reached about the need for urgent action to combat climate change. Yet official CO_2 emission reduction targets are clearly insufficient given the magnitude of the problem. International climate negotiations have been transformed into trade agreements which grant Northern countries and their corporations the right to pollute through the increased use of market-based 'solutions'. The responsible profiteers are several coalitions of extremely powerful and influential transnational corporations (TNCs). These lobbies – which include well-known oil, automotive, mining and chemical companies in the United States, Europe, Australia and Japan – have made use of a number of different strategies in order to protect and inflate their climate-damaging profits.

According to the 2,500 scientists participating in the Intergovernmental Panel on Climate Change (IPCC), 'The balance of evidence suggests that there is a discernible human influence on global climate.'[1] Their warning is echoed by the two thousand economists who have confirmed that the threat of warming is enough to warrant 'preventative steps'.[2] Yet greenhouse gas emissions continue to be spewed into the atmosphere at an ever-increasing rate. Years of negotiations have resulted in a mere 39 industrialised countries agreeing to a pitifully low collective reduction of 5.2 per cent by 2012.[3] In fact, a global reduction of 60 per cent is needed in the first half of the next century in order to avoid cataclysmic climate change.

The 1997 Kyoto Protocol was celebrated by the nations of the world as the first legally binding treaty which sets limits to greenhouse gas emissions. But not only are the reductions written into the Protocol paltry, the agreement also helps to turn greenhouse gases into a commodity. Emissions trading, joint implementation (JI) and the Clean Development Mechanism (CDM), the three industry-inspired market-based 'solutions' enshrined in the Protocol, will allow industrialised countries and their corporations to avoid real measures to combat climate change. By sidestepping government regulation, these commercial escape mechanisms exclude the participation of social and environmental organisations and will delay real improvement.

Profitable Solutions

Emissions trading allows the 39 governments committed to collective reductions under the Protocol to trade the right to pollute among themselves. This can potentially lead to very dangerous scenarios. For example, Russia and the Ukraine committed to stabilising their emissions at 1990 levels in Kyoto, and the dismantling of inefficient Soviet industries has already led to a drop of more than 30 per cent in CO_2 emissions. Under emissions trading, this reduction could be 'bought' by an industrialised country which could then increase its own emissions proportionately. Joint implementation and the Clean Development Mechanism involve the trading of 'emissions reduction units' obtained in special projects aimed at reducing greenhouse gas emissions. These projects can be carried out among industrialised countries (JI) or between one industrialised and one Southern country (CDM). The CDM will supposedly facilitate the transfer of funding and technology for energy efficiency measures to Southern countries. However, it also permits rich countries and TNCs to evade their own climate responsibilities by dumping reduction burdens on the Third World.

Since the introduction of these market-based solutions in 1997, subsequent international climate negotiations have been deadlocked around their implementation rather than addressing the urgent matter of the insufficiency of current reduction commitments. The November 1998 negotiations in Buenos Aires[4] were bogged down by the divisive question of the extent to which these so-called 'flexible mechanisms' can be utilised. Industry and countries including the United States hope to avoid any ceiling on the amount of their reductions that can be achieved 'abroad'. Southern countries and the European Union, on the other hand, are wary of the risk that the US will not take any measures at home, and prefer to set limits on the use of such schemes.

Climate Spoilers Around the World

An unprecedented global offensive launched by oil, automotive, mining, chemical and nuclear interests is behind the adoption of market-based solutions to the climate crisis. Long before Kyoto, these lobbies were already busy orchestrating their multi-billion dollar campaign. Urgent warnings were issued that economic disaster, massive unemployment and loss of competitiveness would ensue if climate commitments were adopted. Industry claimed to have the climate situation under control. They argued that carbon and energy taxes and other regulations should be avoided at all costs in the name of international competitiveness. The solutions, they claimed, lay in voluntary agreements between governments and industry and an unimpeded free market permitting the development of new and improved technology. The climate lobbies managed to shift the debate into a realm dominated by technocratic solutions and corporate concerns like securing profits and strengthening global dominance.

The following is a sample of the preponderance of powerful coalitions, public misinformers and phoney scientists that make up the climate disruptors club.

The USA: the Boldest Offensive

The United States, responsible for 25 per cent of the world's greenhouse gas emissions, has been the headquarters of the most aggressive attempts to avoid binding commitments. Industry lobby groups have poured millions of dollars into PR campaigns denying the existence of climate change and confusing public opinion. Moreover, they have insisted that any binding agreement should also include Southern countries, despite the fact that these nations emit only a fraction of total global greenhouse gases and the historical responsibility for emissions rests on the industrialised world.[5] Hypocritically, corporate groups have also lobbied Southern countries to reject any environmental obligations that could hinder their development. Since the 1997 Kyoto Conference, US lobby groups have focused both on preventing the ratification of the Protocol and simultaneously fighting against a ceiling in the use of flexible mechanisms – securing a 'win–win' situation for industry no matter what happens.

The most outspoken and confrontational US-based lobby group battling the climate agreement and reduction commitments is the Global Climate Coalition (GCC). Created in 1989 by the infamous PR company Burson-Marsteller, the GCC's membership includes the American Petroleum Institute, Amoco, Chevron, Chrysler, Dow Chemical, Du Pont, Exxon, Ford, General Motors, Mobil, the National Mining Association, Texaco, Union Carbide, and until recently, British Petroleum and Shell.[6] Over the past several years, the GCC has waged an extensive, multimillion-dollar disinformation campaign. Its dirty tactics have included creating public scepticism through scientifically dubious glossy reports featuring dire warnings about mass unemployment resulting from emissions reduction. Its members attend climate negotiations meetings *en masse*, and demand that Southern countries commit to the same reductions.

The GCC also funds and promotes sceptical scientists to sow confusion about the very existence of climate change. This is a common tactic used by US industry in the climate debate: investing large sums in supporting global-warming sceptical 'scientists' to counter well-reviewed evidence put forward by the IPCC and other legitimate experts. In addition to taking part in extensive speaking tours across the nation, the sceptics have been put on stage as expert witnesses in state and federal legislatures. The prominence given by the media to these fake scientists lends them automatic public credibility.

In the aftermath of Kyoto, which the GCC described as 'unilateral economic disarmament'[7] for the United States, the coalition has slightly changed its strategy to openly campaign against US ratification of the Protocol. In an attempt to further perplex the public, the GCC has portrayed the EU's relatively more progressive climate policies and highly-developed clean technologies as a deliberate attack on the US economy. The EU, it claims, 'appears less interested in preventing harmful interference with the global climate than in engineering restrictions on the US economy and more favourable economic conditions for its own member countries which have failed to sustain viable economies'.[8]

The US-based Business Roundtable (BRT), comprising the CEOs of more than two hundred large corporations including Amoco, Chevron, Chrysler, Exxon, Ford, General Motors, Shell and Texaco, has played multiple cards in the climate debate. They have harped on the uncertainty of climate science and pushed for 'long-term approaches' which involve emissions reductions by Southern countries, voluntary industry agreements and flexible mechanisms. In June 1997, well in time for Kyoto, the BRT launched a million-dollar advertising campaign on climate change which urged the US administration not to rush headlong into restrictive policy commitments. The Roundtable's arguments have been reinforced by large donations to the Democratic Party (more than US$11 million in 1996) and a total disbursement of $57 million to members of Congress during the past two elections.[9] Not surprisingly, President Clinton's climate policies neatly mirror BRT viewpoints.

The BRT regularly conveys its demands to Clinton and other US authorities through personal meetings and letters. One letter, addressed to top US negotiator Stuart Eizenstat and leaked to Friends of the Earth, spells out the Roundtable's demands for the 1998 Climate Summit in Buenos Aires. Among other things, the message bluntly instructs the US delegation not to accept limits on emissions trading, suggesting that 80 per cent or more of the national commitment could be met in this way.

The BRT also demands full involvement in the Protocol for Southern countries, particularly China and India which currently emit one-twentieth as much carbon as the United States. Even so, the letter makes no secret of the fact that 'participation in full global trading actually puts southern countries at a competitive disadvantage.'[10] The letter also warns of the danger of loss of competitiveness with the EU if the use of the Kyoto market-based 'solutions' is limited: 'The more restrictions on trading, the more Europe improves its competitive position, which is probably not a surprise to you and your delegation who are veterans in dealing with the EEC.'[11]

Another player on the US scene is the Global Climate Information Project (GCIP). This enormous industry coalition, run by PR firm Shandwick (see Chapter 2), consists of groups such as the American Petroleum Institute, the American Plastics Council, and mining and trade unions including the United Mine Workers of America and the AFL-CIO. In September 1997, the GCIP launched a US$13-million-dollar advertising campaign designed to spread misinformation about climate change. One series of ads portrayed the GCIP as global environmentalists concerned about growing CO_2 emissions in the South and stressing the unfairness of exempting these countries from binding commitments.

In fact, many of these climate coalitions are no more than PR front groups, lending a fake neutrality to the corporate players behind them. Such is the case with the Information Council for the Environment (ICE). Created in 1991 by a coalition including the National Coal Association, the Western Fuel Association and the Edison Electrical Institute and managed by PR firm Bracy Williams, the ICE put $500,000 into an advertising blitz to 'reposition global warming as theory (not fact)'.[12] One of its members, coal company Western Fuel Association, produced its own $250,000 video, *The Greening of Planet Earth*, which argues that one benefit of climate change would be an extended growing season.

One of the most cynical aspects of the climate debate is the double role played by Northern-based TNCs in their dealings with Third World countries. In October 1997, Exxon Chair Lee Raymond addressed the 15th World Petroleum Congress in Beijing about the urgent need for Asian governments to continue to fight emissions regulations for at least the next two decades. Talking on behalf of the American Petroleum Institute (which includes British Petroleum, Chevron, Elf, Exxon and Shell), Raymond cautioned that Southern countries would lose foreign investment if binding targets were adopted at the upcoming Kyoto conference. On the home front, however, the oil industry's gloomy message is that commitments will mean massive job losses and reduced economic growth in the US due to industry's forced relocation to less-regulated countries.

International: Trading with Climate

Two groups operating at the international level have been very diligent in lobbying for the right climate for industry. The World Business Council for Sustainable Development (WBCSD, see Chapter 16), a coalition of 125 CEOs of transnational corporations founded in 1990, specialises in the strategic deflection of the growing challenge of the environmental movement on climate and other issues. By promoting self-regulation and spouting out sustainable development rhetoric, the WBCSD has helped its member TNCs to simultaneously green their images and push for unregulated economic growth and free market globalisation. It is worth noting that the corporations active in the supposedly green WBCSD – including Dow Chemical, Shell and Du Pont – have also been involved in aggressive campaigning against agreements on greenhouse gas emission reductions.

Together with the Japanese industry lobby Keidanren, the WBCSD and ICC organised an International Conference on Business Initiatives for Mitigating Climate Change in Kyoto. Björn Stigson, then President of the WBCSD, expressed his pleasure with the outcome of the Climate Summit: 'One of the major outcomes of Kyoto was the recognition that business is a key engine that will drive us towards a more sustainable future.'[13] Both the WBCSD and the ICC tout the clean development mechanism (CDM) as the most promising solution to the climate crisis. This is not surprising, as it will provide ample possibilities for TNCs to win new markets in Southern countries.

The WBCSD has kept busy on various fronts since Kyoto. It runs the International Business Action Plan on Climate Change which promotes CDM projects between its members and Southern countries; it cooperates closely with the UN Conference on Trade and Development (UNCTAD) in the creation of a mechanism for trading greenhouse gas emissions and is simultaneously advising the World Bank on its planned carbon investment fund. Some of these activities can truly be said to contribute to climate mitigation; however, the Business Council's proposals never go beyond those that are profitable for industry.

The International Chamber of Commerce (ICC, see Chapter 18), probably the most powerful corporate lobby group on earth, has similar strategies and demands: voluntary action from industry, global commitments which include Southern countries, market instruments, and nuclear energy as a viable and sustainable solution. The group's enormous resources give it a formidable lobbying capacity. In October 1998, two weeks before the Buenos Aires Climate Summit, the ICC sent a 30-person delegation to Dakar, Senegal. The mission, which included representatives from Shell, LaFarge, Texaco, Mobil and Chevron, met with energy and environmental ministers from more than twenty

African countries in order to tempt them with promises of technology transfer and foreign investment in exchange for support for the CDM.

Hot Air: the European Corporate Lobby Groups

European corporate lobby groups operate under rather different political circumstances than do their US colleagues. In the EU, environmental policies are generally higher on the political agenda than they are on the other side of the Atlantic. Energy taxes (not even under consideration in the US) have already been introduced in a number of countries, although on a very limited scale. The EU is currently discussing an energy tax, although this is accompanied by a decided lack of ambition and plenty of foot-dragging. Finally, the existence of climate change is undisputed in the European political arena.

Given these more challenging conditions, the most influential European business lobby groups such as the European Roundtable of Industrialists (ERT), the employers' organisation UNICE and the chemical industry federation CEFIC, decided upon a subtler approach to the climate debate. European industry has yet to accept binding targets for greenhouse gas reductions. Instead, it has concentrated on promoting voluntary action, industry's alternative to government regulation. Business claims that if the responsibility for solving environmental problems were left to them, the result would be the swift introduction of technological improvements to increase energy efficiency. The Clean Development Mechanism, joint implementation and tradable emissions are also promoted as the wisest solutions to the climate change problem.

UNICE: Fighting Binding Targets

When asked to comment on the US Global Climate Coalition's offensive against climate commitments, a spokesperson from UNICE, the European employers' confederation (see Chapter 4), took a softer approach: 'UNICE is not questioning the scientific aspects in such an aggressive way. We have a completely different approach – climate change has really become a matter of public concern, and we consider preventive measures necessary.'[14] None the less, UNICE (as well as the ERT and CEFIC) considered the EU's proposal for Kyoto for a 15 per cent reduction in CO_2 emissions by 2010 unreasonable. 'The Commission's very partial and very simplistic analysis greatly underestimates the cost to industry of meeting the EU's greenhouse gas reduction targets,' explained Zygmunt Tyszkiewicz, former UNICE Secretary-General.[15] UNICE argues that any international agreement should include Southern countries, and prefers a more relaxed target of 2020 for the CO_2 emissions reductions agreed in Kyoto. 'The fight against climate change will take 50 years,' says UNICE spokesperson Daniel Cloquet.[16]

ERT: Sessions Behind Closed Doors

The European Roundtable of Industrialists (see Chapter 3), which includes numerous companies with vested interests in climate change accelerating sectors, worked hard to avoid emissions reductions. As Assistant Secretary-General Caroline Walcot put it, 'We want to scrap discussions on percentage cuts ... There are people among us with some conscience stirred, but we do not want a quick-fix solution.'[17] In the run-up to Kyoto, representatives from the ERT's Environmental Watchdog Group held a series of meetings with European decision makers, making the point that 'the best agreements are those proposed by industry'.[18]

High-level meetings behind closed doors are an ERT speciality. At a preparatory meeting for the Kyoto Summit in October of 1997, the ERT met with other corporate groups and top politicians 'to work on the "bracketed text" of the Convention'.[19] NGOs were not invited, so as not to 'impede progress'.[20] The ERT has also called for a common corporate agenda for Kyoto, pushing for a 'positive action' approach which would allow industry to reap the full potential economic benefits of an agreement. As Caroline Walcot explains: 'The International Petroleum Industry Environmental Conservation Association has been pushing for a harder stance. We have been trying to persuade them, and the Americans and Australians, to be less rigid.'[21] The group apparently feels more satisfied with the results of Kyoto than does UNICE: 'It is a very good outcome for the EU, because we know we can deliver.'[22] The ERT's main pursuit now is to continue promoting voluntary initiatives by industry as a means of reaching emissions reductions.

CEFIC: Protecting HFCs

CEFIC, which consists of national chemical industry federations as well as companies like Bayer, British Petroleum, ICI, Monsanto Europe, Norsk Hydro, Novartis, Repsol, Rhône-Poulenc, Shell, Solvay and Union Carbide, initiated a special mission to prevent HFCs (hydrofluorocarbonate compounds) from being included in the Kyoto agreement.[23] Although alternatives to these dangerous chemicals are currently available, CEFIC proposed leakage reductions and efficiency improvements rather than a phase-out. Chemical industry pressure persuaded the EU to exempt HFCs from its greenhouse gas reduction goals, but in the end, the Kyoto Protocol included them in the 'basket' of gases to be reduced. CEFIC bitterly complained: 'This does not properly take into account the efforts of industry to substitute HFCs for CFCs and HCFCs in the early nineties in order to protect the ozone layer.'[24]

Fighting Ecological Taxes

The three major European industrial lobby groups all oppose a Europe-wide energy tax, a proposal that would greatly help to reduce greenhouse gas emissions. UNICE argues that such a tax would destroy industry's global competitiveness and would neither create jobs nor significantly reduce CO_2 emissions.[25] In the case that the EU decides to proceed with the implementation of an energy tax, however, UNICE demands the impossible: 'International conditionality and ... a total tax exemption for sectors with sharp exposure to international competition.'[26] The ERT's Caroline Walcot is equally clear: 'Governments should understand that tax schemes will only hurt industry. If you help industry to be more competitive, we would be better able to invest in solutions. We are saying "no taxes".'[27] CEFIC has also successfully dodged the imposition of an energy tax over the past years. CEFIC's Director for Climate Issues Bent Jensen recalls attempts by then Environment Commissioner Carlo Ripa de Meana to introduce such a tax back in 1991: 'We took a very hard step on that. He left Brussels in a hurry. Really, industry did not want this taxation.'[28]

Consequently, there is scant hope for an EU-wide energy tax. Weak attempts in 1992, 1995 and 1997 were quickly snuffed out by the unbending opposition of industry and a few member states. The most recent move, a watered-down compromise known as the Monti Proposal, forged in 1998,[29] was surprisingly rejected in the European Parliament by a coalition of conservatives and New Labour MEPs.[30] Ironically, a recent Parliament resolution on climate change states that the Monti Proposal would not even be sufficient to achieve Kyoto's greenhouse gas reductions. Without a CO_2/energy tax, the EU's commitments for greenhouse gas emissions reduction seem impossible, as measures proposed by member states are clearly insufficient to achieve the level of cuts required. Moreover, EU plans like the Trans-European Networks (TENs, see Chapter 8), a programme costing 400 billion euro for new transport infrastructure projects, and the liberalisation of energy markets, will make it almost impossible to achieve the proposed targets. The TENs alone are predicted to increase CO_2 emissions from the transport sector by 15 to 18 per cent.[31] In addition, newly liberalised energy markets will reduce energy prices and consequently increase consumption and CO_2 emissions.

Avoiding Regulation

CEFIC has a long tradition of introducing voluntary commitments in order to avoid government regulation of the chemical industry's environmental performance.[32] Like the ERT and UNICE, the chemical lobby umbrella promotes voluntary agreements on energy efficiency and joint implementation – particularly with Central and Eastern European countries – as an alternative to regulation.[33] But the most active and sophisticated approach to promoting self-regulation in the climate debate has come from the ERT. In preparation for the Kyoto Summit, the ERT's Environmental Watchdog Group issued a glossy report outlining 'how to choose the right policies for Europe'.[34] In the report, the ERT calls for voluntary action by industry and market-based solutions for reducing greenhouse gas emissions. As encouragement, the report presents a number of factories in which ERT member corporations have invested in new technology and reduced CO_2 emissions. However, overall figures on the status of global CO_2 emissions by the TNCs united in the ERT are suspiciously absent. Based on these isolated examples, the report recommends technological development, joint implementation and tradable emission rights as the ways forward. Alarmingly, it also concludes that the market should 'enable the further use of nuclear power as a source for carbon-free energy'.[35]

The ERT seems very confident that its strategy of corporate environmentalism will take the wind out of the environmental movement's sails. As Caroline Walcot puts it: 'The green groups are creaking with age ... The lesson from COP-2 [Second Conference of the Parties to the Climate Convention] was that they just don't recognise that it is a different world, with different needs. All they succeed in doing is making it more difficult for industry to take positive action on a voluntary level.'[36] UNICE's post-Kyoto demands prioritise long-term voluntary agreements as well as the unlimited use of flexible mechanisms. The employers want to be fully involved in the implementation of the Clean Development Mechanism, joint implementation and emissions trading, demanding not only that no ceiling is imposed in the use of these instruments, but that the 'emission reductions units' are fully tradable between all three. From the UNICE perspective, this should remove any need to further regulate or tax European industry.[37]

Climate Change: a Comeback for Nuclear Energy?

Climate change offers the last chance for a nuclear comeback in Europe, where many countries are intending to shut down nuclear power plants and the Swedish and German governments have committed to complete nuclear energy phase-outs. Both the ERT and UNICE promote nuclear energy as a viable solution to climate change, and the nuclear industry has its own active lobby groups which claim that investments in nuclear energy, and a new generation of 'inherently safe' power plants, are the best way to reduce greenhouse gas emissions. By institutionalising the Clean Development Mechanism (CDM), the Kyoto Protocol breathed new life into the future of European nuclear companies. The sector is lobbying for nuclear technology to be included as one of the possible CDM options so that its activities can be expanded to new markets. With this goal in mind, the nuclear lobby registered more than 150 lobbyists at the Buenos Aires Climate Summit.

What the nuclear lobby neglects to mention is that nuclear power indirectly causes enormous CO_2 emissions through energy-intensive activities such as the construction and decommissioning of reactors, the extraction, processing, transport and reprocessing of nuclear fuel, and the storage and treatment of nuclear waste. Furthermore, nuclear power is the least cost-effective – not to mention the most dangerous – method of producing electricity. Foratom, the European nuclear industry lobby, cynically insists that energy efficiency and renewables will not be sufficient to avert climate change. Predictably, the nuclear industry myopically views climate change as 'the best friend we have had in the past 40 years'.[38]

Economic Globalisation versus Climate Policies

Global climate negotiations are just one of the many arenas which have been captured and are being controlled by the corporate sector. The economic and political power of TNCs has become a serious barrier to effective action against global warming. As countries' economies are reoriented from local, regional and national markets towards production for the global economy, the TNC threat to relocate has become a common theme, and 'international competitiveness' the paramount objective.

The burden is now on social movements all over the world to increase pressure on governments to adopt real solutions to the climate crisis rather than caving in to corporate threats, misinformation and 'greenwash'. A closer look at TNC attempts to appear environmentally responsible exposes the irreparable damage that would result if corporations were left to their own devices in countering climate change. In fact, it is the corporate strategy of consolidating and globalising unsustainable Northern lifestyles and consumption patterns that constitutes one of the most serious threats to the earth's ecosystems today. And it is the deregulated global economy that has created such a dramatic political dependency on TNCs, making it ever more difficult for governments to reject the corporate climate agenda.

The Corporate Cooptation of the United Nations

The International Chamber of Commerce (ICC) has long been a triumphant lobbyist for global economic deregulation in fora such as the World Trade Organization, the G-8 and the OECD. Its latest coup, however, has been the solidification of a snug relationship with the United Nations. 'We have improved our relations and expanded the amount of work we do in collaboration with UN organisations with which we may not have been as close in the past,' says Stefano Bertasi from the ICC's Paris headquarters. 'Certainly I think there has been an opening on the UN's part, in the way it uses business and the way it considers the potential contribution of business to its work.'[1]

Forging a New Alliance

The UN's glasnost towards the corporate world is an important victory for lobby groups like the International Chamber of Commerce. According to ICC Secretary-General Maria Livanos Cattaui, UN Secretary-General Kofi Annan signalled that the time was ripe for consultation between the UN and business. 'The way the United Nations regards international business has changed fundamentally. This shift towards a stance more favourable to business is being nurtured from the very top,' Cattaui noted with satisfaction in a February 1998 *International Herald Tribune* column.[2]

Cattaui's optimism was entirely justified. Just days later, 25 ICC business leaders met with a heavyweight UN delegation headed by Kofi Annan. Cattaui heralded the 9 February 1998 meeting as the first step in 'a systematic dialogue'[3] between the two global actors. The ICC delegation – which included captains of industry from Coca-Cola, Goldman Sachs, McDonald's, Rio Tinto Zinc and Unilever – was encouraged by Annan's receptiveness to their ideas. As one ICC representative told the *Wall Street Journal*, 'I was impressed by the willingness and openness.'[4] In a joint statement resulting from the meeting, the ICC and the UN Secretary-General stated: 'Broad political and economic changes have opened up new opportunities for dialogue and cooperation between the United Nations and the private sector.' The newfound allies agreed to 'forge a close global partnership to secure greater business input into the world's economic decision-making and boost the private sector in the least developed countries'.[5] Industry representatives took advantage of the occasion to argue for the establishment of 'an effective regulatory framework for globalisation, including investment, capital markets, competition, intellectual property rights and trade facilitation'.[6]

Geneva Business Dialogue

The next high-profile event marking the budding romance between the ICC and the United Nations was the Geneva Business Dialogue in late September 1998. ICC President Helmut Maucher,[7] also the top dog in Nestlé as well as in the European Roundtable of Industrialists (ERT, see Chapter 3), was the undisputed central figure at this meeting. In his eyes, the Geneva Business Dialogue was convened in order to 'bring together the heads of international companies and the leaders of international organisations, so that business experience and expertise is channelled into the decision-making process for the global economy'.[8]

Geneva Business Dialogue participants included EU Finance Commissioner Yves-Thibault de Silguy, World Trade Organization Director-General Renato Ruggiero, high-level World Bank officials, prominent UN representatives like Under Secretary-General Vladimir Petrovsky and UNCTAD Secretary-General Rubens Ricupero, and presidents, prime ministers and other top decision makers from Finland, Hungary, Thailand, Switzerland and the United States. Among the 450 global business leaders in attendance were the CEOs of BASF, Goldman Sachs, ICI, Lyonnaise des Eaux, Mitsubishi, Norsk Hydro, Siemens, Shell and Unilever.

In his welcoming speech, Maucher explained that apart from 'socialising, networking and making friends', the Geneva Business Dialogue was intent upon achieving concrete results: specifically, 'action points' for how to 'establish global rules for an ordered liberalism'.[9] Two days later, he concluded: 'The ICC is in the front of the discussion, as the voice of business, dialoguing with the WTO and the UN.' Explaining that global problems required the delegation of power to the global level, Maucher called both for a strengthened WTO and for an overhaul of the UN's structure to facilitate the stronger involvement of business. 'A strong UN', he stressed, 'is good for business'.[10] In a satellite address to the Business Dialogue, UN Secretary-General Kofi Annan agreed that 'the UN and the private sector need each other', and pledged to 'build on the close ties between the UN and the ICC'.[11]

Managing Globalisation

'Building a truly global framework for cross-border investment and worldwide business activities'[12] was the central theme of discussion in Geneva. The global economic crisis, then spreading from South-east Asia through Russia and Latin America, was a source of great anxiety for participants. Sensing an upcoming backlash against trade and investment liberalisation, business leaders clearly feared that not only the financial crisis but also the debate about regulating the runaway global economy could move beyond their control and turn against them. Consequently, industry captains from the largest corporations on earth, businessmen from the South and various political leaders agreed on the need to regulate 'hot money' flows, to counter 'globaphobia' and to establish a global framework for 'managing globalisation'.

The Geneva Business Dialogue was the ICC's attempt to take the reins in the debate about the regulation of the global economy. The challenge of 'managing globalisation' had also been discussed at the 1998 World Economic Forum (see Chapter 15), but the Geneva Business Dialogue strove to surpass mere elite consensus building and to result in concrete cooperation. The need for 'managing globalisation' as signalled by business leaders was used as an argument for granting more regulatory powers to international bodies like the UN and the WTO; at the same time, close cooperation with the ICC as the representative of global business interests could be established. 'Currently, too much duplication and inadequate coordination are preventing intergovernmental bodies from handling effectively the complex and interrelated problems of the late 20th century,' concluded the conference declaration. 'Intergovernmental organisations will need additional authority, but with the proviso that they must pay closer attention to the contribution of business and competition to wealth creation.'[13]

ICC–UN Cooperation in Practice

The dialogue between the ICC and the UN is an ongoing one, and includes regular meetings at the highest level. During the World Economic Forum in January 1999, for example, UN Secretary-General Annan met again with Helmut Maucher to discuss 'avenues to pursue further the partnership between the United Nations and the private sector'.[14] Practical cooperation between business and UN agencies like the UN Conference on Trade and Development (UNCTAD) and the UN Development Programme (UNDP) is also becoming routine.

UNCTAD Secretary-General Rubens Ricupero provided an illustration of this collaboration during the Geneva Business Dialogue. Pointing to the number of African countries that have liberalised their economies yet still receive little foreign investment, he noted that UNCTAD and the ICC have started working on a set of guidelines to assist Less Developed Countries (LDCs) in attracting corporations. The project has been launched with six countries (Bangladesh, Ethiopia, Madagascar, Mali, Mozambique and Uganda) and involves TNCs like British-American Tobacco, British Petroleum, Cargill, Coca-Cola, DaimlerChrysler, Nestlé, Novartis, Rio Tinto, Shell, Siemens and Unilever. The corporations will assist in 'the identification of past practices and optimal conditions to create a favourable climate for FDI'.[15] ICC Secretary-General Cattaui concluded in the conference press release: 'The project gives practical expression to the closer working relationship between ICC and the UN system agreed with Secretary-General Annan almost a year ago.'[16]

The ICC–UNCTAD project is part of a larger effort which includes a joint series of business investment guides to the least developed countries. These guides aim to increase foreign direct investment flows into the 48 countries considered as 'least developed' by the UN, 38 of which are African. According to an UNCTAD press release, 'An important part of the process will be the identification of best practices and optimal conditions to create a favourable climate for FDI.'[17] This newfound cooperation between UNCTAD and business has become increasingly controversial. During a two-day consultation meeting with NGOs and trade unions in June 1998, UNCTAD was sharply criticised for 'losing its direction and spirit', and in particular for its close links with the ICC.[18] NGOs criticised several specific UNCTAD projects, for example, one on biotrade which facilitates 'transnational corporations making deals on access to biodiversity resources with developing countries'.[19]

Integrating Two Billion People into the Global Economy?

In March 1999, a coalition of campaign groups challenged what is probably the most ambitious joint project between the UN and business: the Global Sustainable Development Facility (GSDF). According to leaked documents, the proposed project, set up by the United Nations Development Programme (UNDP), aims to 'eradicate poverty, create sustainable economic growth and allow the private sector to prosper through the inclusion of two billion new people in the global market economy' by the year 2020.[20] The awkward nickname given to the project by its creators is '2B2M-2020' – meaning 'two billion to the market by the year 2020'. The GSDF involves 20 well-known corporations, including many with seriously flawed social and environmental records such as ABB, British Petroleum, Novartis, Rio Tinto, Shell and Statoil.[21] Each of the corporate project partners is charged a participation fee of US$50,000. Among the six senior advisers to the GSDF are ICC Secretary-General Cattaui and Björn Stigson of the World Business Council for Sustainable Development (see Chapter 16).

The companies involved in the GSDF will be granted access to UNDP offices in over 135 countries. Through their collaboration with the UN body, 'corporations will gain valuable insights into local conditions, key priorities and issues in developing countries, which will help them shape corporate strategies and products for these emerging markets.'[22] The UNDP boasts that the project will provide TNCs with 'worldwide recognition for their cooperation with the UN/UNDP', and that a special GSDF logo will allow business to highlight this relationship. The project will be kicked off with a feasibility phase of up to ten pilot projects jointly funded by UNDP and the corporations involved, followed by an official launch. Regarding the projects themselves, which should 'contribute to the overall strategy of creating opportunities for poor people to become active participants in the global economic system', the UNDP proposal is quite vague. Examples include 'rural telephony and electrification', 'developing products and services adapted to "emerging markets" of the poor', 'access to technology' and 'connecting the microfinance industry with the global financial markets'.[23]

On behalf of campaign groups from around the world, the US-based Transnational Resource and Action Center (TRAC) wrote an open letter to UNDP Executive Director James Gustave Speth, urging him to cancel the GSDF project. Speth defended the GSDF, stating that the UNDP's goal is 'to ensure that at least some investments occur in ways that are pro-poor, pro-environment, pro-jobs and pro-women'.[24] Despite these soothing words, TRAC Executive Director Joshua Karliner feels that the GSDF should be halted. 'We fear that these global corporations care more about "greenwashing" their own tarnished public images than about meeting the pressing needs of the world's poor,' he said. 'The UN should not be building collaborative projects with corporations which are the architects of a system that is usurping the UN's authority, and which are the perpetrators of human rights and environmental problems which so hinder sustainable human development.'[25] The UNDP's alternative vision, however, is that 'in the long term, a strong relationship exists between sustainable human development and the growth of shareholder value'.[26]

Today, close to half of the world's population survives outside of the global market economy. Although this enormous group, which includes traditional farmers, self-sufficient communities and indigenous peoples, is poor judged by neoliberal economic standards, they do not necessarily want to become active participants in the global economic system as

UNDP claims. In fact, there are many who categorically do *not* want this, including the indigenous peoples around the world whose traditional lifestyles are incompatible with the 'global market economy' and the farmers' movements in India and Latin America which have identified economic globalisation as the main threat to their livelihoods. It is hardly surprising that large corporations with an unlimited need to expand their market shares would be happy to have these people added to the global pool of consumers and producers.

Maucher's Ambitions

The new partnership with the UN is part and parcel of the ICC's general strategy to relaunch and reinvigorate its image in order to acquire increased visibility and influence. The reorganisation process began in 1995, when Helmut Maucher took the helm as ICC Vice-President. He brought in a new Secretary-General, Maria Livanos Cattaui, who had organised the World Economic Forum in Davos for many years and has an extensive network of elite international contacts (see Chapter 15).

Maucher used his own personal network of business contacts to recruit additional industry leaders for ICC membership. Feeling that the ICC had hitherto not been sufficiently influential or visible in the international press,[27] he prioritised a heightened emphasis on media outreach. He also focused on streamlining the organisation's activities and creating and lubricating ICC channels to decision makers.[28] This included securing unencumbered access to top-level UN officials. Observing the effective work of environmental and human rights NGOs within the UN system, he warned: 'We have to be careful that they do not get too much influence.'[29] Arguing that industry deserves a privileged place at the head of the UN table, Maucher stressed: 'Governments have to understand that business is not just another pressure group but a resource that will help them set the right rules.'[30]

There are several reasons why the ICC wants to establish 'partnerships' with international institutions like the WTO, UNCTAD and the UN General Secretariat. The joint statement issued in February 1998 by the UN Secretary-General and the ICC provides some insight: 'Business has a strong interest in multilateral cooperation, including standard-setting through the United Nations and other intergovernmental institutions and international conventions on the environment and other global and transborder issues.'[31] In these partnerships lurk the attractive potential of gaining control over international rule setting and influencing global regulatory institutions so that the business agenda is promoted and liberalisation locked in. By encouraging the setting of global rules, the ICC hopes to avoid the emerging backlash against globalisation, which could well turn against its members.

Secondly, this 'partnership' strategy would prevent the positioning of these global bodies against business, which, according to the ICC, NGOs have successfully accomplished in the past within various UN institutions. The ICC's attempt to establish strong working relations with UNCTAD, for example, will discontinue the historic role of this organisation in promoting the interests of Third World people and civil society movements. Finally, a third advantage of working closely with international organisations and particularly the UN is the legitimacy gained in working with these respected bodies. As the US *Journal of Commerce* put it, the UN's name 'offers a highly desirable endorsement in a brand-crazy world'.[32]

Shared Vision?

'Building a stronger relationship with the business community is part of Kofi Annan's "quiet revolution" to renew the United Nations for the twenty-first century', announced the UN's Department of Public Information in a recent leaflet.[33] Although the UN has sought contact with the Business Consultative Council (established by the World Economic Forum), the Prince of Wales Business Leaders' Group and other international business coalitions, the ICC seems to have emerged as the 'preferred dialogue partner' according to Maucher.[34]

The big question is why the UN is so eager to enter into such a partnership, which has already proven controversial. In fact, there are a number of pragmatic reasons. Support of the ICC might help the UN to regain a central position in global policy making, which during the last years of intense economic globalisation has been predominantly controlled by the Bretton Woods financial institutions.[35] Also, working with the ICC changes the UN's image, which in some countries, particularly the United States, is seen as a weak, ineffective bureaucracy.[36] Finally, the ICC has already returned some favours by asking G-8 leaders for new funding for the UN at their 1998 and 1999 summits.[37]

The UN's close cooperation with the ICC and its individual TNC members reflects its ideological transformation over the past decades. In a clear departure from its original vision, it now promotes economic globalisation and TNC investment as the best ways to combat poverty. This metamorphosis explains ICC Secretary-General Cattaui's claim to have UN support for her organisation's vision: 'What makes the dialogue possible is the perception by both sides that open markets are a precondition for spreading more widely the benefits of globalisation, for integrating developing countries into the world economy, and for improving living standards of all the world's peoples, and in particular the poor.'[38]

The joint UN–ICC statement appears to confirm a wide-ranging consensus, as it emphasises the importance of 'the effective functioning of the global market place and the existence of open, equitable, inclusive economic systems, based on the free flow of trade, investment for economic growth and development and the avoidance of protectionist pressures.'[39] The UN's embrace of this world view was reconfirmed at the 1999 World Economic Forum in Davos, where Annan promoted a vision of 'a global market ... with a human face' and 'a world which offers everyone at least a chance of prosperity, in a healthy environment' as an alternative to the current world 'which condemns a quarter of the human race to starvation and squalor'.[40]

The UN seems to have renounced its concerns about the growing economic dominance of TNCs worldwide. Until 1993, it had a Centre on Transnational Corporations (UNCTC), which carried out research and worked with the Commission on Transnational Corporations, an intergovernmental body with the mandate to develop a code of conduct for TNCs. Corporations were extremely hostile to the UNCTC, which also developed environmental guidelines for industry and promoted the restriction of foreign investment in South Africa during the apartheid regime. In 1993, the UNCTC was dismantled as part of an internal 'reorganisation', and UNCTAD became the new UN focal point for work on TNCs. UNCTAD, however, has not addressed the regulation of TNC activities, but rather works closely with them in order to stimulate foreign investment flows to the Third World. UN work on a code of conduct for TNCs has stopped entirely.

Maucher and His Critics

Maucher is clearly sensitive to the fact that the ICC's attempts to coopt the UN are vulnerable to critique. He launched a fierce attack on his critics at the Geneva Business Dialogue in September 1998. 'Let me take the bull by the horns,' he told the conference. 'We have heard the last days about people opposing and criticising the Geneva Business Dialogue, just because for the first time business gets involved in talking with the UN. It is disgusting that some people say that Annan and the UN are dominated by business.'[41] In fact, Maucher has a long history of conflict with citizens' organisations, primarily due to the decades-long consumer boycott against Nestlé because of its unethical promotion of infant formula.[42]

During the final press conference of the Geneva Business Dialogue, Maucher again complained to journalists about demonstrations by activist groups the previous night: 'We feel that these groups realise that the ICC is now organised more efficiently as the business voice in contact with the UN ... It is difficult for them to digest that the business voice is also important.' More aggressively, he asserted that NGO activities should be transparent: 'How are they financed, and what do they stand for? We will insist on answers, and that they follow the normal democratic process and stick to the rules.'[43]

Maucher's question about the funding of protests against the Geneva Business Dialogue is symptomatic of his elitist detachment from the public realm. The peaceful and colourful protests – several hundred people enjoying music, food, banners and speeches – were organised by enthusiastic volunteers on an almost non-existent budget. This type of event is obviously well beyond the imagination of an industrialist from a corporation with a global advertising budget of around two billion dollars, and for whom multimillion-dollar acquisitions of competing companies are a regular occurrence.

It is also remarkable that Maucher emphasises the difference between 'responsible NGOs' and 'activist pressure groups'. Clearly, the ICC feels seriously threatened by these less delineated, grassroots-based movements and is taking action to marginalise them. When the ICC met with Tony Blair in May 1998 to present its message to the G-8 Summit, it suggested a similar 'weeding out' of certain NGOs. The ICC statement to the G-8 proposes that it would 'be useful for the UN and other inter-governmental bodies to establish rules to clarify the legitimacy and accountability of many new non-governmental organisations engaged in the public policy dialogue which proclaim themselves to represent particular interests or significant sections of civil society'.[44]

The ICC has taken an offensive position to deal with thorny questions about its ambitions to shape a TNC-friendly 'global regulatory framework'. The most fundamental question of all, however, is whether or not corporations should leave the shaping of rules – local, national or global – to democratically elected governments in cooperation with civil society.

Part IV

Challenging Corporate Power

Challenging Corporate Power

The previous chapters have provided an overview of the diverse methods of political pressure used by corporations. The massive resources which TNCs and their lobby groups have at their disposal for lobbying decision makers and manipulating perceptions through PR campaigns is one key factor behind corporate influence in the political realm. Additionally, the political power held by TNCs is connected to their privileged access to politicians and civil servants in national and international political institutions. Finally, the current elite consensus around the expediency of a global economy dominated by TNCs provides fertile ground for corporate lobbying.

Some of the negative impacts of political dominance by transnational corporations have also been touched upon. Protective policies of all kinds are increasingly being subordinated to corporate clamours for international competitiveness, with the predictable result that social and environmental priorities are crowded out. The global 'free market' policies pursued by industry lobby groups result in a further concentration of economic power in the grip of a limited number of global corporations. This causes the destruction of local economic structures all around the world, at enormous social and environmental cost.

This book argues that the potent cocktail of economic and political power wielded by mega-corporations is a serious matter, meriting urgent attention in the political debate. In this final chapter, we identify some of the political and structural factors that have encouraged the growing corporate influence over politics, and put forward some proposals for how to minimise the disproportionate political influence of TNCs in Europe and beyond.

The EU: a Corporate Lobbyist's Paradise

The accelerated process of European unification has resulted in a fundamental democratic gap, which provides an ideal environment for corporate lobbying. The powers of the European Parliament remain far too limited to compensate for the loss of democratic control created as more and more decision-making power shifts from national capitals to Brussels.

This transfer in policy formulation upwards to the EU level tends to shift the balance of power between corporate and other societal interests within individual member states. Wealthy corporations and their lobby groups have the means to set up well-staffed offices in Brussels and to hire external consultants and PR agencies. This enables them to keep track of the details of relevant EU policies and to position lobbyists to best influence decision making.

By contrast, European-level umbrella NGOs are often underdeveloped, disconnected and lacking in resources. Social movements are organised primarily on the local and national levels, and the political debates in which they are engaged usually unfold within a national context where European questions receive little attention.

Furthermore – and this phenomenon is apparent both at the national and EU levels – top managers in Europe's largest corporations enjoy privileged access to key decision makers. This access is fully exploited by elite groupings like the European Roundtable of Industrialists (ERT) and the Transatlantic Business Dialogue (TABD). In matters such as foreign economic policy, the European Commission regards TNCs as a natural constituency that supports its quest for power in exchange for a say in policy matters.

These cosy connections between European decision makers and corporate lobby groups must be challenged as deeply undemocratic. In particular, semi-institutionalised corporate-government alliances like the TABD and the Competitiveness Advisory Group (CAG), in which unelected corporate representatives are granted illegitimate powers, must be brought into question.

The complex and opaque institutional set-up of the EU makes it almost impossible to track who is lobbying whom on which issues and with what effect. In this book, we have tried to provide some insight into the corporate lobbying scene in Brussels and elsewhere, but the picture is obviously far from complete. More investigative research and media reporting on the nature and extent of corporate political influence is sorely needed.

Corporations out of Politics?

Clearly, the first steps to diminish corporate political power would be to expose the extent of the political influence wielded by the corporate sector and to hold TNCs publicly accountable. This would necessitate measures such as reporting obligations for the political activities of corporations, corporate lobbyist registration systems, mandatory transparency about financial donations to political parties and so forth. The implementation of such measures might help to catalyse a debate about whether or not corporations should be directly involved in politics.

Currently, there is scant transparency around the political activities of European TNCs. The corporations active within the political groupings described in this book are almost without exception unwilling to inform the public about their lobbying operations. This is the indisputable conclusion of *Ending Corporate Secrecy*, a study by Corporate Europe Observatory based on corporate annual reports, web sites and other publicly available information as well as extensive correspondence with over fifty European TNCs.[1] Many well-known corporations refuse to disclose any information at all about their political activities, and many others divulge only very limited information. Some acknowledge their membership in 'business associations' but not lobby groups, while others claim that involvement in corporate lobby groups does not constitute a political activity.

Shell and Unilever, for example, failed to give anything but very general information when questioned about their membership in multiple lobbies, referring all questions to the secretariats of the corporate groups. Bayer, Bosch and Hoechst admitted their involvement in lobby groups, but explicitly refused to elaborate any further. The same goes for Nestlé, Siemens, Petrofina, Société Générale de Belgique and others which denied that their work in business associations constitutes a political activity. ABB, Carlsberg, Krupp, Pilkington and others refused to provide any information whatsoever.

Whether or not the corporate political activities described in this book are legitimate, there is no doubt that the secrecy of the involved corporations is not legitimate. TNCs that find it appropriate to dedicate vast financial resources towards influencing political processes should live up to basic standards of transparency and accountability. They should voluntarily publicise information about their political positions and activities in their annual reports and on their web sites, and should respond openly and conclusively to queries. This would make it possible to hold corporations accountable for environmentally and socially harmful political lobbying, for instance by boycotting products until a change in behaviour has been implemented. Unfortunately, the results of *Ending Corporate Secrecy* suggest that corporations are by no means disposed to agreeing voluntarily to even a basic level of transparency.

The introduction of binding rules for information disclosure about corporate political activities would seem to be an obvious step, but corporate lobbying on the European and international levels remains seriously under-regulated. The European Parliament is gradually strengthening provisions in this field, but progress is painfully slow and the results insufficient. In 1997, the Parliament introduced the obligatory registration of lobbyists attempting to influence MEPs as well as some minimal rules for regulating lobbyist behaviour. The rules were made somewhat stricter in March 1999; in particular, MEPs are now obliged to submit annual reports on extracurricular employment as well as on financial and other support received from outsiders, including from corporate sources. A peek at the register between the years of 1996 and 1998, however, reveals that a substantial number of MEPs submitted nothing, and those who used the register often failed to declare everything.[2] The lobbyist register is largely a list of names, and contains no details about whom the lobbyists represent nor what their business in the Parliament entails.

The European Parliament's rules are much less stringent than the US Lobbying Disclosure Act, which forces corporations and lobby groups to report on their lobbying-related expenses every six months. Although this has reduced neither the level of lobbying nor the influence of lobbyists in the US, it has significantly increased transparency in the political realm. Based on the information disclosed in the US register, the media and campaign groups are able to obtain a far more precise picture of corporate lobbying than is possible in the European Union. The Washington-based Centre for Responsive Politics, for instance, publishes overviews of corporate lobbying directed at the Congress, with details about individual sectors, corporations and lobby groups.[3]

Though weak, the European Parliament's regulations are still better than those governing the European Commission and the Council of Ministers. Within these institutions, the only real possibility to monitor corporate lobbying is provided by the 'Access to Information' rules. Corporate Europe Observatory's repeated requests for information have met with unpredictable and often unreliable responses from the Commission.[4] This is discouraging, and will likely deter many people from further pursuing information.

Rolling Back Corporate Economic Power

The increasing bargaining power of TNCs in the European and global economies, a result of decades of 'free trade' and deregulation policies that facilitate corporate mobility, is a recurring theme in the case studies presented in this book. These policies, which include trade liberalisation, privatisation, deregulation of labour markets and so forth, have also shifted the power balance on the national level to favour business and have simultaneously decreased the countervailing forces of trade unions and social movements. In addition, governments have abandoned many of the policy instruments previously devised to regulate business. All in all, economic dependency on international trade and investment and thereby on TNCs has increased dramatically. This is a fundamental reason for the firm corporate grasp on European politics.

Ultimately, then, the key to reducing corporate political power is the dissolution of this dependency, thereby making room for genuine democratic control over the economy. Politicians are enslaved to the erroneous idea that there is no alternative to the current economic reliance on TNCs; consequently, it is critical that they are provided with viable and realistic alternatives. One condition for any such transformation is the discontinuation of the European Commission's ongoing offensive for deregulation inside and outside of the EU, and the parallel creation of space for new political ideas.

Optimists believe that the EU could be transformed and used as an instrument to achieve democratic control and regulate the market forces that have been unleashed by years of deregulation and economic globalisation. The evidence put forward in this book, however, generally does not support such an optimistic position. The reality of the past few years in fact indicates that national governments pressured by civil society are more likely to take the lead in introducing progressive market regulations. Examples are the French government's reduction of the working week to 35 hours, however limited in scope, and the ecological taxes introduced by several northern European governments, although these remain far below the magnitude needed to achieve ecological sustainability.

The European unification process of the last decades was built upon the pursuit of greater economic growth, and this heritage continues to dominate EU policies. Despite the self-orchestrated green and pro-jobs image, existing European Union regulations often undermine rather than further the fulfillment of social and environmental goals. The economic foundations of the EU, the Single Market and the single currency, are rock solid, whereas many social and environmental regulations amount to little more than vague words and voluntary agreements. The rigid legislation of the internal market, for instance, *de facto* blocks countries from proactively introducing new environmental policies, because they might be interpreted as barriers to free trade. Similarly, the single currency and the harsh requirements of the stability pact are serious road-blocks for governments wanting to increase public expenditure to create new employment.

Turning the Tide

There is no ultimate blueprint for an alternative to economic globalisation and the ever fiercer global competition it entails. However, it is possible to chart a course towards a future world with more democratised and sustainable societies, including high social and environmental standards.

Turning the tide would begin with the rejection of policies that increase the economic dominance of TNCs and the adoption of measures to restrict their power. Gaining genuine democratic control over finance and capital would constitute a first step in that direction, and would help governments and communities to improve social conditions and job opportunities. Realistic proposals already exist, such as taxes on international financial transactions,[5] stringent restrictions on short-term speculative capital flows, and international action to combat corporate tax evasion. The regulation of corporate investment is equally crucial. This could happen through the restriction of access in the case of natural resource exploitation, or by imposing performance requirements decided upon by the affected communities, such as job creation, the use of local suppliers and adherence to high environmental standards.

The urgently needed rebuilding of local economies is possible through the introduction of community reinvestment legislation and with direct public investment in sustainable agriculture, public transport, urban renewal, social services, education and health care. But rather than waiting for governments to act, many local communities have discovered ways of recapturing their lost vitality. Local credit unions and other small-scale savings schemes with clear social and environmental objectives can be created, breaking public dependency upon conventional profit-driven banks. Community Supported Agriculture programmes encourage local food production and allow farmers to escape from the drawbacks of industrial agriculture.[6] A growing number of decentralised Local Exchange and Trade Schemes (LETS) promote economic and social activities outside of the mainstream economy.[7] All of these alternative economic systems contribute to the disempowerment of TNCs, at the very least by withholding from them the profits they need to survive.

The power of individual consumers should not be underestimated. Ethical consumption – buying products that are socially and environmentally benign and leaving others on the shelves – has enormous potential, as do boycotts that force companies to listen to the bottom line set down by consumers. In many parts of Europe and the world, shareholders' actions and international alliances against specific corporations and their malpractices have produced significant, albeit reluctant, change in corporate behaviour. A number of campaigns have succeeded in forcing companies to modify certain practices, or to withdraw hazardous products from the market.

The last years have seen an encouraging upsurge of campaigns against corporate misbehaviour and for corporate accountability. Campaigns addressing the political activities of corporations are also on the rise. One encouraging example is the increasingly successful campaign to pressure corporations to leave the controversial Global Climate Coalition (GCC), a business grouping lobbying against government action to reduce atmosphere-damaging CO_2 emissions. British Petroleum and Shell left the GCC in 1997 and 1998 respectively, and pressure is now building up to force corporations like Exxon do the same.

In the era of European and global restructuring and increasing corporate power, it is time to evaluate the traditional strategies, tools and skills used by social movements. In his book *The Corporate Planet,* Joshua Karliner calls for 'grassroots globalisation' and stresses: 'The old 1960s slogan "think globally, act locally" is no longer sufficient as a guiding maxim ... Civil society must confront the essential paradox of the twenty-first century by developing ways of thinking and acting both locally and globally at the same time.'[8] Rather then merely aiming to reform individual corporations to make them more socially responsible or more accountable, the ultimate goal must be to dismantle the macro-structures of corporate political power.

Social movements have an increasing awareness about the shift of power from national governments to international institutions, and the role played by corporations in the shaping of the whole spectrum of public policies from food and health to employment and education. By campaigning against flawed global and regional free trade and investment agreements, groups are attacking the structures of corporate power. Campaigns such as that against the Multilateral Agreement on Investment (MAI) helped movements to develop skills to challenge the political power of TNCs. The increased use of the Internet has also facilitated a new model of cooperation. The international campaign which killed the MAI in the OECD (see Chapter 12) provides an example of how different actors, including environmentalists, international solidarity campaigners, feminists, artists and many others, worked together to create an extraordinary exchange of information, analysis and common strategies, and at the same time conducted a diverse range of local and national campaigns. Crucially, opportunistic alliances with right-wing groupings, which would have undermined the moral authority of the campaigns, were avoided.

Inspiring examples of local people who have challenged the legitimacy and dominance of corporations through direct action and civil disobedience are accumulating. Growing consciousness about the socially destructive impacts of market liberalisation embodied in the WTO has led to massive resistance by Indian farmers fighting to protect their livelihoods and traditional community agricultural practices. In the United Kingdom, thousands of people were mobilised to resist the government's massive road-building plans using non-violent direct action. The UK is also home to a vibrant movement against genetically engineered crops. The uprooting of fields containing genetically manipulated plants and the exposure of corporate interests behind transgenic food have inspired a heated national debate and a corresponding loss of legitimacy for biotech companies such as Monsanto (figure 4).

Figure 4   Activists uproot genetically modified crops in England. Some estimates measure public opinion in the UK as 70 per cent against genetically modified foods. (Photo: genetiX snowball)

The surge in campaigns against genetic manipulation in the UK and in other EU member states shows an inspiring way forward. In several countries, these campaigns have forced governments to introduce bans on genetically modified organisms and moratoriums on approving new genetically modified products, thereby breaching the rules of the EU's Single Market. Those achieving these important victories are often not aware that they have forced their governments to violate EU regulations, but are simply demanding that democratically-elected governments prioritise environmental, social and ethical concerns over corporate interests.

As these motivating victories continue to multiply, people at the individual, local, national and international levels are becoming empowered to claim the precedence of their rights over corporate privileges. Today's increasingly footloose TNCs and the global marketplace within which they operate are neither economically necessary nor immune to change. Viable and fulfilling alternatives do exist. As people all over the world continue to reject the corporate agenda, its powerful grasp on people's work, communities and lives will begin to crumble.

Part V

Appendices

Navigating the Brussels Labyrinth: The European Union and its Institutions

> Brussels isn't a true democracy inasmuch as it's not a political system where you have politicians or public servants who are dealing with voters and citizens. It's kind of one level away. The democracy comes from the member states, almost irrespective of the European Parliament.
>
> *John Russell, EU Committee of the American Chamber of Commerce*[1]

On 15 March 1999, in an unprecedented act, the entire executive of the European Union – all 20 European Commissioners – stepped down after the publication of a damning report by an independent investigative committee into fraud, nepotism and mismanagement within the Commission.[2]

The report concluded that 'it is becoming difficult to find anyone who has even the slightest sense of responsibility' within the Commission. No commissioner was personally accused of lining his or her own pockets, but they were collectively accused of having lost control of an increasingly corrupt bureaucracy. As power continues to seep away from national member states and flows into the institutions of the European Union, this 'loss of control' is cause for alarm.

In this book, it is argued that this lack of democratic accountability and loss of control within the European Union's institutions enables corporate lobby groups to exercise a disproportionate influence on European Union policies. This appendix provides some general information on the main EU institutions.

European Commission

The European Commission serves as the nucleus, the clearing-house and the engine for the European Union. It has the ability to initiate new legislation, and oversees the implementation of legislation that has been approved by the Council of Ministers (and in most cases, the European Parliament).

The Commission is presumed to be an 'institution whose vocation is the completely impartial representation of the general interest'.[3] However, nationality plays an important role in the composition of the Commission: each member state is entitled to at least one of the twenty commissioners, whereas the larger states have a maximum of two. The Commission and its President are appointed for five-year periods through a unanimous decision by the 15 member state governments. Under the Amsterdam Treaty, which came into force on 1 May 1999, the European Parliament may withdraw the mandate of the Commission as a whole, but it cannot dismiss individual commissioners. The Commission oversees the work of the EU's 16,500 civil servants in the 23 directorates in Brussels.

Not all of the commissioners and their respective directorates have equal political power. For example, DG I (External Commercial Policy), DG III (Industry) and DG XV (Single Market) are much more influential in shaping EU policies than are DG V (Social Affairs) or DG XI (Environment). These inequalities within the Commission are very beneficial to industry, which has good access to the directorates for industry and Single Market, whereas the environmental movement and trade unions work primarily with the less powerful directorates for social affairs and environment.

Council of Ministers

The democratic gap in Europe, which is a matter of real concern, is there basically because of the Council of Ministers. And the real democratic danger that I see is that governments will be only too happy to make decisions on the European level, because they are decisions behind closed doors which they can then interpret from a particular angle for their own national electorates rather than being much more under scrutiny if they have to do it in the national framework.
Alan Watson, Burson-Marsteller[4]

Whereas the European Commission is probably the most well-known EU institution, the real power resides with the lower-profile Council of Ministers. The Council – composed of ministerial representatives from all member states[5] – has the final say in whether or not legislative proposals by the Commission will be approved.[6] To accomplish this task, it convenes in various sectoral compositions. The national ministers of agriculture, gathered in the Agriculture Council, decide on issues related to agriculture; transport issues are decided by transport ministers in the Transport Council, and so forth. Meetings are prepared by Brussels-based working groups of the Council and the Committee of Permanent Representatives (COREPER).

In some fields, like taxation, Council decisions must be unanimous; other areas depend upon qualified majority voting. The votes of ministers from different member states carry different weights depending roughly upon national population. In what is among the gravest 'democratic deficits' of the European Union, the proceedings of the Council of Ministers are only to a very limited extent open to the public.

COREPER, the Committee of Permanent Representatives, adds yet another non-transparent layer to the EU decision-making apparatus. COREPER ambassadors from each member country are vested with considerable amounts of decision-making power by national ministers, who are generally too busy to spend time in Brussels. These relatively anonymous civil servants, who include very few women among their ranks, have set up a true 'old boys' network' in which they 'negotiate big deals, often informally over lunch'.[7] Every day, the COREPER ambassadors and their deputies split into some twenty working groups on various subjects. Thus, according to *The Economist*, 'about 90 per cent of Council decisions are taken before ministers ever get entwined.'[8]

European Council

The Council of Ministers of the EU has a rotating presidency. The member state which holds the six-month presidency hosts at least one EU Summit. During these Summits, also dubbed 'European Councils', the 15 heads of state or government plus the president of the European Commission decide on the medium- and long-term political goals of the European Union. More detailed decisions on EU legislation are not dealt with during European Councils, but fall within the domain of the Council of Ministers.

European Parliament

> Parliament has always taken any crumbs that have fallen off the table. Like a good dog, very pleased with anything that is given to it.
> *Michael Hindley, Member of the European Parliament*[9]

Next to the Council and the Commission, the European Parliament (EP) is the third leading EU institution. The EP has 626 members. Each member state has a fixed number of representatives in the Parliament based on the size of its population. Members of the European Parliament (MEPs) are chosen in national direct elections, held every five years.

Unlike national parliaments, the European Parliament cannot draft legislation; it can only revise or in some cases block legislation drafted by the Commission. Only in limited policy areas – the 'first pillar', where the so-called co-decision procedure applies[10] – can the European Parliament veto Council decisions. But in most cases, the final decision lies with the Council of Ministers and takes place in secret.

The Parliament's power remains limited, although it has increased with the Maastricht and Amsterdam Treaties. 'MEPs are lonely people,' according to one lobbyist. 'They are flattered when you take an interest in them. You give them information about an issue that helps them look and sound good. But they are still trivial in terms of decision-making power. Cultivating them is an investment in the future.'[11]

A Condensed History of the EU

The first major step in the process of European unification was the 1957 Treaty of Rome, which created the European Economic Community (EEC). The central feature of the treaty was the creation of a common market, with free movement of goods, services, people and capital. The initial six members of the EEC (Belgium, France, Germany, Italy, Luxembourg and the Netherlands) were joined by the UK, Denmark and Ireland in 1973 and later by Greece (1981), Spain (1986) and Portugal (1986). With the 1987 Single European Act, the powers of the EEC institutions, particularly the European Commission and the Council of Ministers, were expanded significantly. The EEC countries committed themselves to removing all remaining barriers to trade and investment, which entailed European directives replacing national environment and consumer protection legislation. The European Court of Justice was granted the authority to decide if national legislation should be considered a barrier to trade.

The 1991 Maastricht Treaty contained a plan of action for Economic and Monetary Union (EMU), to result in a Single European Currency replacing the national currencies. The European Parliament received expanded powers in a number of policy areas (including transport, environment, etc.). In 1994, the EEC changed name to the European Union (EU) and three new countries joined (Sweden, Finland and Austria), bringing the total to 15.

After almost two years of negotiations, the EU Summit in June 1997 in Amsterdam agreed on a new treaty. The Amsterdam Treaty expanded the EU's powers in the areas of Justice and Home Affairs, and constitutes a further step towards the creation of an EU-wide defence and foreign policy. The European Parliament's mandate was further expanded to include co-decision power (veto right) on employment incentives, customs cooperation, social policy, equal opportunities, public health, transparency and countering fraud. Many important policy areas (for example, harmonisation of legislation, agriculture, transport, taxation, industry, cohesion, Common Foreign and Security Policy and Justice and Home Affairs) however remain under the consultation procedure, with very limited power for the European Parliament. In 1998, the EU started negotiations about membership for five new countries, including four from Central and Eastern Europe, which might be included in the EU beginning in 2003. On 1 January 1999 a huge leap forward in European unification was taken with the launch of the euro, the EU's single currency. According to plan, the euro will replace eleven national currencies by the year 2002.

1957:   Treaty of Rome creates the European Economic Community (EEC) with six member states (Belgium, France, Germany, Italy, Luxembourg, the Netherlands).

1962:   The start of the Common Agricultural Policy (CAP): market and price guarantees and various protectionist measures, coordinated and financed by the EEC.

1973:   United Kingdom, Denmark and Ireland join the EEC.

1979:   European Monetary System established, including the European Currency Unit (ECU).
        First direct elections for the European Parliament.

1981:   Greece joins the EEC.

1986:   Spain and Portugal join the EEC.

1987:   Single European Act in operation.

1991:   Maastricht Treaty signed.

1992:   Official start of the European Single Market (31 December).

1994:   Sweden, Finland and Austria join the EU (Norway says no in referendum).
        Maastricht Treaty starts operating (EEC becomes European Union – EU).

1995:   EU Summit in Madrid (December) agrees on time plan for the launch of the Single Currency.

1997:   Treaty of Amsterdam signed.

1999:   Single currency (euro) launched (1 January), run by the European Central Bank.
        Amsterdam Treaty starts operating.

Appendix 3

ERT Members and their Companies

The following list reflects the ERT membership as of June 1999. The latest, updated version of this list (including links to the web sites of ERT companies) is available on the Corporate Europe Observatory web site: <http://www.xs4all.nl/~ceo/eurinc/ertlist.html>
Please note that only a selection of brands and subsidiaries is listed.

Chairman

Helmut O. Maucher
Nestlé (Switzerland)
Activities: Food, biotechnology, pharmaceuticals, cosmetics.
Subsidiaries, brands: Rowntree, Perrier, Findus, Chambourcy.
Associated Companies: L'Oreal, Lanvin.
Comments: Boycotted in 18 countries due to its promotion of breastmilk substitutes in Third World countries, violating the International Code of Breast Milk Substitutes (reversing the decline in breastfeeding could save the lives of 1.5 million infants every year, according to UNICEF). Nestlé Chair Helmut Maucher is also chair of the ERT, and until early 1999 headed the ICC (International Chamber of Commerce).

Vice-Chairmen

Gerhard Cromme
Friedrich Krupp (Germany)
Activities: Machines, electronics, telecommunications, steel (including for the auto industry), building products.
Subsidiaries, brands: Hoesch, Polysius.
Comments: One-quarter of Krupp's shares are owned by Iranian Ayatollahs. Krupp merged with Thyssen in 1999, and is now called ThyssenKrupp. Thyssen subsidiaries Blohm & Voss and Thyssen Nord-

seewerke produce warships for Indonesia and Turkey, among other countries. During the Nazi regime, Krupp used slave labour from prison camps; survivors are still awaiting compensation.

Morris Tabaksblat
Unilever (Netherlands/UK)
Activities: Food, household products, personal care products.
Subsidiaries, brands: Vinamul, UML, Crosfield, Lipton, Lux, Timotei, Ola, Magnum.
Comments: Aggressive promoter of biotechnology. Poor record of compliance with environmental regulations: for example, Crosfield fined £7,500 in 1993; UML fined £35,000 and Vinamul fined £19,000 in 1995; Unilever fined £30,000 in 1996 after spilling seven tonnes of oil in Cheshire, UK. The company has admitted that it has no regulations against the use of child labour, and cannot guarantee equal opportunities for women. Owns subsidiaries in Bahrain, China, Colombia, Indonesia, Nigeria and Sri Lanka, among other countries.

Other Members

Américo Amorim
Amorim Group (Portugal)
Activities: Production, processing and distribution of cork, banking, mobile phones, hotels.
Subsidiaries, brands: Corticeira Amorim, Telecel-Comunicaoes Pessaoais, Banco Comercial Portugues.
Comments: Exploitation of cork trees exclusively outside Portugal, as Portuguese cork forests were burned in the 1970s in order to claim insurance money. Interests in over forty hotels in Cuba. In 1998, Américo Amorim was involved in a scandal in which the Portuguese government gave high-level jobs in the public sector to big business leaders.

Percy Barnevik
AB Investor (Sweden)
Activities: Long-term investments.
Subsidiaries, brands: leading owner of AstraZeneca, Ericsson, Scania, ABB, Stora Enso, Atlas Copco, Electrolux and Saab AB, among many others.
Comments: Represents the interests of the Wallenberg family, founders of SEB (Skandinaviska Enskilda Banken), which did business with the Nazi regime during the Second World War.

Jean-Louis Beffa
Saint-Gobain (France)
Activities: Glass, paper, building materials.

Subsidiaries, affiliates, brands: Norton Co., TSL Group, CertainTeed, Solaglas, Isover, Vicasa.
Comments: Criticised for asbestos production in Brazil. CertainTeed is listed in the US as one of the major producers of toxic PVC chemicals. Norton Co. supplies the arms and nuclear industries.

Peter Bonfield
BT (United Kingdom)
Activities: Telecommunications.
Subsidiaries, brands: Syncordia Solutions, Syntegra, Viag Interkomand Telfort. Global joint venture with AT&T.
Comments: Between 1985 and 1996, massive job cuts reduced the number of employees from 235,000 to 125,000.

Cor Boonstra
Philips (Netherlands)
Activities: Electrical goods.
Subsidiaries, brands: Grundig.
Comments: Affiliates in 60 countries. Subsidiaries in China, Colombia, El Salvador, Ethiopia, Indonesia, Iran, Nigeria, the Philippines, Rwanda and Zaire, among many others. Supplies the nuclear industry, and appears in the Toxics Watch 1995 list of the top 300 parent companies having the largest total amount of carcinogenic waste resulting from production in the US. François Xavier Ortoli (Total) and André Leysen (Gevaert) are board members.

Bertrand Collomb
Lafarge Coppée (France)
Activities: Cement, building materials.
Subsidiaries, brands: Cementia Holding AG, Ennemix plc.
Comments: Second largest producer of cement worldwide. Lafarge appears in the list of the top 300 parent companies having the largest total amount of carcinogenic waste resulting from production in the US.

François Cornélis
Petrofina (Belgium)
Activities: Oil, petrochemicals, electricity.
Subsidiaries, brands: Sigma Coatings, Fina, Beverol.
Comments: Drilling for oil in Vietnam, Angola and Siberia, among many other places. Former EU commissioner Etienne Davignon and former Canadian Prime Minister Brian Mulroney are board members. Taken over by Total in 1998. Cornelis is also president of the Catholic University of Louvain, which in December 1998, on the same day as the Total-Petrofina merger hit the headlines, presented an award to Burmese opposition leader and Nobel Peace Prize winner Aung san Suu Kyi.

Alfonso Cortina
Repsol (Spain)
Activities: Oil, chemicals, gas, electricity.
Subsidiaries, brands: Gas Natural, Petronor, CLH, Astra.
Comments: Enormous investments in Latin America. Eighth largest oil company in the world after buying up the Argentinian oil company YPF in 1999. Violates rights of and agreements with indigenous and local people in Bolivia. Repsol's honorary chairman Oscar Fanjul is the former Secretary of State for Industry and a member of the second Competitiveness Advisory Group.

Dimitris Daskalopoulos
Delta Dairy (Greece)
Activities: Dairy products.
Subsidiaries, brands: Delta Classic, Princesa.
Comments: Family company of the Greek Daskalopoulos dynasty. It has a very strong presence in the Balkans region.

Etienne Davignon
Société Générale de Belgique (Belgium)
Activities: Banking.
Holdings: Energy, public utilities, financial services, industry.
Subsidiaries, brands: CBR Cimenteries, Gechem, Union Minière, Arbed (steel), Tractabel (energy), Electrabel (gas, electricity), Recticel (polyurethane foams), Coficem/Sagem (electronics, also for military).
Comments: Old colonial enterprise, founded in 1822 by William of Orange. Tenth biggest commercial and savings bank in the world (1997). Davignon was former EU Commissioner for Industry. Company partly owned by Suez Lyonnaise des Eaux.

Carlo De Benedetti
Cofide-Cir Group (Italy)
Activities: Insurance, buildings, food, media.
Subsidiaries, brands: La Republica, L'espresso.
Comments: Financial holding of the De Benedetti family (Cofide, Compagnia Finanziaria de Benedetti). In 1998, the family sold their last shares of Olivetti, a veteran ERT company. Olivetti's accounts for 1994, 1995 and 1996 were investigated, and charges were brought against Carlo de Benedetti by the Attorney General of Ivrea in March 1999. A trial is forthcoming.

Thierry Desmarest
Total (France)
Activities: Oil, petrol, gas, nuclear, chemicals.
Subsidiaries, brands: Hutchinson, Bostik.

Comments: Maintains links with Iraq and Burma. Operates in Indonesia, Iran, Kuwait, Yemen, Burma, Angola, Libya and Colombia, among many other places. Total has bought up the Belgian oil company Petrofina. In May 1998 the EU agreed not to challenge US extra-territorial laws (the D'Amato and Helms-Burton bills which respectively punish companies investing in Iran, Libya and Cuba) in return for a guarantee that Total not be punished for its investments in Iran. Unocal, Total's business partner in Burma, has been charged with human rights violations in a US court for its operations in that country.

Jean-René Fourtou
Rhône-Poulenc (France)
Activities: Biotechnology, pharmaceuticals, chemicals, insecticides, herbicides.
Subsidiaries, brands: Rhône-Poulenc Rorer, Pasteur Merieux Connaught, Rhodia, Fisons.
Comments: Present in 160 countries. The 1998 annual report claims that the company played an active role in promoting the EU life patents directive. Rhône-Poulenc works with the controversial public relations company Burson-Marsteller. In June 1998, it won permanent approval to spray the herbicide bromoxynil on its cotton crops in the US, which have been genetically manipulated to be resistant to this herbicide. This was after bromoxynil, a known carcinogenic which causes birth defects in mammals, was banned in December 1997 in the US. In 1999, Rhône-Poulenc merged with the German company Hoechst to create the 'life sciences' (biotechnology) giant Aventis.

Paolo Fresco
Fiat (Italy)
Activities: Automobiles, aviation, robotics, publishing, insurance.
Subsidiaries, brands: Lancia, Alfa Romeo, Iveco, New Holland (agricultural and construction equipment), Teksid (metallurgical), Snia BPD (chemicals and biotechnology), Fiat Ferroviaria (railway systems), Impregilo, Fiat CIEI, Fiat SpA.
Comments: Part of Agnelli's dynasty-led, government-fed empire. Fiat CIEI supplies the nuclear industry. Seven officials from Valsella, taken over by Fiat in 1984, were arrested in 1991 for illegally selling US$180 million worth of munitions to Iraq, including $9 million worth of anti-personnel and anti-tank mines, the largest sale ever reported. Impregilo is part of a consortium which in 1999 bid for the contract to construct the Ilisu dam in Turkey. This project would wipe out 52 villages and 15 towns; the World Bank believes that the dam would also violate the UN convention aimed at preventing border disputes and wars between states sharing water resources. Fiat also has operations in Iran, Turkey, Mexico and Morocco, among other countries.

José Antonio Garrido
Iberdrola (Spain)
Activities: Electricity, nuclear, construction, telecommunications, real estate.
Subsidiaries, brands: Iberener, Iberinco, Coelba.
Comments: Very strong presence in Latin America. Second largest power company in Spain, and largest nuclear power company with seven nuclear plants. Blocking the introduction of solar energy.

Fritz Gerber
F. Hoffmann-La Roche (Switzerland)
Activities: Pharmaceuticals, biotechnology, chemicals, vitamins, diagnosis, fragrances and flavours.
Subsidiaries, brands: Genentech, Boehringer Mannheim, De Puy.
Comments: Parent holding company is Roche Holding AG. Advocates gene patenting and human genetic engineering. Genentech has been accused by US-based NGO Foundation on Economic Trends of using a private charity, the Human Growth Foundation, to help recruit thousands of healthy children of short stature for potential treatment with its human growth hormone Protropin. Irresponsible marketing of drugs such as the sedative Versed, the diet pill Xenical and the anti-Parkinson medication Tasmar.

Ronald Hampel
ICI (United Kingdom)
Activities: Chemicals, plastics.
Subsidiaries, brands: Chlor-Chemicals and many others. In 1993, ICI sold off Zeneca (agrochemicals, genetically engineered crops).
Comments: ICI has an extraordinary record of chemical pollution, and is considered as one of the worst polluters in the UK. Between 1995 and 1997, its infamous Runcorn plant in the UK breached the law no less than 472 times.

Ulrich Hartmann
Veba (Germany)
Activities: Electricity, oil, chemicals, health (pharmaceuticals, biotechnology, animal health), transport systems, telecommunications.
Subsidiaries, brands: Preussen Elektra AG, Sydkraft AB, Aral, Degussa AG, Schenker AG, BTL and some 680 other companies.
Comments: Operates nuclear power plants. Has mining concessions in Venezuela on Bari and Yupka tribal lands.

Daniel Janssen
Solvay (Belgium)
Activities: Chemicals, oil, transport, finance.

Subsidiaries, brands: Interox, Venilia, Solvay Polymers Inc.

Comments: Producer of persistent organic pollutants, chemicals suspected of disrupting hormones in human and animal species. Fined for polluting the Mersey river in the UK (1993) and the Llobregat river in Spain (1996), among others. In 1998, two Solvay PVC manufacturing plants in Argentina and Brazil were proven to be discharging high levels of heavy metals and organochlorines, including dioxin, directly into the environment. Solvay Polymers Inc. provided funding for the industry lobby group the Council for Solid Waste Solutions.

Alain Joly
Air Liquide (France)

Activities: Supply of industrial and medical gases.

Subsidiaries, brands: Carbagas, Air Liquide America Corp, Cryospace, Aqualung, Schüllke & Mayr.

Comments: The world's largest industrial gas company. Also supplies chemical, food, and oil companies such as Rhône-Poulenc, Monsanto, GE, ICI, Shell, Bayer and Dow Chemical. Air Liquide America Corp, together with the British Oxygen Company and Liquid Carbonic Industries Corporations, was sued in 1993 for fixing prices and other violations of the federal Sherman Antitrust Act. The case was settled out of court and the three companies paid $100,000,000 compensation. The same US subsidiary in 1996 supplied contaminated oxygen to the US Temple Veterans Affairs Hospital in Texas.

Jak Kamhi
Profilo Holding (Turkey)

Activities: Electronics, construction, tourism, transportation, mobile phones.

Subsidiaries, brands: Saba, Telefunken, SGS, VB, Müessillik.

Comments: Twenty per cent owned by Thomson multimedia. Links with Israel's national secret service agency Mossad.

Cees van der Lede
Akzo Nobel (Netherlands)

Activities: Pharmaceuticals, coatings, chemicals, fibres, automotive products, 'defence equipment', waste management, helicopters, armoured vehicles.

Subsidiaries, brands: Akcros Chemicals, Organon, Courtaulds Aerospace Ltd.

Comments: Eleventh largest chemical producer worldwide (1997). Fined repeatedly for discharging, among other substances, oestrogenic compounds into rivers. Organon has been accused of double standards in its drug-marketing practices. Akzo Nobel is a military supplier, and is contracted for the EU's Eurofighter jet project.

David Lees
GKN (United Kingdom)
Activities: Aerospace (military and civil), automotive and agritechnical components, industrial services.
Subsidiaries, brands: Westland, Walterscheid, Joseph Sanky, Cleanaway, Meineke.
Comments: Involved in a major scandal with the previous Tory government and then defence minister Michael Heseltine. Sells military aerospace equipment to the Indonesian government, among many others.

André Leysen
Gevaert (Belgium)
Activities: Financial holding company.

Flemming Lindelov
Carlsberg (Denmark)
Activities: Beverages.
Subsidiaries, brands: Allied/Tetley, Nordic Beverages (together with Coca-Cola).
Comments: Operates in countries such as China, Malawi and Croatia. Following a pressure campaign, Carlsberg dropped its plans to establish a brewery in Burma in 1996.

Jérôme Monod
Lyonnaise des Eaux-Dumez (France)
Activities: Utilities, transport, finance, communications.
Subsidiaries, affiliates, brands: Dumez SA, SITA, GTM, France Déchêts, Northumbrian Water.
Comments: Present in more than 120 countries. France Déchêts has a monopoly in dealing with industrial byproducts such as arsenic, mercury and asbestos. After burying 40,000 tonnes of toxic waste per year in France over a 30-year period, the company left the community to deal with it. Northumbrian Water is linked to the release of endocrine-disrupting chemicals into rivers in the UK. Lyonnaise owns 29 per cent of ERT member company Société Générale de Belgique.

Mark Moody-Stuart
Royal Dutch/Shell (Netherlands/UK)
Activities: Oil, petrol, coal, plastic, chemicals, renewable energy.

Subsidiaries, brands: Shell Chemicals, Nigeria LNG Limited, Royal Additives, Montell, etc.

Comments: Involved in crimes against the Ogoni people in Nigeria through its funding of the former Nigerian military regime. Despite plenty of green rhetoric, Shell's investment in solar energy does not exceed the amount that the company recently invested in a single coal-fuelled power plant in Australia.

Egil Myklebust
Norsk Hydro (Norway)

Activities: Dams, light metals, petrochemicals, oil, gas, seafood, fertilisers, insurance.

Subsidiaries, brands: Fison Fertilisers, Utkal Alumina.

Comments: Utkal Alumina has been associated with human rights violations against local people in India, according to Norwegian NGO Norwatch. Responsible for environmental damage related to oil drilling in northern Norway and north-west Russia. World's foremost manufacturer of PVCs. Involved in financing Angolan civil war. CEO Myklebust was elected chairman of the World Business Council for Sustainable Development (WBCSD) in 1997.

Jorma Ollila
Nokia Group (Finland)

Activities: Telecommunications.

Subsidiaries, brands: Salcomp Oy.

Comments: Until recently, exported information technology used by the Indonesian government in its war against East Timor. Earns one-fifth of the country's export income. Leading supplier of mobile phones. Lobbied the European Parliament for lax technical requirements for electronic commodities.

Heinrich von Pierer
Siemens (Germany)

Activities: Electrical, arms, nuclear.

Subsidiaries, brands: Osram, Nixdorf, Arco Solar, Plessey.

Comments: The sole German manufacturer of nuclear power technology. During the Nazi regime, Siemens used slave labour from prison camps; survivors are still awaiting compensation.

Lars Ramqvist
L.M. Ericsson (Sweden)

Activities: Communications, health care (medical engineering), household products.

Subsidiaries, brands: Ericsson Microelectronics, Ericsson Defense Electronics, etc.

Comments: Has 40 per cent of global sales in mobile telephone systems, which are suspected of causing brain tumours. Peter Sutherland, former GATT head and current chair of both British Petroleum and Goldman Sachs, is on Ericsson's board.

Franck Riboud
Danone (France)
Activities: Food (fresh dairy products, beverages, biscuits).
Subsidiaries, brands: HP Foods, BSN, Evian, Lu, Britannia, San Miguel.
Comments: In 1994, the company changed its name from BSN to Danone. Products contain genetically manipulated food. HP Foods was the seventh biggest offender in the 'industrial processes' sector according to the Environment Agency's 'Hall of Shame'. Operates in China, Indonesia, Pakistan and Turkey, among other places. BSN has repeatedly violated the International Code of Marketing of Breast Milk Substitutes.

Nigel Rudd
Pilkington (United Kingdom)
Activities: Glass, building products, automotive products, oil, gas, plastics, chemicals.
Subsidiaries, brands: SOLA.
Comments: Provides glass products to the auto industry. Military supplier. Large-scale ambitions for sales in Central and Eastern Europe.

Richard Schenz
OMV (Austria)
Activities: Oil, gas, plastics, chemicals.
Comments: 49.9 per cent owned by Österreichische Industrieholding AG, which is itself owned by the Republic of Austria. Its oil exploration activities near Rockall (island placed 289 miles from the Scottish mainland, in the middle of the Atlantic Frontier) have been criticised for disrupting pristine areas of the Atlantic Ocean, rich in bird and marine life.

Manfred Schneider
Bayer (Germany)
Activities: Health care (pharmaceuticals, consumer care, diagnosis), plastics, agriculture (crop protection, animal health), chemicals, transport systems, photographic equipment.
Subsidiaries, brands: Haarmann & Reiner, H.C. Starck, Dystar, Millennium, AGFA-Gevaert.
Comments: Prosecuted in Brazil for poisoning coffee plantation workers with the pesticide Baysiston, forbidden in Germany for the past 20 years. Its growth hormone Olaquindox has been forbidden in the EU for being a carcinogenic as well as genetically damaging. Bayer was sued by

holocaust survivors for its collaboration with Auschwitz Doctor Mengele in experiments with Jews during the Nazi regime. Developed, mass-produced and marketed heroin as a children's cough medicine beginning at the turn of the century and continuing until 1958.

Jürgen Schrempp
DaimlerChrysler (Germany)
Activities: Automobiles, arms.
Subsidiaries, brands: AEG, Messerschmidt, Dornier, MTU.
Comments: After 1998 merger with Chrysler, renamed DaimlerChrysler. Germany's largest producer of arms.

Louis Schweitzer
Renault (France)
Activities: Automobiles, lorries, aerospace, telecommunications, media, rail systems, financial services, insurance, banks.
Subsidiaries, brands: Mack Trucks.
Comments: The company was privatised in 1996. Found guilty by the US Environmental Protection Agency in 1998 of deliberately including deceptive 'defeat devices' to avoid emissions reductions in its engines. In 1997, the French Court of Appeals concluded that Renault's lack of consultation with its European works council before closing its factory in Vilvoorde, Belgium was 'manifestly unlawful'. Some 3,000 workers were fired with this plant closing. Board of directors includes Jean-Claude Paye (former OECD boss and head of the Competitiveness Advisory Group).

George Simpson
General Electric Company (UK)
Activities: Aircraft engines, appliances, capital services, lighting, medical systems, plastics, power systems (nuclear, gas), electricity distribution.
Subsidiaries, brands: Kidder Peabody Brokerage, GE Capital, NBC, Utah Construction, RCA.
Comments: In the US, GE has been convicted of bribery, employment discrimination, insider trading, price fixing and criminal fraud for cheating the Army, Navy and Air Force. It has contaminated a huge number of areas, and four of its US factories were on the EPA's list of the most dangerous sources of air pollution. None the less, GE is the top US and the world's sixth largest manufacturer of air pollution control equipment. It finances politicians in both US political parties. It is a leading member of the Business Roundtable (BRT), and is active in political education and propaganda. GE has funded numerous tax-exempt front groups and think-tanks that promote their corporate perspective, including the Brookings Institution and the American Enterprise Institute. GE was the biggest single winner from Reagan's 1981 tax cuts. In collaboration with Hitachi and Toshiba, GE has built more than twenty nuclear plants in

Japan. Through its ownership of NBC, one of the top three commercial television networks in the United States, GE is able to filter programme and news content.

Michael Smurfit
Jefferson Smurfit (Ireland)
Activities: Paper and packaging.
Subsidiaries, brands: Cellulose du Pin, SCC (Smurfit Cartón de Colombia), Cartón y Papel.
Comments: Subject of an Irish campaign for its human rights abuses due to forest-related activities in Colombia. Conflicts with the Paez indigenous peoples in Colombia, where Smurfit owns pine and eucalyptus plantations. A report done by Smurfit shareholders highlights the 'unfair dismissal of unionists, displacement of peasant farmers, reduction of bio-diversity and acceleration of soil erosion'.

Peter Sutherland
British Petroleum (United Kingdom)
Activities: Oil, plastics, chemicals, mines.
Subsidiaries, brands: Gulf, Kennecott, Purina, Distillers.
Comments: Active in the corporate climate change lobby. Involvement with Colombian paramilitary in order to secure access to oil in strategic areas. BP's pressure on the Colombian government resulted in the modification of the expropriation clause of the country's new constitution 'to favour foreign investments'.

Marco Tronchetti Provera
Pirelli (Italy)
Activities: Tyres, cables.
Subsidiaries, brands: Standard Motor.
Comments: Subject of a national boycott in the US in support of the Brazilian Rubber Workers Union. Pirelli's operations endanger the livelihood of Amazonian rubber tappers, who generate income by extracting latex in a sustainable manner. Major sponsor of Formula One motor racing.

Mark Wössner
Bertelsmann (Germany)
Activities: Media, publishing, entertainment (film, radio, music), multimedia, industry (printing, paper, services).
Subsidiaries, brands: Random House, Grunner&Jahr (G&J), Stern, Circulo de Lectores, BMG, Compuserve, AOL, Lycos, Arista records, RCA.
Comments: Biggest publisher/printer in the world, with a revenue of US$ 14 billion in 1997. Printed Nazi literature during the Nazi regime.

Resources

The latest, updated version of this resource list is available on the Corporate Europe Observatory web site: <http://www.xs4all.nl/~ceo/eurinc/resources.html>

Some Recommended Organisations

A SEED Europe
Network of European youth groups campaigning against ecological destruction and social injustice.
PO Box 92066
1090 AB Amsterdam
Netherlands
Tel: +31–20–668–2236
Fax: +31–20–468–2275
E-mail: aseedeur@antenna.nl
http://www.antenna.nl/aseed/

ATTAC
Network for democratic control over international finance.
9 bis, rue de Valence
F-75005 Paris
France
Tel: +33–1–55439643
Fax: +33–1–43362626
E-mail: attacint@attac.org
http:/www.attac.org/

CEE Bankwatch
Central and Eastern European NGO Network for Monitoring the Activities of International Financial Institutions.
Regional Coordinator: Jozsef Feiler
c/o MTVSz

Ulloi u. 91/b, III/21
H-1091 Budapest
Hungary
Tel: +36–1–2167297
Fax: +36–1–2167295
E-mail: jozseff@bankwatch.org
http://www.bankwatch.org/

Coordination against Bayer-Dangers
Critical watchdog and campaign group on German-based chemical giant
Bayer.
Postfach 150418
D-40081 Düsseldorf
Germany
Tel: +49–211–333911
Fax: +49–211–333940
E-mail: CBGnetwork@aol.com

The Cornerhouse
UK-based research and campaign group which aims to support the
growth of a non-discriminatory civil society in which communities have
control over the resources and decisions that affect their lives and means
of livelihood. The Cornerhouse produces highly recommended briefings.
PO Box 3137
Station Road
Sturminster Newton
Dorset DT10 1YJ
United Kingdom
E-mail: cornerhouse@gn.apc.org
http://www.icaap.org/Cornerhouse/

Corporate Watch
UK-based group researching and exposing crimes and hypocrisies of cor-
porations that refuse to act in a responsible manner.
Box E, 111 Magdalen Road
Oxford OX4 1RQ
United Kingdom
Tel/fax: +44–1865–791391
E-mail: corporatewatch@i-way.co.uk
http://www.oneworld.org/cw/

Transnational Resource and Action Center

US-based research and campaign group exposing corporate greed by documenting the social, political, economic and environmental impacts of transnational giants. Maintains a highly recommended web site.
PO Box 29344
San Francisco, CA 94129
United States
Tel: +1–415–5616568
E-mail: corpwatch@igc.org
http://www.corpwatch.org/

Critical Shareholders Association

Umbrella of over thirty German shareholder activist groups demanding environmental protection, social justice and respect for human rights from corporations like Krupp, Siemens and Daimler.
Schlackstrasse 16
D-50737 Cologne
Germany
Tel: +49–221–5995647
Fax: +49–221–5991024
E-mail: critical_shareholders@compuserve.com
http://ourworld.compuserve.com/homepages/critical_shareholders/whatdowe.htm

Ethical Consumer

Publishes an excellent magazine and maintains a database on the social and environmental records of major TNCs.
Unit 21, 41 Old Birley Street
Manchester M15 5RD
United Kingdom
Tel: +44–161–2262929
Fax: +44–161–2266277
E-mail: ethicon@mcr1.poptel.org.uk
http://www.ethicalconsumer.org/

Friends of the Earth International (FoEI)

Global umbrella of nearly sixty groups campaigning for sustainability.
PO Box 19199
1000 GD Amsterdam
The Netherlands
Tel: +31–20–6221369
Fax: +31–20–6392181
E-mail: info@foeint.antenna.nl
http://www.xs4all.nl/~foeint/
http://www.foe.org/
http://www.foeeurope.org/

GRESEA (Groupe de Récherche pour un Stratégie Economique Alternative)

Belgian research and campaign group focussing on TNCs and global economic justice.
Rue Royale 11
B-1000 Brussels
Belgium
Tel: +32–2–2197076
Fax: +32–2–2196486
E-mail: gresea@innet.be

IBFAN (International Baby Food Action Network)

A partnership of over 150 groups in more than 90 countries aimed at improving infant health. It monitors corporate practices relating to baby food and maintains a successful boycott against Nestlé.
PO Box 157
CH-1211 Geneva 19
Switzerland
Tel: +41–22–7989164
Fax: +41–22–7984443
E-mail: philipec@iprolink.ch
http://www.gn.apc.org/ibfan/

International Forum on Globalization (IFG)

Coalition of activists and scholars opposed to neoliberal globalisation.
PO Box 12218
San Francisco, CA 94112
United States
Tel: +1–415–7713394
Fax: +1–415–7711121
E-mail: ifg@ifg.org
http://www.ifg.org/

McSpotlight Web Site

The single most extensive resource on the web on McDonald's. Includes links to many other progressive sites, but also to the web sites of companies like Nestlé and Unilever.
E-mail: info@mcspotlight.org
http://www.mcspotlight.org/

The Multinationals Resource Center

The US-based Multinationals Resource Center (MRC) is a project of Multinational Monitor magazine. The MRC is designed to help activists, journalists, academics and others who need information on the activities of corporations operating in their communities.

PO Box 19405
Washington, DC 20036
Tel: +1–202–3878030
E-mail: mrc@essential.org
http://www.essential.org/mdc/

Norwatch (The Future in Our Hands)
Research and campaign group which monitors TNCs based in Norway.
PO Box 4743
Sofienberg
N-0506 Oslo
Norway
Tel: +47–22201045
Fax: +47–22204788
E-mail: norwatch@fifi.no
http://www.ngo.grida.no/ngo/fivh/eng_norw.htm

Observatoire de la Mondialisation
Scholars and activists campaigning against neoliberal globalisation
projects like the MAI, the proposed WTO Millennium Round and the
Transatlantic Economic Partnership (TEP).
40, rue de Malte
F-75011 Paris
France
Tel: +33–1–43383817
Fax: +33–1–43383788
E-mail: ecoropa@magic.fr
http://www.ecoropa.org/obs/

Oilwatch Europe
Oilwatch Europe connects the southern Oilwatch network with the home
base of corporations like Elf, Agip, Shell and BP. Oilwatch Europe also
informs the European public and facilitates cooperation between
European NGOs.
c/o A SEED Europe
PO Box 92066
1090 AB Amsterdam
Netherlands
Tel: +31–20–6682236
Fax: +31–20–4682275
E-mail: oilwatch@aseed.antenna.nl
http://www.antenna.nl/aseed/oilwatch/

Peoples Global Action (PGA)
Global network of groups and movements opposing the WTO and 'free trade'.
E-mail: pga@agp.org
URL: http://www.agp.org/

Polaris Institute
Canadian institute which aims to strengthen citizens' movements against corporate power.
4 Jeffrey Avenue
Ottawa, Ont. K1K 0E2
Canada
Tel: +1–613–7468374
E-mail: tclarke@web.net
URL: http:/www.nassist.com/

Project Underground
Exposes corporate environmental and human rights abuses, and supports communities facing the mining and oil industries.
1847 Berkeley Way
Berkeley, CA 94703
United States
E-mail: project_underground@moles.org
URL: http://www.moles.org/

Public Citizen – Global Trade Watch
Campaigns against unfair, unsustainable international trade and investment policies.
215 Pennsylvania Ave SE
Washington, DC 20003
United States
Tel: +1–202–5464996
E-mail: mstrand@citizen.org
URL: http:/www.citizen.org/pctrade/

Third World Network
Network of groups and individuals in the South that campaigns for a fair distribution of the world's resources and for just and sustainable development models.
228 Macalister Road
10400 Penang
Malaysia
Tel: +60–4–2266159
Fax: +60–4–2264505
E-mail: twn@igc.apc.org
URL: http://www.twnside.org.sg/

Transnational Institute (TNI)
Progressive international network of scholars and activists
Paulus Potterstraat 20
1071 DA Amsterdam
The Netherlands
Tel: +31–20–6626608
Fax: +31–20–6757176
E-mail: tni@tni.org
URL: http://www.tni.org

Women's Environment and Development Organization (WEDO)
Global organisation working to increase women's visibility, roles and
leadership in public policy making through peace, gender, human rights,
environmental and economic justice campaigns.
355 Lexington Avenue, 3rd Floor
New York, NY 10017
United States
Tel: +1–212–9730325
Fax: +1–212–9730335
E-mail: wedo@igc.org
URL: http://www.wedo.org/

Women In Development Europe (WIDE)
The WIDE network works to influence European and international
policies and to raise awareness on gender and development issues, with
the objective of empowering women worldwide.
70, rue du Commerce
B-1040 Brussels
Belgium
Tel: +32–2–5459070
Fax: +32–2–5127342
E-mail: wide@gn.apc.org
URL: http://www.eurosur.org/wide/porteng.htm

Books

*Corporations are Gonna Get Your Mama – Globalization and the Downsizing
of the American Dream*
Kevin Danaher, Global Exchange (ed.), Monroe, ME: Common Courage
Press, 1996.

Dismantling Corporate Rule
Tony Clarke, San Francisco: International Forum on Globalization,
1996.

Gender Mapping the European Union Trade Policy
WIDE, Brussels, 1997.

Global Dreams: Imperial Corporations and the New World Order
Richard Barnet and John Cavanagh, New York: Simon and Schuster, 1994.

Global Spin: The Corporate Assault on Environmentalism
Sharon Beder, Devon: Green Books, 1997.

Green Backlash: Global Subversion of the Environmental Movement
Andrew Rowell, London: Routledge, 1996.

Green Capitalists – a Report on Large Corporations and the Environment
Mikael Nyberg, Friends of the Earth Sweden, 1998.

Greenwash – the Reality Behind Corporate Environmentalism
Jed Greer and Kenny Bruno, TWN & Apex Press, 1996.

Hijacking Environmentalism: Corporate Responses to Sustainable Development
Richard Welford, London: Earthscan, 1997.

Silent Coup – Confronting the Big Business Takeover of Canada
Tony Clarke, Ottawa: CCPA & Lorimer, 1997.

The Case Against the Global Economy and For a Turn Toward the Local
Jerry Mander and Edward Goldsmith (eds), San Francisco: Sierra Club Books, 1996.

The Corporate Planet: Ecology and Politics in the Age of Globalization
Joshua Karliner, San Francisco: Sierra Club Books, 1997.

The Earth Brokers: Power, Politics and World Development
Pratap Chatterjee and Matthias Finger, London: Routledge, 1994.

The New European Economy Revisited
Loukas Tsoulakis, Oxford: Oxford University Press, 1997.

The Myth Behind European Union
Ash Amin and John Tomaney (eds), London: Routledge, 1995.

Toxic Sludge Is Good For You! Lies, Damn Lies and the Public Relations Industry
John Stauber and Sheldon Rampton, Monroe, ME: Common Courage Press, 1995.

When Corporations Rule the World
David C. Korten, New York: Kumarian Press, 1995.

Magazines and Periodicals

Adbusters
Published by: Adbusters Media Foundation
1243 West 7th Avenue
Vancouver, British Columbia
Canada V6H 1B7
URL: http://www.adbusters.org/adbusters/

Corporate Europe Observer
Published by: Corporate Europe Obervatory
Paulus Potterstraat 20
1071 DA Amsterdam
The Netherlands
E-mail: ceo@xs4all.nl
URL: http://www.xs4all.nl/~ceo/observer/

Corporate Watch
Published by: Corporate Watch
Box E, 111 Magdalena Road
Oxford OX4 1RQ
United Kingdom
E-mail: corporatewatch@i-way.co.uk
URL: http://www.oneworld.net/cw/pages/magazine.html

Multinational Monitor
Published by: Essential Information, Inc.
1530 P Street NW
Washington, DC 20005
United States
E-mail: monitor@essential.org
URL: <http://www.essential.org/monitor/>

PR Watch
Quarterly on the US PR/Public Affairs industry
Center for Media and Democracy
3318 Gregory Street, Madison, WI 53711
United States
Tel: +1 608 233 3346
Fax: +1 608 238 2236
E-mail: 74250.735@compuserve.com
URL: http://www.prwatch.org/

SPECTRE
Quarterly full of progressive EU-critical news
BP5, Bxl46, rue Wiertz
1047 Brussels
Belgium
Tel: +32 2 511 8428
Fax: +32 2 284 9505
E-mail: spectre@sp.nl
URL: http://www.sp.nl/spectre/

The Ecologist
Subscriptions: RED Computing
The Outback, 58–60 Kingston Road
New Malden, Surrey, KT3 3LZ
United Kingdom
E-mail: ecologist@gn.apc.org
URL: http://www.gn.apc.org/ecologist/

Third World Resurgence
Third World perspectives on environment, politics, economy, culture
and much more.
Published by: Third World Network
228 Macalister Road
10400 Penang
Malaysia
E-mail: twn@igc.apc.org
URL: http://www.twnside.org.sg/souths/twn/

Some Industry Lobby Sites

AmCham (EU Committee of the American Chamber of Commerce)
URL: http://www.eucommittee.be/

AMUE (Association for the Monetary Union of Europe)
URL: http://amue.lf.net/

Burson-Marsteller
URL: http://www.bm.com/

BRT (Business Roundtable)
URL: http://www.brtable.org/

CEFIC (European Chemical Industry Association)
URL: http://www.cefic.be/

CEPS (Centre for European Policy Studies)
URL: http://www.ceps.be/

EPC (European Policy Center)
URL: http://www.TheEPC.be/

ERT (European Roundtable of Industrialists)
URL: http://www.ert.be/

EuropaBio
URL: http://www.europa-bio.be/

FIEC (European Construction Industry Federation)
URL: http://www.fiec.be/

Financial Leaders Group
URL: http://www.uscsi.org/

GCC (Global Climate Coalition)
URL: http://www.globalclimate.org/

ICC (International Chamber of Commerce)
URL: http://www.iccwbo.org/

IRF (International Road Federation)
URL: http://www.irfnet.org/

TABD (Transatlantic Business Dialogue)
URL: http://www.tabd.com/

Trilateral Commission
URL: http://www.trilateral.org/

UNICE (European Employers' Confederation)
URL: http://www.business-cohesion.org/resource/links/social.htm

USCIB (United States Council for International Business)
URL: http:/www.uscib.org/

WBCSD (World Business Council for Sustainable Development)
URL: http://www.wbcsd.ch/

WEF (World Economic Forum)
URL: http://www.weforum.com/

Some Web Addresses of EU and Other International Institutions

Starting point for EU institutions
URL: http://europa.eu.int/index-en.htm

EIB (European Investment Bank)
URL: http://www.eib.org/

OECD (Organization for Economic Cooperation and Development)
URL: http://www.oecd.org/

UN (United Nations)
URL: http://www.un.org/

WTO (World Trade Organization)
URL: http://www.wto.org/

Addresses of Some EU Institutions

European Commission
200 rue de la Loi
B-1049 Bruxelles
Belgium
Tel: +32 2 2991111
Fax: +32 2 2950166
URL: http://europa.eu.int/en/comm.html

Council of Ministers
175 rue de la Loi
B-1048 Bruxelles
Tel: +32 2 2856111
Fax: +32 2 2857397 / +32 2 2857381
URL: http://ue.eu.int/angl/summ2.htm

European Parliament
97–113 rue Belliard
B-1047 Bruxelles
Belgium
Tel: +32 2 2842111
Fax: +32 2 2306933
URL: http://www.europarl.eu.int/sg/tree/en/

Notes

Chapter 1

1. 'Lobbyists Swarm to Europe's Washington DC', *The European*, 15 June 1998, p. 10.
2. The US-based Centre for Responsive Politics estimated that the Washington DC lobbying scene included 11,500 professionals in 1997, some 21 lobbyists per US Congressperson. The DC lobbying industry had a turnover of US$1.26 billion that same year. Source: <http://www.opensecrets.org/pubs/lobby98/summary.htm>
3. David Coen, 'The European Business Interest and the Nation State: Large Firm Lobbying in the European Union and Member States', *Journal of European Public Policy*, 4:1, March 1997, pp. 91–108.
4. Ibid.
5. The *European Public Affairs Directory* (published annually by Landmarks Publications, Belgium) provides a good overview.
6. Maria Green Cowles, 'The EU Committee of AmCham: the Powerful Voice of American Firms in Brussels', *Journal of European Public Policy*, 3:3, September 1996, pp. 339–58. Commissioner Spinelli's proposals were outlined in the document *Multinational Undertakings in the European Community*. During the same period, large US corporations were brought before the European Court of Justice for abusing power from their dominant market positions, and the EC worked on regulating TNC behaviour in fields like taxation, employment and development policy.
7. Personal interview with MEP Glyn Ford, 26 January 1999.
8. Davignon was Commissioner for Industry between 1977 and 1984, and Perissich was Director-General of the same directorate in the 1980s.
9. 'Pressure on Schröder for Sweeping Changes', *International Herald Tribune*, 24 March 1999.
10. *Handelsblatt*, 10 March 1999. Electronics giant Ericsson is moving part of its headquarters to London and still threatens to leave Sweden completely. Other examples are the Finnish-Swedish forest product and paper producer Stora Enso, the British-Swedish pharmaceutical giant Astra-Zeneca, and the Merita and Nordbanken banks. The Swedish corporate tax rate is actually a low 28 per cent, but business is also demanding cuts in the progressive income tax system (up to 60 per cent for the highest incomes) and taxes on income from shares. A special government-commissioned 'Growth Working Group' with representatives of large corporations and

trade unions recommended a general lowering of income tax rates (and improved education) to make Sweden 'internationally competitive'.

11. 'Lafontaine Fights a Rear Guard Action to Defend Tax Ambitions', *Financial Times*, 6–7 March 1999. Due to these tax reliefs, allowances and other loopholes, Germany in fact has the lowest level of corporate income tax revenues as a percentage of GDP in the G-7, despite relatively high official corporate tax rates of between 30 and 45 per cent. The government's proposal included decreasing parts of the corporate tax and a further drop in the basic income tax rate in combination with the introduction of a new ecotax on energy and the closing of several corporate tax loopholes. It was these last proposals which infuriated corporate Germany.

12. 'Lafontaine Fights a Rear Guard Action to Defend Tax Ambitions', *Financial Times*, 6–7 March 1999; 'Pressure on Schröder for Sweeping Changes', *International Herald Tribune*, 24 March 1999; 'Taxes Drive Corporate Flight', *The European*, 7 December 1998. The merger of chemical producer Hoechst with the French Rhône-Poulenc into the new company Aventis is partly a relocation. By moving parts of its operations to France, Hoechst wants to avoid taxes and the German system of *Mittbestimmung* (co-determination), which gives trade unions a number of seats in the advisory boards of large corporations. The advisory board of Aventis will have no labour representatives.

13. A letter leaked to the press revealed that a group of 22 CEOs had tried hard to make Chancellor Schröder act 'to rein in' Lafontaine.

14. Gunther Hofmann, 'Wer Regiert die Republik?', *Die Zeit*, 18 March 1999 (1999/12).

15. The comment was made at the Bayer annual shareholders meeting in Cologne, 30 April 1999. Source: personal communication with Philip Minkes, Coordination Against Bayer Dangers, Germany.

16. 'Irish Reined In by Brussels', *The European*, 30 October 1997. For example, Boston Scientific closed down its Danish operations and expanded its activities in Ireland, and several airlines plan to close down other European offices and open central ticketing offices in Dublin.

17. *The New European Economy Revisited*, Loukas Tsoukalis, Oxford: Oxford University Press, 1997.

18. Two hundred and thirty seven mergers and acquisitions took place in Europe in 1998, compared to 100 in 1995. Over 25 per cent of the 1998 mergers were European crossborder deals, up from 17 per cent in 1995. Source: Jürgen Schrempp (CEO of DaimlerChrysler), 'Why We Believe in the Euro', *Newsweek*, Special Issue, November 1998–February 1999, p. 38.

19. US$69.4 billion in 1995. Source: 'The Atlantic Century? Once Again, the US and Europe are the Twin Drivers of the World Economy', *Business Week*, 8 February 1999.

Chapter 2

1. For the sake of simplicity, the entire constellation of public relations, public affairs and related political consultancies will be referred to as the 'PR' sector.

2. Personal interview with Laurentien Brinkhorst, Brussels, 17 February 1999.

3. Personal interview with Frank Schwaba-Hoth, Brussels, 17 February 1999.
4. John Stauber and Sheldon Rampton, *Toxic Sludge Is Good For You! Lies, Damn Lies and the Public Relations Industry*, Monroe, ME: Common Courage Press, 1995.
5. Sharon Beder, *Global Spin: The Corporate Assault on Environmentalism*, Devon: Green Books, 1997.
6. Claudia Peter, 'The Clandestine Threat: Astroturf Lobbying in Europe', unpublished speaking text for *Next Five Minutes* conference in Amsterdam, 12–14 March 1999.
7. Personal interview with Frank Schwaba-Hoth, Brussels, 17 February 1999.
8. 'Lobbyists Swarm to Europe's Washington DC', *The European*, 15 June 1998, p. 10.
9. Personal interview with Laurentien Brinkhorst, Brussels, 17 February 1999.
10. Quote taken from: VPRO Television, *Europa BV*, originally broadcasted on Dutch television on 19 October 1997.
11. Ibid.
12. Ibid.
13. Ibid.
14. Corporate Europe Observatory, *CEObserver*, Zero Issue, October 1997.
15. Personal interview with Laurentien Brinkhorst, Brussels, 17 February 1999.
16. Brinkhorst is the daughter of MEP Laurens-Jan Brinkhorst and was previously employed as Stanley Crossick's assistant at the European Policy Centre.
17. Personal interview with Laurentien Brinkhorst, Brussels, 17 February 1999.
18. Ibid.
19. Ibid.
20. Ibid.
21. Ibid.
22. Ibid.
23. Ibid.
24. Ibid.
25. Invitation to Entente conference 'Pressure Politics: Industry's Response to the Pressure Group Challenge', 4 June 1998.
26. Maria Laplev (Director of consultancy firm GPC Market Access Europe), 'Lobbyists Count the Cost of Influence' in 'The European Union in 1998', a special edition of the *European Voice*.
27. See McLibel web site: <http://www.mcspotlight.org/>
28. Peter Hamilton, Board Director of Entente, speech at 'Pressure Politics' conference, 4 June 1998.
29. Ibid.
30. Quote taken from Rory Watson, 'Crossing the Business and Political Divide', *European Voice*, 9 July 1998.
31. Ibid.
32. CEPS, 'CEPS Corporate and Inner Circle Members', CEPS web site.
33. See CEPS web site: <http://www.ceps.be/>
34. Quote taken from Rory Watson, 'Crossing the Business and Political Divide', *European Voice*, 9 July 1998.

35. Mr Crossick, a British corporate lawyer who set up his lobby firm in Brussels in 1977, managed to add to the Maastricht Treaty a 68-word paragraph worth US$1–2 billion per word in savings to the European pension industry. Without these words, pension funds could have been forced to equalise the pension payments they had made to men and women since 1957. Source: Charlemagne, 'EU: The Brussels Lobbyists and the Struggle for Ear-Time', *The Economist*, 14 July 1998.
36. See European Policy Centre web site: <http://www.theepc.com>
37. Keith Richardson is also special advisor to the Centre. Other advisors include Julian Oliver, former chairman of the American Chamber of Commerce's EU Committee.
38. *After Cardiff: Which Way for the European Union?*, European Policy Centre, 30 June 1998.
39. Rory Watson, 'Crossing the Business and Political Divide', *European Voice*, 9 July 1998.

Chapter 3

1. Keith Richardson, quoted in Hållen, J. and Thoren, R., 'Det hänger pa kontakterna', *Metallarbetaren*, April 1993.
2. ERT web site, 1999: <http://www.ert.be/pc/enc_frame.htm>
3. Keith Richardson, *Managing Europe: the Challenge to the Institutions*, February 1998.
4. Caroline Walcot, Assistant Secretary-General of the European Roundtable of Industrialists, quoted in *Kritiska EU Fakta*, 24 October 1994.
5. Personal interview with Keith Richardson, Brussels, 21 February 1997. The chapters on the ERT in this book are based heavily on interviews with Keith Richardson and Wim Philippa because it proved impossible for us to arrange interviews with ERT members or their direct assistants.
6. Pehr Gyllenhammar, quoted in Maria Green Cowles, 'Setting the Agenda for a New Europe: The ERT and EC 1992', *Journal of Common Market Studies*, 33:4, December 1995, p. 503.
7. The Business Roundtable (BRT) is a US-based coalition of more than 200 CEOs from large corporations, established in the 1970s.
8. Cowles, 'Setting the Agenda for a New Europe: The ERT and EC 1992' p. 504.
9. Then called the 'Roundtable of European Industrialists'.
10. Bastiaan van Apeldoorn, *Transnational Capitalism and the Struggle over European Order*, Dissertation, European University Institute, Florence, January 1999, pp. 131–2. After retiring from the Commission a few years later, both Davignon and Ortoli moved to the corporate world and became ERT members as CEOs of the Belgian holding company Société Générale de Belgique and the French oil company Total respectively.
11. Letter to ERT member Jacques Solvay, Solvay et Cie, from Paul Winby, ICI, 7 June 1984, quoted in Cowles, 'Setting the Agenda for a New Europe: The ERT and EC 1992' p. 514.
12. ERT, *Changing Scales: A Review Prepared for the Roundtable of European Industrialists*, Paris, 1985.
13. Personal interview with Keith Richardson, Brussels, 21 February 1997.

14. Cowles, 'Setting the Agenda for a New Europe: The ERT and EC 1992' pp. 519–20.
15. Bastiaan van Apeldoorn and Otto Holman, 'Transnational Class Strategy and the Relaunching of European Integration: The Role of the European Roundtable of Industrialists', paper presented at the 35th Annual Convention of the International Studies Association, Washington DC, 28 March–1 April 1994, p. 21.
16. ERT brochure, September 1993.
17. ERT, *Missing Networks*, Brussels, 1991, p. 17.
18. Bastiaan van Apeldoorn, *Transnational Class Strategy and European Integration: The Strategic Project of the European Round Table of Industrialists*, Master's Thesis, University of Amsterdam, August 1994, p. 94.
19. Keith Richardson, quoted in *Europa BV*, VPRO Television, originally broadcasted on Dutch television on 19 October 1997.
20. Agence Europe, 12 December 1993. Quoted in Bastiaan van Apeldoorn, 'Transnational Capitalism and the Struggle over European Order', p. 246.
21. Caroline Walcot, Assistant Secretary-General of the European Roundtable of Industrialists, quoted in *Kritiska EU Fakta*, 24 October 1994.
22. Caroline Walcot, interviewed for *dERTy business* (video), Small World Media Ltd, London, 1993.
23. Cowles, 'The European Roundtable of Industrialists: the Strategic Player in European Affairs', in J. Greenwood (ed.), *European Case Book on Business Alliances*, 1995.
24. Personal interview with Keith Richardson, Brussels, 21 February 1997.
25. Letter sent by Jacques Santer to Jérôme Monod, dated 10 January 1996.
26. Letter sent by Jacques Santer to Jérôme Monod, dated 5 July 1995.
27. Including Carlo de Benedetti (Olivetti), Etienne Davignon (Société Générale de Belgique), Jan Timmer (Philips), Candido Velazquez (Telefónica) and Pehr Gyllenhammar (former CEO of Volvo).
28. ERT web site, 1999. <http://www.ert.be/>
29. Ibid.
30. Personal interview with Wim Philippa, Brussels, 16 December 1998.
31. ERT web site, 1999. <http://www.ert.be/>
32. Ibid.
33. There are currently eleven working groups. The ERT constantly adapts the themes addressed by these groups to focus on timely issues in which it has a special interest.
34. Over the past few years, the ERT seems to have worked regularly with the UK-based consultancy Business Decisions Limited. This consultancy was also hired by the biotech industry lobby group EuropaBio (see Chapter 9) to produce its 1997 report *Benchmarking the Competitiveness of Biotechnology in Europe*.
35. ERT web site, 1999. <http://www.ert.be/>
36. Personal interview with Keith Richardson, Brussels, 21 February 1997.
37. ERT, *Benchmarking for Policy-Makers: The Way to Competitiveness, Growth and Job Creation*, Brussels, 1996.
38. 'Much of the impetus and, indeed, substance of the Commission's benchmarking proposal originated from the original work of the European Round Table – endorsed later by the Competitiveness Advisory Group. Let me say how important I think it is for the Commission to continue to receive 'pioneering' forward-looking ideas like this which can really help advance

the policy drive to improve Europe's competitiveness', letter to Keith Richardson by David Wright, Adviser to Commission President Santer, Brussels, 10 October 1996.

39. Letter from Jacques Santer to Daniel Janssen, 20 December 1996.

40. Personal interview with Keith Richardson, Brussels, 21 February 1997.

41. ERT, *Investment in the Developing World: New Openings and Challenges for European Industry*, Brussels, November 1996, p. 12.

42. Ibid.

43. ERT, *Benchmarking for Policy-Makers*, p. 2.

44. Phone interview with Keith Richardson, 11 March 1997.

45. 'ERT Warning to European Council Over Enlargement', *European Report*, 10 December 1997, III, p. 3.

46. Ibid.

47. The ERT report gives 16 case studies of win–win situations, each of which links an ERT company with a CEE host country. The companies involved are the following: B.A.T., Lyonnaise des Eaux, Philips and Shell in Hungary; Bertelsmann, BP, GKN and Saint-Gobain in Poland; Krupp and Unilever in Romania; Lafarge, Lyonnaise des Eaux and Shell in Czech Republic; Profilo Group in Lithuania; Renault in Slovenia; Siemens in the Slovak Republic; Solvay in Bulgaria and Veba in Latvia.

48. CEECAP, 'Report on the Impacts of Economic Globalisation and Changes in Consumption and Production Patterns', 1998, pp. 32–7.

49. And cumulative investment since 1989 of over 50 billion euro. Source: European Bank for Reconstruction and Development, *Transition Report Update*, April 1998.

50. UNCTAD, *World Investment Report* (1998), as quoted in ERT, *The East–West Win–Win Business Experience*, Brussels, 1999.

51. Personal interview with Wim Philippa, Brussels, 16 December 1998.

52. Eberhard von Koerber, 'The Voice of Experience', *Business Central Europe*, annual 1997/98, p. 19. Koerber is the current president of Asea Brown Boveri, (ABB). ABB was an ERT member company for many years under the presidency of Percy Barnevik. Barnevik, now president of Investor AB, is still an ERT member.

53. The Phare Programme is the main channel for the European Union's financial and technical support for the countries of Central and Eastern Europe (CEE). Set up in 1989 to support economic and political transition, Phare had by 1996 been extended to include 13 partner countries from the region. Originally allocated 4.2 billion euro for the 1990–94 period, the Phare budget was increased to 6.693 billion euro for the 1995–99 period. For a critical view on the Phare programme, see Jo Brew, 'EU Aid or Asset Stripping', in Corporate Europe Observatory (ed.), *Europe, Inc.*, Amsterdam 1997, pp. 62–5.

54. ERT, *The East–West Win–Win Business Experience*, Brussels, February 1999, p. 25.

55. Personal interview with Keith Richardson, Brussels, 21 February 1997.

56. And cumulative investment since 1989 of over 50 billion euro. Source: EBRD, *Transition Report Update*, April 1998.

57. Eurostat, 1998.

58. CEECAP, 'Report on the Impacts of Economic Globalisation and Changes in Consumption and Production Patterns', 1998.

59. ERT, *Job Creation and Competitiveness through Innovation*, Brussels, November 1998.
60. Ibid.
61. Ibid., p. 18.
62. 'Life-long learning' implies that employees should be flexible and prepared for re-education throughout their lives to follow the changing employment needs of industry. The concept of life-long learning and other educational reforms were introduced in two earlier ERT reports: *Education for Europeans* (1995) and *Investing in Knowledge* (1997).
63. ERT, *Job Creation and Competitiveness through Innovation*, Brussels, November 1998, p. 29.
64. Personal interview with Wim Philippa, Brussels, 16 December 1998.
65. Nicholas Hildyard, Colin Hines and Tim Lang, 'Who Competes? Changing Landscapes of Corporate Control', *The Ecologist*, 26:4, July/August 1996, p. 131.
66. Competitiveness Advisory Group, *Capital Market for Competitiveness: Report to the President of the European Commission, the Prime Ministers and Heads of State*, Brussels, June 1998.
67. Magnus Grimond, 'Pilkington Lops 1500 More Jobs in Costs Drive', *Associated Newspapers Ltd*, 29 October 1998.
68. Jacques Santer, Introduction to the first CAG report *(Enhancing European Competitiveness)*, June 1995.
69. Ibid.
70. The German state agency responsible for the privatisation of former East German state enterprises.
71. When Ciampi re-entered the Italian government as Treasury Minister in May 1996, he retreated from the CAG. His position as president of the CAG was taken over by former ERT member Floris Maljers (Unilever).
72. Personal interview with Keith Richardson, Brussels, 21 February 1997.
73. Competitiveness Advisory Group, *Enhancing European Competitiveness. Third Report to the President of the Commission, the Prime Ministers and Heads of State*, June 1998.
74. Ibid.
75. Personal interview with Keith Richardson, Brussels, 21 February 1997.
76. Personal interview with Zygmunt Tyszkiewicz, Brussels, 18 March 1997.
77. Personal interview with Keith Richardson, Brussels, 21 February 1997.

Chapter 4

1. UNICE promotion leaflet.
2. Personal interview with Christophe de Callatäy, Brussels, 18 November 1998.
3. Ibid.
4. Ibid.
5. Ibid.
6. Personal interview with Zygmunt Tyszkiewicz, Brussels, 18 March 1997.
7. Ibid.
8. Personal interview with Christophe de Callatäy, Brussels, 18 November 1998.
9. Ibid.

10. Ibid.
11. The Treaty on European Union requires the European Commission to consult with management and labour, the so-called 'social partners'. The Commission should solicit opinions or recommendations from the 'social partners' before it submits legislative proposals to the Council. The 'social partners' may also choose to negotiate an agreement to implement the proposal, which is then adopted at their request as a Council decision. All these processes are encompassed under the heading 'Social Dialogue'. As of June 1999, UNICE, UEAPME, CEEP and ETUC are officially recognised as 'social partners' in the Social Dialogue.
12. Personal interview with Christophe de Callatäy, Brussels, 18 November 1998.
13. Ibid.
14. Personal interview with Zygmunt Tyszkiewicz, Brussels, 18 March 1997.
15. Personal interview with Christophe de Callatäy, Brussels, 18 November 1998.
16. Personal interview with Zygmunt Tyszkiewicz, Brussels, 18 March 1997.
17. Economic and Financial Affairs, External Relations, Social Affairs, Industrial Affairs and Company Affairs.
18. Personal interview with Zygmunt Tyszkiewicz, Brussels, 18 March 1997.
19. Ibid.
20. UNICE, *Benchmarking Europe's Competitiveness: From Analysis to Action*, Brussels, December 1997.
21. For an explanation of 'benchmarking', see Chapter 3.
22. UNICE, *Benchmarking Europe's Competitiveness*.
23. Ibid.
24. Personal interview with Christophe de Callatäy, Brussels, 18 November 1998.
25. The Stability and Growth Pact is a rigid set of economic criteria put in place at the Amsterdam Summit of June 1997 in order to keep budget deficits below 1 per cent of GDP in 'normal times' and below 3 per cent during a recession after the coming into force of EMU. Countries exceeding these benchmark values face fines, but an escape clause exempts countries 'in severe recession', and finance ministers of the EMU countries have to vote on the imposition of such fines. See European Council, *Amsterdam European Council, 16 and 17 June 1997 Presidency Conclusions, Annex I, European Council resolutions on Stability, Growth and Employment*, Brussels, 17 June 1997.
26. Personal interview with Christophe de Callatäy, Brussels, 18 November 1998.
27. UNICE, *Benchmarking Europe's Competitiveness*.
28. Personal interview with Christophe de Callatäy, Brussels, 18 November 1998.
29. Ibid.
30. Ibid.
31. Ibid.
32. UNICE position on the implications for business of EU enlargement to Central and Eastern European countries, 2 December 1997.
33. The term 'acquis communautaire' refers to all principles, policies, laws, practices, obligations and objectives that have been agreed or that have developed within the European Union. The 'acquis communautaire'

includes judgments by the European Court of Justice and thereby establishes the primacy of Community law over national law.

34. Personal interview with Christophe de Callatäy, Brussels, 18 November 1998.
35. Ibid.
36. Ibid.
37. UNICE, 'Preliminary UNICE comments on the Commission communication concerning the creation of a New Transatlantic Marketplace', Brussels, 23 April 1998.
38. Ibid.
39. UNICE, 'Forthcoming WTO multilateral negotiations. Preliminary UNICE objectives', Brussels, 16 July 1998.
40. Ibid.
41. Confidential source, Brussels, 21 February 1997.
42. Personal interview with Zygmunt Tyszkiewicz, Brussels, 18 March 1997.

Chapter 5

1. Personal interview with John Russell, Manager for European Affairs, EU Committee of the American Chamber of Commerce, 16 December 1998. The exceptions include Northern Telecom, SmithKline Beecham and Rhône-Poulenc, corporations that are normally regarded as Canadian, British and French. As Mr Russell explains, 'It is a matter of globalisation of industry and mergers, so obviously we have to adapt.'
2. EU Committee of AmCham web site: <http://www.eucommittee.be/pages/prof1.htm>
3. In early 1999, Mr Russell quit his function at the EU Committee of AmCham and became Managing Director for Shandwick Public Affairs in Brussels.
4. Personal interview with John Russell, Brussels, 16 December 1998.
5. Ibid.
6. Ibid.
7. Keith Chapple, Chairman of the EU Committee of the American Chamber of Commerce in Belgium, *European Voice*, 30 April 1998.
8. Ibid.
9. Ibid.
10. An example is its 1988 publication *Countdown 1992* which gave a complete overview of the legislative process for all 282 original Single Market directives and over 500 other pieces of Single Market legislation.
11. Personal interview with John Russell, Brussels, 16 December 1998.
12. Ibid.
13. Maria Green Cowles, 'The EU Committee of AmCham: the Powerful Voice of American Firms in Brussels', *Journal of European Public Policy*, 3:3, September 1996, pp. 339–58.
14. 'EU Recycling Support Plan Worries US Firms', *ENDS Daily*, 1 March 1999.
15. Personal interview with John Russell, Brussels, 16 December 1998.
16. Ibid.
17. Cowles, 'The EU Committee of AmCham: the Powerful Voice of American Firms in Brussels'.
18. Personal interview with John Russell, Brussels, 16 December 1998.
19. Ibid.

Chapter 6

1. The AMUE currently has almost three hundred members, sixteen of which are represented in the ERT. Figures derived from AMUE membership and board composition as of November 1998, and ERT membership as of January 1999. Sources: <http://amue.lf.net/aboutus/about.htm> and <http://www.ert.be/pc/enc_frame.htm>
2. Phone interview with Bertrand de Maigret, 11 March 1997.
3. Personal interview with Etienne Davignon, Brussels, 20 February 1997.
4. ERT, *Reshaping Europe*, Brussels, 1991, p. 2.
5. Personal interview with Etienne Davignon, Brussels, 20 February 1997.
6. Speech by Jacques Santer to the board of directors of the AMUE, 26 February 1998.
7. Phone interview with Bertrand de Maigret, 11 March 1997.
8. Personal interview with Etienne Davignon, Brussels, 20 February 1997.
9. AMUE, 'Taking Stock of 9 Years of Euro Conferences', *Euro Newsletter*, No. 38, January/February 1999.
10. Ibid.
11. Ibid.
12. Ibid.
13. AMUE, Annual Report of the President for the Year 1997.
14. AMUE, *Preparing the Changeover to the Single Currency*, May 1994.
15. Etienne Davignon (Société Générale de Belgique), Philippe Lagayette (Caisse des Dépôts et Consignations) and Tom Hardiman (IBM Europe). Source: 'Composition of the Expert Group on the Introduction of the Euro as the Single Currency', European Commission press release IP/94/600, 1 July 1994.
16. Commission Green Papers are documents intended to stimulate debate and launch a process of consultation at the European level on a particular topic (such as social policy, the single currency, telecommunications). These consultations may then lead to the publication of a White Paper, translating the conclusions of the debate into practical proposals for Community action. Source: European Commission, *Glossary: The Institutional Reform of the European Union: 200 Concepts for a Better Understanding of the Challenges Facing the European Union ...*, SCADPlus Database.
17. The European Monetary Institute (EMI) was the forerunner to the European Central Bank (ECB). It focused on the technical preparations needed to introduce the single currency and establish a European system of central banking, and prepared the ECB's monetary policy.
18. Green Paper on the Practical Arrangements for the Introduction of the Single Currency, European Commission, 31 May 1995; *The Changeover to the Single Currency*, European Monetary Institute, 14 November 1995.
19. In Madrid, the European Council agreed on the scenario and calendar for EMU. The euro was to come into existence on 1 January 1999, with exchange rates between the euro and the national currencies of EMU members to be irrevocably fixed on that day. The year 2002 will see the total replacement of EMU countries' currencies by the euro.
20. AMUE, *The Sustainability Report: Report of the AMUE Working Group on Sustainability of the Euro and the Convergence Criteria*, Paris, February 1998.

21. For example, the AMUE was awarded a major contract with the Parliament after the 1992 monetary crisis; its advice was to change the European monetary system and move towards a single currency.
22. Phone interview with Bertrand de Maigret, 11 March 1997.
23. Personal interview with Etienne Davignon, Brussels, 20 February 1997.
24. Ibid.
25. Phone interview with Bertrand de Maigret, 11 March 1997.
26. 'An Awfully Big Adventure', *The Economist*, in a special survey on the EMU, 11 April 1998.
27. AMUE, *The Sustainability Report*.
28. The European Central Bank (ECB) was established on 1 June 1998, replacing its predecessor, the European Monetary Institute (EMI, see note 17). The ECB is responsible for monetary policy in the European Union and has competence for carrying out foreign exchange interventions.
29. Phone interview with Bertrand de Maigret, 11 March 1997.
30. Personal interview with Etienne Davignon, Brussels, 20 February 1997.
31. 'The Euro – Special Report', *Business Week*, 27 April 1998.
32. 'US Raiders Lay Siege to Euroland', *The European*, 15–21 June 1998.
33. Ibid.
34. Statement signed by seventy Dutch economists, published in *De Volkskrant*, 13 February 1997.
35. Ravi Bulchadani, quoted in 'The Euro – Special Report', *Business Week*, 27 April 1998.
36. Jürgen Schrempp (CEO of DaimlerChrysler), 'Why We Believe in the Euro', *Newsweek*, Special Issue, November 1998–February 1999, p. 38.
37. The current contribution to the EU by member states is 1.25 per cent of GDP.
38. After Lafontaine had resigned, the ECB in fact lowered the interest rate for the euro-zone countries. Duisenberg opposed Lafontaine's motivation for lowering interest rates (lowering unemployment). When the ECB lowered the interest rate, this was motivated by strictly monetarist reasons.
39. David Bowers, European equity strategist for Merrill Lynch & Co., quoted in 'The Euro – Special Report', *Business Week*, 27 April 1998.

Chapter 7

1. *Maastricht Treaty*, Title VII, Final Provisions, Article N2, 1991.
2. The Reflection Group, presided over by Carlos Westendorp, then Spanish Secretary of State for EU Relations, was composed of 15 representatives from the EU member states, one from the European Commission and two members of the European Parliament. It officially started functioning on 2 June 1995.
3. Final Report Westendorp Group, 5 December 1995.
4. Personal interview with Keith Richardson, Brussels, 21 February 1997.
5. Ibid.
6. Jérôme Monod, Chairman of Lyonnaise des Eaux and Gerhard Cromme of Krupp later took over the chairmanship of the ERT's IGC working group.
7. Personal interview with Keith Richardson, Brussels, 21 February 1997.
8. Ibid.
9. Personal interview with Zygmunt Tyszkiewicz, Brussels, 18 March 1997.

10. François Perigot, letter to Irish President John Bruton, 23 September 1996, p. 2.
11. Keith Richardson, *Managing Europe: the Challenge to the Institutions*, February 1998.
12. UNICE, 'Contribution to the Intergovernmental Conference', Brussels: ERT, 15 March 1996, p. 4.
13. Co-decision is one of the decision-making procedures set up in the Maastricht Treaty. Under co-decision, the European Parliament can put forward amendments to Council proposals. In the case that the Council does not agree, the proposal goes back to the Parliament for a second reading. If the Parliament sticks to the amendments, a conciliation procedure begins, and continues for a maximum of three months. This gives the Parliament a kind of veto right.
14. Personal interview with Keith Richardson, Brussels, 21 February 1997.
15. Qualified majority voting in the Council was extended to some areas including employment, customs cooperation, adoption of research programmes and protection of privacy.
16. The co-decision procedure has been extended to include decisions on employment incentives, customs cooperation, social policy, equal opportunities, public health, transparency and countering fraud. Large policy areas, such as harmonisation of legislation, agriculture, taxation, industry, cohesion, and Common Foreign and Security Policy and Justice and Home Affairs, remain under the consultation procedure, with very limited power for the European Parliament.
17. Keith Richardson, *Managing Europe: the Challenge to the Institutions*, February 1998.
18. UNICE, 'Contribution to the Intergovernmental Conference', p. 1.
19. European Commission, 'Single Market: Action Plan Bears Fruit', press release IP/99/128, Brussels, 23 February 1999.
20. Personal interview with Keith Richardson, Brussels, 21 February 1997.
21. Personal interview with Zygmunt Tyszkiewicz, Brussels, 18 March 1997.
22. UNICE, 'Contribution to the Intergovernmental Conference', p. 1.
23. Phone interview with Keith Richardson, 11 March 1997.
24. Ibid.
25. Ibid.
26. Presidency Conclusions from the Amsterdam Summit (SN 150/97), Annex, p. 10.
27. 'Employment Chapter Offers Few Ideas', *European Voice*, 26 June 1997, p. 15.
28. Amsterdam Treaty, Article 109n.
29. 'Employment Chapter Offers Few Ideas', p. 15.
30. Zygmunt Tyszkiewicz, 'Employment and Competitiveness' in *Challenge Europe: Making Sense of the Amsterdam Treaty*, the European Policy Centre, Brussels, July 1997, p. 51.
31. Presidency Conclusions from the Amsterdam Summit (SN 150/97), Annex, pp. 10–13.
32. Keith Richardson, 'Business Viewpoint' in *Challenge Europe: Making Sense of the Amsterdam Treaty*, p. 53.
33. Phone interview with Keith Richardson, 11 March 1997.
34. Personal interview with Zygmunt Tyszkiewicz, Brussels, 18 March 1997.

35. ERT position paper on the Intergovernmental Conference, 28 October 1996.
36. Letter from Jacques Santer to the heads of state and government on the eve of the Amsterdam Summit, 16–17 June 1997.
37. 'Extra Trade Deals Powers Left Open', *European Voice*, 26 June 1997, p. 19.
38. Keith Richardson, *Managing Europe: the Challenge to the Institutions*.
39. The Amsterdam Treaty was approved by a majority of voters in referendums in Ireland (55 per cent) and Denmark (62 per cent). It was ratified by all national Parliaments in the EU and came into force on 1 May 1999.
40. UNICE press statement, 18 June 1997.
41. Personal interview with Christophe de Callatäy, Brussels, 18 November 1998.
42. Keith Richardson, 'Business Viewpoint' in *Challenge Europe: Making Sense of the Amsterdam Treaty*, p. 53.
43. See for example the ERT's 1991 publication *Reshaping Europe*, p. 58.
44. Keith Richardson, 'Business Viewpoint' in *Challenge Europe: Making Sense of the Amsterdam Treaty*, p. 53.

Chapter 8

1. European Commission, *1998 Report on the Implementation of the Guidelines and Priorities for the Future*, Brussels, 1998.
2. This amount will come from various pre-accession funds, as well as from the EU's structural and cohesion funds. Source: *T&E Bulletin*, May 1998.
3. Greenpeace Switzerland, *Missing Greenlinks: Examination of the Commission's Guidelines for a Decision about the Trans-European Networks and Proposal for Ecological Restructuring*, Zurich, 1995.
4. ERT, *Missing Links*, Brussels, 1984; ERT, *Missing Networks*, Brussels, 1991.
5. Pehr Gyllenhammar, letter to Hans Merkle, Chair of the German engineering company Bosch, quoted in Maria Green, 'The Politics of Big Business in the Single Market Program', leaflet, May 1993, p. 3.
6. ERT, *Beating the Crisis*, 1993, p. 22.
7. Interview with Keith Richardson, then ERT Secretary-General, 21 February 1997.
8. ERT, 'ECIS: An Invitation to Participate', Brussels, 1993.
9. 'At a suitable distance from Brussels, the region hosts first-rate research institutions and provides model solutions to the complex problems of collective investment in a modern society.' Source: ECIS leaflet, 1994.
10. ERT, 'ECIS: An Invitation to Participate', Brussels, 1993. The strategy behind setting up ECIS had already been introduced in the 1989 ERT report *The Need for Renewing Transport Infrastructure in Europe*. In that report, the ERT had emphasised the importance of bringing together the public sector, industry, banks, service enterprises and private institutions to overcome obstacles in infrastructure implementation.
11. For example, DG VII (Transport) requested a December 1994 seminar for an audience of 45 representatives from Central and Eastern Europe. The seminar, entitled 'Attracting Private Finance for Transport Infrastructure in Central and Eastern European Countries', was financed by the EU's Phare Programme.

12. This working group consisted of civil servants from the EU member states. Its chairman, then Commission Vice-President Henning Christophersen, left the European Commission in 1995. In 1996, he became a member of the board of ECIS.

13. 'An entity operating under a private legal statute would define projects and then seek funds from both the public and private sector ... even where – as in the case of high-speed trains – the public stake may approach 70 per cent.' Source: *ECIS Newsletter*, October 1994, p. 2.

14. Ibid.

15. These proposals were published by ECIS under the title *Making It Happen: Building and Financing TENs*. Another ECIS publication in the busy autumn of 1994 was *Investment in Transport Infrastructure: The Recovery in Europe*, which was discussed the following month at a workshop in Rotterdam with 'a panel of senior government officials from the UK, France and the Netherlands'.

16. *ECIS Newsletter*, October 1994.

17. Ibid.

18. PBKAL refers to the Paris–Brussels–Cologne–Amsterdam–London high-speed train connections which the EU hopes can become the base of an EU-wide network.

19. *ECIS Newsletter*, December 1994. The report was heavily criticised in the 1995 Greenpeace study *Missing Greenlinks*.

20. European Commission, *The Likely Macroeconomic and Employment Impact of Investments in Trans-European Transport Networks*, (SEC(97)10), 1997.

21. The decision to close down ECIS was taken at its fourth Annual Assembly after 'careful assessment' of 'its chances to maintain the critical mass in financial and human resources'. Source: *ECIS Newsletter*, June 1997.

22. FIEC represents 30 contractors' organisations in 22 countries, involving a total of 1.9 million enterprises and 10 million employees. The FIEC secretariat in Brussels employs a staff of eight, but a large amount of the work is done in numerous 'sub-commissions' consisting of representatives of the national organisations. Source: FIEC web site <http://www.fiec.be/>

23. The European Construction Forum consists of FIEC (contractors) and includes ACE (architects), EFCA (consulting engineers), UEPC (developers and house builders), CEPM, CEMBUREAU and EAPA (construction material producers) and FETBB (construction workers). Source: FIEC web site <http://www.fiec.be/>

24. 'The IRF has provided leadership for the development of a new coalition of Europe's leading road and transport organisations into a new umbrella group called the European Coalition for Sustainable Transport (ECST).' Source: *IRF Annual Report*, 1998.

25. ERF press release, 2 February 1999.

26. Peter Chapman, 'TENs Funding Faces Uphill Struggle', *European Voice*, 4, 19 March 1998.

27. 'The Transport Challenge', *Frontier-free Europe*, November–December 1996, p. 10.

28. Tim Jones, 'Commission Urges Euro Area to Boost Investment', *European Voice*, 4, 26 November 1998.

29. Peter Chapman, 'Private Sector Help Sought for TENs', *European Voice*, 4, 29 January 1998.

30. Tim Jones, 'Commission Urges Euro Area to Boost Investment', *European Voice*, 4, 26 November 1998.

31. MEPs also called on the Commission 'to propose new forms of long-term funding and ways to make venture capital more easily available'. Source: Rory Watson, 'MEPs Warn of Funding Shortfall Threat to TENs', *European Voice*, 4, 5 November 1998.

32. T&E, *Roads and the Economy*, Brussels, 1996.

33. *Transport Investment, Transport Intensity and Economic Growth*, Interim Report by the Standing Advisory Committee on Trunk Road Assessment (SACTRA), published 9 February 1998 by the UK Department of the Environment, Transport and the Regions.

34. European Commission, *1998 Report on the Implementation of the Guidelines and Priorities for the Future*, Brussels, 1998, p. 5.

35. T&E, *Transport & Environment Bulletin*, October 1998.

36. EUROPIA, established in 1989, in its own words 'informs the European Commission, the Council of Ministers, the European Parliament and other European institutions and the general public on matters of interest to the European downstream industry'. The president of EUROPIA is François Cornelis, CEO of Petrofina and an active ERT member. Source: EUROPIA web site <http://www.europia.com/>

37. On 6 July 1998, only a few days after the Auto-Oil Programme was finally passed, Elf announced that it would that same autumn start supplying its service stations in the UK with diesel produced according to the 2005 standards of the Auto-Oil programme, with 90 per cent less sulphur content. Source: Interview with Frazer Goodwin, Communications Manager, Transport & Environment, 17 February 1999.

38. Decision making on the Auto-Oil Programme followed the so-called co-decision procedure.

39. Personal interview with Annette Hauer, assistant at the Green Group in the European Parliament, Brussels, 26 January 1999.

40. T&E, *Transport & Environment Bulletin*, August/September 1998.

41. Ibid.

42. 'Commission Outlines Measures to Reduce Carbon Dioxide Emissions from Transport', Brussels, 31 March 1998. Source: Commission web site <http://europa.eu.int/>

43. Currently only 14 per cent of freight is transported by rail in the EU, down from 30 per cent in 1970.

44. Chris Johnston, 'No Smooth Ride for Transport Sector', *European Voice*, 5, 24 January 1999.

Chapter 9

1. Niccolo Sarno, 'Poll Finds Europeans Mistrust State and Science', Inter Press Service, Brussels, 6 October 1997.

2. The sample, taken among 16,000 people all over the EU, showed that 74 per cent of the population wanted labelling on such products and only 28 per cent thought regulation should be left to the industry. Sixty per cent thought that only traditional breeding methods should be used for farm animals.

3. EuropaBio, *European Bionews*, Special Issue, December 1993. EuropaBio's predecessor, the Senior Advisory Group on Biotechnology (SAGB) was set up in 1989 'to provide a senior industrial forum for addressing policy issues affecting biotechnology in the European Community' and 'to promote a supportive climate for biotechnology in Europe'.

4. Club de Bruxelles conference, 'The Future of Biotechnologies in Europe: From Research and Development to Industrial Competitiveness', 26–27 September 1996.

5. EuropaBio, *European Bionews*, Issue 10, November 1996.

6. Other founding members were Akzo Pharma, Du Pont, Eli Lilly, Ferruzi Group, Gist-Brocades, Hoechst, Hoffmann-La Roche, ICI, Sandoz, Schering and SmithKline Beecham.

7. SAGB report titles include: *Community Policy for Biotechnology: Priorities and Actions* (January 1990), *Economic Benefits & European Competitiveness* (July 1990), *Creation of a Community Task Force and Independent Consultative Body* (October 1990) and *Benefits & Priorities for the Environment* (November 1991).

8. EuropaBio, *European Bionews*, Issue 2, May 1994.

9. 'At a time when the European biotech sector is fighting to maintain its competitive position, the regulatory situation in the European Union seems to have taken a step backward towards fragmented national markets. The ERT underscored this problem in a meeting with Commission President Jacques Santer last month when it questioned how companies can operate efficiently where the EU may decide on a specific policy, but where individual member states can impose their own – often contradictory – controls. The recent example of genetically modified maize in which an EU marketing authorization was rapidly followed by a series of national measures restricting the marketing illustrates this. EuropaBio will work closely with the EU and national authorities to seek to find a solution.' Source: EuropaBio, *European Bionews*, Issue 11, March 1997.

10. Jacques Delors, White Paper on Growth, Competitiveness and Employment, 1993.

11. Ibid.

12. 'Communications Programmes for EuropaBio', Burson-Marsteller, January 1997.

13. Ibid., p. 3.

14. Ibid., p. 8.

15. Ibid., pp. 15–16.

16. Jacob Langvad, 'Biotech Industry has Slept During Classes', *Berlingske Tidende*, 27 June 1997.

17. Quote from the declaration made by Italian playwright Dario Fo during the Nobel Prize ceremony at the Academy of Science in Stockholm in 1997.

18. On 1 March 1995, the European Parliament rejected the draft Directive for the Legal Protection of Biotechnological Inventions against the will of the European Commission and the Council of Ministers. This is the only time the Parliament, to date, has used its veto powers (a power granted to it in the Maastricht Treaty) to reject draft EU legislation.

19. International Research Associates conducted a poll for the European Commission in which 61 per cent of those polled thought that biotechnology posed a risk and believed that it could result in dangerous new diseases. Source: Niccolo Sarno, 'Poll Finds Europeans Mistrust State and Science'.

20. Ibid.
21. This 'specially commissioned independent study' was commissioned by EuropaBio and carried out by a team of researchers from Business Decisions Limited and biotechnology experts from the Science Policy Research Group of the University of Sussex. Business Decisions Limited, 'a consultancy specialising in competitiveness and regulatory reform issues', was also responsible for the last two ERT reports.
22. FEBC includes AMEEP (food and feed enzymes), CEFIC (chemicals), CIAA (food), COMASSO (plant breeders), EDMA (diagnostic products), ECPA (plant protection products), EFPIA (pharmaceuticals), FAIP (farm animals), FEDESA (animal health products), FEFAC (compound feed), FEFANA (foodstuffs additives) and GIBIP (plants and seeds). EuropaBio hosts the FEBC Secretariat.
23. FEBC, *FEBC's Views on the 'Directive on the Legal Protection of Biotechnological Inventions'*, Brussels, 1997.
24. 'Western Europe is the world's largest market for chemicals. The European chemical industry should, therefore, operate with an advantage over other regions whose home markets are not as significant. However, the difficulties in securing effective patent protection in the region mean that this market is not as easily exploitable by high technology business as it should be, putting European-based chemical companies at a disadvantage to their American counterparts, for example.' Source: CEFIC Position Paper, 'Patents: Key to Innovation in Europe', November 1996, p. 3.
25. European Campaign on Biotechnology Patents (ECOBP), 'The Big Mirage: The Misuse of the Patient with Hereditary Diseases Before the EP's Vote in 1997', an ECOBP Background Paper, March 1998, p. 4.
26. Ibid., p. 7.
27. GIG, 'Position on the European Biotechnology Directive', 19 November 1997.
28. Rural Advancement Foundation International (RAFI), 'The Life Industry 1997; The Global Enterprises that Dominate Commercial Agriculture, Food and Health', *RAFI Communiqué*, November/December 1997.
29. 'Seeds of Discontent: The Pros And Cons Of Gene-Spliced Food', *Business Week*, 2 February 1998, pp. 62–3.
30. John Arlidge, 'Brit Advertising Standards Authority Slams Monsanto', *Observer*, London, 28 February 1999.

Chapter 10

1. Josh Karliner, *The Corporate Planet: Ecology and Politics in the Age of Globalization*, San Francisco: Sierra Club, 1998, p. 6.
2. 'Acting in Harmony on World Trade', *European Voice*, 16–22 January 1997.
3. Before the Amsterdam Treaty came into force on 1 May 1999, the 133 Committee was known as the '113 Committee'.
4. Interview with MEP Michael Hindley, Brussels, 17 February 1999.
5. John Cavanagh, *Background to the Global Financial Crisis*, Washington, DC: Institute for Policy Studies, September 1998.
6. 'World Bank Estimates 200 Million "Newly Poor"', *Associated Press*, 3 June 1999.

7. UNCTAD, *World Investment Report 1997*.
8. See, for instance, *European Economy: Reports and Studies*, No. 3, 1997.
9. Josh Karliner, *The Corporate Planet*, p. 5.
10. *Jobs and the Giants*, London: World Development Movement, February 1998.
11. If the investments of local TNC subsidiaries are included, the total volume of foreign investment reached US$1,600 billion in 1997. UNCTAD, *World Investment Report 1997*.
12. UNCTAD, *World Investment Report 1997*.
13. The packages included requirements for indebted governments to guarantee the following: the right for all foreign investors to establish investments in every sector of the economy; the weakening of labour and environmental standards to attract investment; the removal of safeguards in stock markets that limit flash sell-offs and capital flight; and prevention against the adoption of regulations which would restrict or control foreign investment in their countries.
14. In Brazil, for instance, Spanish Telefónica bought up large parts of the newly privatised phone company Telebras, Dutch ABN AMRO purchased Banco Real, and French supermarket giant Carrefour took over the department store chain Lojas Americanas to strengthen its position in the competition on the Brazilian market with Portuguese retailer Sonae and US giant Walmart. Only one of the eight largest Argentinian banks is still locally owned, compared to five in 1994. The wave of international acquisitions is expected to continue as new sectors, for instance, water and sewage, are privatised. 'Snapping up South America', *Business Week*, 18 January 1999.
15. UNCTAD, *World Investment Report 1997*.
16. Roy Jones, 'MAI: Unions Seek Safeguards', *International Union Rights*, 5(1), 1998, p. 5.
17. Hilary F. French, *Investing in the Future: Harnessing Private Capital Flows for Sustainable Development*, Washington, DC: Worldwatch Institute, 1998.

Chapter 11

1. European Commission, *The New Transatlantic Marketplace*, Communication, Brussels 11 March 1998.
2. EU/United States: 'France Confirms to Council its Rejection of Sir Leon Brittan's Ideas on New Transatlantic Market', *Agence Europe*, Brussels, 30 March 1998.
3. An internal communiqué from the EU/US Senior High Level Group indicates that the French government was in fact not fundamentally opposed to launching NTM-style negotiations; their fierce language at the EU Ministers' meeting was for 'public consumption'. Source: Public Citizen, 'Alert: New Transatlantic Marketplace (NTM) Lives', 9 May 1998 on <http://www.citizen.org/>
4. As an EU source put it: 'It is saving face for everyone. France gets to kill the NTM, but the summit will still discuss trade liberalisation, so the pieces of the NTM will live on.' Source: *Inside US Trade*, 1 May 1998, p. 5.
5. 'New Transatlantic Economic Partnership to Accelerate Trade Growth', White House press statement, 18 May 1998.

6. 'Declaration of the EU–US Summit on the Transatlantic Economic Partnership', London, 18 May 1998.

7. European Commission, *Transatlantic Economic Partnership Action Plan* (an agreement between the US and EU administrations), Brussels, 9 November 1998.

8. Ibid.

9. 'Declaration of the EU–US Summit on the Transatlantic Economic Partnership', London, 18 May 1998.

10. European Commission, 'We will set up a regular dialogue between us in order to ensure closer cooperation in the run-up to the 1999 Ministerial Conference in the WTO, with a view to providing leadership and facilitating preparations initiated in May 1998. This dialogue will be realised in a pragmatic way and piloted by a series of meetings at ministerial and official level from now until the 1999 WTO Ministerial meeting.' *Transatlantic Economic Partnership Action Plan*, Brussels, 9 November 1998.

11. For examples, see for instance: 'US Barriers to Trade and Investment', *CEObserver*, April 1998.

12. European Commission, *Transatlantic Economic Partnership Action Plan*, Brussels, 9 November 1998.

13. 'New Transatlantic Economic Partnership to Accelerate Trade Growth', White House press statement, 18 May 1998.

14. Testimony of Mary C. Sophos, Senior Vice-President of Government Affairs, Grocery Manufacturers of America, Inc. before the House of Representatives, Committee on Ways and Means, Subcommittee on Trade, 28 July 1998.

15. Ibid.

16. Under-Secretary of Commerce for International Trade David Aaron, testimony on US–EU Trade Relations, before the House of Representatives, Committee on Ways and Means, Subcommittee on Trade, 28 July 1998.

17. Ibid.

18. Ibid.

19. Testimony of Mary C. Sophos, Senior Vice-President of Government Affairs, Grocery Manufacturers of America, Inc. before the House of Representatives, Committee on Ways and Means, Subcommittee on Trade, 28 July 1998.

20. Ibid.

21. Declaration of the EU–US Summit on the Transatlantic Economic Partnership', London, 18 May 1998.

22. Letter from Community Nutrition Institute to the US Trade Representative commenting on the TEP, 6 July 1998.

23. Ibid.

24. Loukas Tsoulakis, *The New European Economy Revisited*, Oxford: Oxford University Press, 1997.

25. 'Completion of these mutual recognition agreements has been a long-standing priority of the United States and the European Union,' State Secretary Daley added. 'I also want to give credit to the Trans-Atlantic Business Dialogue. The TABD said the MRA was important; we heard them and acted.' Source: TABD, 'U.S. and EU Reach Agreement on Mutual Recognition of Product Testing & Approval Requirements', press release, 13 June 1997.

26. Paula Stern, 'The Trans-Atlantic Business Dialogue: a New Paradigm for Standards and Regulatory Reform Sector-by-Sector', article prepared by the Council on Foreign Relations, Washington, 1996, on TABD web site <http://www.tabd.com/>

27. TABD, '1997 Rome Communiqué', Rome, 7 November 1997.

28. EuropaBio, *European Bio-News*, Issue 11, March 1997.

29. Dr Horst Langer, Member of the Managing Board of Siemens AG in an address to the European-American Chamber of Commerce in the US: 'Transatlantic Business Dialogue (TABD): A Step Toward Better Economic Relations', New York, 10 March 1998.

30. Sir Leon Brittan, 'Globalisation: Responding to New Political and Moral Challenges', speech at the World Economic Forum, Davos, 30 January 1997. The New Transatlantic Agenda was adopted at the 1995 Madrid Summit which laid out an 'action plan' to enhance political and economic relations between the EU and the US. Central to it is the Transatlantic Business Dialogue.

31. TABD web site: <http://www.tabd.com/>

32. Sir Leon Brittan in his speech 'Investment Liberalisation: A New Issue for WTO. Europe and the Challenge of the Global Economy' at the CBI Conference, Harrogate, 11 November 1996.

33. TABD, *Chicago Declaration*, 9 November 1996, p. 3.

34. Brian Coleman, 'Trans-Atlantic Business Dialogue Gains Momentum at Rome Talks', *The Wall Street Journal Europe*, 10 November 1997. According to the TABD: '... the TABD process is achieving solid results ... the EU and U.S. Administrations had taken significant, concrete action on one third of the TABD recommendations and the situation has improved since then. Additionally, more than half of the TABD recommendations from Rome were under active discussion between government and the business community.' Source: TABD, *Charlotte Statement of Conclusions*, Charlotte, 7 November 1998.

35. Sir Leon Brittan, quoted by Timothy J. Hauser, Acting Under-Secretary, International Trade Administration, US Department of Commerce in his Statement to the House of Representatives, Committee on Ways and Means, Subcommittee on Trade, delivered on 23 July 1997.

36. Personal interview with Stephen Johnston, Brussels, 26 January 1999.

37. Ibid.

38. Ibid.

39. Declaration of the EU-US Summit on the Transatlantic Economic Partnership, London, 18 May 1998.

40. 'Extracts from a press conference by the British Prime Minister Tony Blair, President Clinton and President Santer', UK Foreign Office Press Release, 18 May 1998.

41. For more information on the Transatlantic Labour Dialogue, see: <http://www.eu-osha.es/publications/conference/eu_us/index.html>

42. The Transatlantic Sustainable Development Dialogue doesn't seem to be very active. For some scanty information, refer to the European Partners for the Environment (EPE) web site: <http://www.epe.be/>

43. For more info on the Transatlantic Consumer Dialogue, see the TACD web site: <http://www.tacd.org/>

44. For more information on the Transatlantic Environmental Dialogue (TAED), see the TAED web site: <http://www.tiesnet.org/environment/taed.htm>

45. Interview with Stephen Johnston, Brussels, 26 January 1999.
46. Ibid.
47. Dutch Prime Minister Wim Kok quoted in 'TABD Participates in the US–EU Summit held in The Hague', *TABD Newsletter*, June 1997.
48. Interview with Stephen Johnston, Brussels, 26 January 1999.
49. Ibid.

Chapter 12

1. This chapter is based on the report *MAIGALOMANIA*, which Corporate Europe Observatory published in February 1998.
2. Tony Clarke, as quoted in personal notes made by Olivier Hoedeman during the occupation of ICC headquarters, Paris, 19 October 1998.
3. Sir Leon Brittan in a speech on investment at a conference organised by the Royal Institute for International Affairs (Chatham House) and the London School of Economics. Quoted in 'Commission Calls on European Business to Intensify Worldwide Investment Efforts', EC press release IP/95/269, 17 March 1995.
4. UNCTAD, *World Investment Report*, 1997.
5. ICC report, *Multilateral Rules for Investment*, 30 April 1996.
6. William H. Witherell, Director for Financial, Fiscal and Enterprise Affairs at the OECD, in 'The OECD Multilateral Agreement on Investment', *Transnational Corporations*, 4(2), August 1995.
7. Sir Leon Brittan in 'Commission Launches Discussion Paper on Worldwide Investment Rules', EC press release IP/95/52, 19 January 1995.
8. The WTO was invited as an observer.
9. Taken from USCIB web site: <http://www.uscib.org/policy/multinat.htm>
10. Ibid.
11. Anneke van Dok-van Weelen, Dutch Foreign Trade Minister, 'Report to the Dutch Parliament', November 1995, p. 4 (our translation).
12. Since early 1998, the draft text of the MAI has been available on the OECD web site: <http://www.oecd.org/daf/cmis/mai/negtext.htm>
13. 'Speaking note: European Commission representative at High-Level Meeting on the MAI', 16–17 February 1998, Paris.
14. Ibid.
15. Ibid.
16. In November 1997 for instance the German office of the OECD replied to an inquiry from interested citizens that 'there must be a misunderstanding. There is a draft text. This is however internal and not available for the public.' Fax from Dr Herbert Pfeiffer, Bonn OECD Centre, 28 November 1997.
17. Van Karnebeek is also chairman of chemical giant AKZO Nobel and the Dutch branch of the International Chamber of Commerce.
18. BIAC consultation, 15 January 1998.
19. 'Speaking note: European Commission representative at High-Level Meeting on the MAI', 16–17 February 1998, Paris.
20. Ibid.
21. Ron Plijter, *Mission Report*, European Commission DG1, Brussels, 19 February 1998.

22. OECD, 'Ministerial Statement on the Multilateral Agreement on Investment (MAI)', Paris, 27–28 April 1998.

23. Helmut Maucher, 'Firm Deadline Needed for MAI', *ICC Business World*, 15 May 1998.

24. Olivier Hoedeman, notes taken during the Geneva Business Dialogue, Geneva, 23–24 September 1998.

25. See also *MAI: the Reality of Six Months of 'Consultation and Assessment'*, Corporate Europe Observatory, Amsterdam, October 1998.

26. An English translation of the report can be found at <http://www.gn.apc.org/negreens/mai-lalu.htm> – the original French text is at <http://www.finances.gouv.fr/pole_ecofin/international/ami0998/am i0998.htm>

27. 'Internet Guerrillas', *Financial Times*, 30 April 1998.

28. 'Katz: Activists use Internet to slow trade liberalisation. US business leader sees free-trade threat', *Journal of Commerce*, 12 October 1998.

29. Ibid.

30. The most elaborate process has taken place in Canada, where the Canadian anti-MAI movement held a 'MAI Inquiry – a Citizens' Search for Alternatives' in the autumn of 1998. During this three-month process, local citizens' groups discussed ways to regain democratic control over the economy. Hearings took place all over Canada. For more information, refer to: <http://www.canadians.org/>

Chapter 13

1. Peter Sutherland, speech given in New York City on 3 March 1994.

2. Public Citizen, *The MAI Shell Game*, Public Citizen web site <http://www.citizen.org/pctrade>

3. Letter from Mickey Kantor to Bob Drake, President of the National Cattlemen's Association, dated 8 February 1996.

4. Ted Bardacke, 'American Boycotts Start to Bite', *Financial Times*, 2 June 1997.

5. Leslie Gevirtz, 'Business Challenges Massachusetts' Myanmar Sanctions', *Reuters News Wire*, 23 September 1998.

6. Anne L. Wexler, a former White House aide, was ranked as one of the capital's ten most influential lobbyists in the January 1998 issue of the *Washingtonian* magazine.

7. The Wexler Group is an independent unit of Hill and Knowlton, Inc., an international public relations firm.

8. Ken Silverstein, 'Doing Business with Despots', *Mother Jones*, May/June 1998.

9. The European Commission even filed a so-called amicus brief on behalf of the NFTC. Source: *Reuters News Wire*, 23 September 1998.

10. 'EU and Japan Urge WTO to Ban Massachusetts Myanmar Boycott', AFP, Geneva, 22 September 1998.

11. Myriam Vander Stichele, *Towards a World Transnationals' Organisation?*, Amsterdam: Transnational Institute (TNI), 30 April 1998.

12. Personal interview with Keith Richardson, Brussels, 21 February 1997.

13. James Enyart of Monsanto, quoted in Vandana Shiva, 'Who are the Real Pirates?', *Third World Resurgence*, Third World Network, Malaysia, 63, November 1995, pp. 16–17.

14. Edmund J. Pratt, 'Intellectual Property Rights and International Trade', *Pfizer Forum*, 1996.

15. James Enyart of Monsanto, quoted in Vandana Shiva, 'Who are the Real Pirates?'

16. Edmund J. Pratt, 'Intellectual Property Rights and International Trade', *Pfizer Forum*, 1996.

17. Myriam Vander Stichele, *Towards a World Transnationals' Organisation?*

18. Stephanie Howard, *Eugenics: a Self-defense Guide to Protecting Your Genes*, A SEED Europe, 1998.

19. The Convention on Biodiversity (CBD) clearly states that there should be benefit-sharing from the use of genetic resources, taking into account the rights of local communities, while TRIPs only gives weight to the right of corporations.

20. Aviva Freudmann and John Maggs, 'Bankers, Insurers Celebrate WTO Pact: Deal Puts Financial-Services Markets Under Global Rules for the First Time', *Journal of Commerce*, 16 December 1997.

21. Sir Leon Brittan in the *Financial Times*, 18 May 1998.

22. 'WTO Financial Services Agreement to Come Into Force on 1 March', *Agence Europe*, 16 February 1999.

23. Ibid.

24. Dutch Ministry of Economic Affairs, 'Financiële Diensten: een Hernieuwde poging', *WTO-NIEUWSBRIEF*, No. 5, November 1997.

25. Sir Leon Brittan, 'Europe's Prescriptions for the Global Trade Agenda', speech to the Coalition of Services Industries, Washington DC, 24 September 1998.

26. Ibid.

27. Sir Leon Brittan, 'Europe and the United States: New Challenges, New Opportunities', address to The Foreign Policy Association, New York, 23 September 1998.

28. Tim Wall, 'New WTO Investment Rules Cause Concern; Major Issues Loom for Countries Already Struggling With Uruguay Round Trade Agreements', *Africa Recovery*, 10(3), December 1996.

29. WTO, 'Report (1998) of the Working Group on the Relationship between Trade and Investment to the General Council', WT/WGTI/2, 8 December 1998 (98–4920).

30. Sir Leon Brittan, 'Europe and the United States: New Challenges, New Opportunities'.

31. Sir Leon Brittan, *The WTO Future Agenda*, speech at the Meeting of the European Community and European Non-Governmental Organisations, Business Federations and Labour Organisations on the WTO Future Agenda, Brussels, 16 November 1998.

32. European Commission DG1A, 'International Rules for Investment and the WTO', public discussion paper distributed at a dialogue meeting between the Commission and non-governmental organisations in Brussels, 27 January 1999.

33. European Commission DG1A, 'WTO New Round: Trade and Investment', note for the attention of the 113 Committee, Brussels, 15 December 1998.

34. Notes made during EC-NGO dialogue meeting, Brussels, 28 January 1999.

35. Commission document 'Minutes of the First Meeting of the Investment Network', Brussels, 27 November 1998.
36. 'Annotated Agenda Investment Correspondent Network', minutes of a meeting held between the Investment Network and the European Commission, Brussels: EC, 5 March 1999.
37. European Services Network leaflet 'GATS 2000 – Opening Markets for Services', Brussels, no date.
38. Sir Leon Brittan in a speech delivered at the first meeting of the European Services Network, Brussels, 26 January 1999.
39. Maria Green Cowles, 'The TABD and Domestic Business-Government Relations: Challenge and Opportunity', draft to be published in Maria Green Cowles, James Caporaso and Thomas Risse (eds), *Europeanisation and Domestic Change*, forthcoming.
40. Helmut Maucher: 'Ruling by Consent', guest column in the *Financial Times*, *FT Exporter*, 6 December 1997, p. 2.
41. ERT, *European Industry – A Partner for the Developing World*, Brussels, 1993.
42. Personal interview with Wim Philippa, Brussels, 16 December 1998.
43. Peter Sutherland is former Irish Justice Minister and was EU Competition Commissioner 1985–89 and GATT/WTO Director-General 1993–95.
44. Personal interview with Wim Philippa, Brussels, 16 December 1998.
45. Personal interview with Stephen Johnston, Brussels, 26 January 1999.
46. Ibid.
47. Phone interview with Stefano Bertasi, 22 February 1999.
48. Ibid.
49. International Chamber of Commerce, *The World Business Organisation in 1997*, brochure, Paris: ICC, p. 4.
50. Phone interview with Stefano Bertasi, 22 February 1999.
51. Dunkel is a former Swiss trade negotiator and chaired the GATT 1980–93.
52. Statement from members of international civil society opposing a Millennium Round or a new round of comprehensive trade negotiations, Geneva, 21 March 1999.

Chapter 15

1. The first Bilderberg meeting was presided over by Prince Bernhard, the husband of Dutch Queen Juliana.
2. Kees van der Pijl, *The Making of an Atlantic Ruling Class*, London: Verso, 1984.
3. Ibid.
4. Stephen Gill, *American Hegemony and the Trilateral Commission*, Cambridge: Cambridge University Press, 1990, p. 127.
5. Ibid., p. 259.
6. Alan Armstrong with Alistair McConnachie, 'The 1998 Bilderberg Meeting', *The Social Creditor, Official Journal of the Social Credit Secretariat*, July/August 1998.
7. Anonymous source quoted in Alan Armstrong with Alistair McConnachie, 'The 1998 Bilderberg Meeting'.
8. 'International Power Brokers Meet to Discuss Global Future; World's Most Secret Society to Meet in Sintra', *The News*, Portugal, 1 May 1999.

9. 'Bilderberg-"summit" Opens in Sintra Under Massive Security; Sampaio Attends Sintra Summit', *The News*, Portugal, 5 June 1999.
10. Official Bilderberg Conference Press release, as quoted in 'Bilderberg-"Summit" Opens in Sintra Under Massive Security; Sampaio Attends Sintra Summit'.
11. Trilateral Commission, 'About the Trilateral Commission', <http://www.trilateral.org/>
12. David Korten, *When Corporations Rule the World*, New York: Kumarian Press, 1995.
13. Trilateral Commission, 'Trilateral Commission Membership', <http://www.trilateral.org/>
14. 'Club Surveys the Global Economy', *International Herald Tribune*, 16 March 1999.
15. Stephen Gill, *American Hegemony and the Trilateral Commission*, p. 157.
16. Ibid.
17. WEF, 'Annual Meeting in Davos'.
18. WEF, *Institutional Brochure*, 'Impact of the World Economic Forum'.
19. Ibid.
20. Samuel P. Huntington, 'Cultures in the 21st Century: Conflicts and Convergences', Keynote Address at Colorado College's 125th Anniversary Symposium, 4 February 1999.
21. WEF, 'Annual Meeting 1998 Summaries', Geneva, 1998.
22. 'Economics and Social Cohesion', interview with Klaus Schwab, *TIME*, 15 February 1999.

Chapter 16

1. WBCSD, 'What is the WBCSD?', WBCSD web site: http:// www.wbcsd.ch/>
2. Pratap Chatterjee and Matthias Finger, *The Earth Brokers*, London: Routledge, 1994.
3. Ibid.
4. ERT member Egil Myklebust, President and former Chief Executive Officer of Norsk Hydro, currently chairs the WBCSD.
5. Stephan Schmidheiny, with the Business Council for Sustainable Development, *Changing Course; A Global Business Perspective on Development and the Environment*, Cambridge, MA: MIT Press, 1992.
6. Personal interview with Björn Stigson, Brussels, 17 January 1997.
7. WBCSD, *Signals for Change: Business Progress for Sustainable Development*, WBCSD, Geneva, 1997.
8. One representative was Larry Summers, Deputy Secretary of the US Treasury. Summers is the former Chief Economist of the World Bank 'who gained public fame for advocating the shipping of more toxic wastes to low income countries because people there die early anyway and they have less income earning potential so their lives are less valuable'. Source: David C. Korten, 'The United Nations and the Corporate Agenda', text circulated on the Internet, July 1997.
9. David C. Korten, 'The United Nations and the Corporate Agenda'.
10. David Korten works with People Centered Development Forum and is the author of *When Corporations Rule the World*, New York: Kumarian Press, 1995.

11. David C. Korten, 'The United Nations and the Corporate Agenda'.
12. Ibid.
13. WBCSD web site: <http://www.wbcsd.ch/>
14. Personal interview with Björn Stigson, Brussels, 17 January 1997.
15. WBCSD web site: <http://www.wbcsd.ch/>
16. Personal correspondence with Tony Juniper, Policy Director, Friends of the Earth England, Wales and Northern Ireland, 22 March 1999. See also the WBCSD web site: <http://www.wbcsd.ch/>
17. Ibid.
18. ERT, *Reshaping Europe*, Brussels, 1991, p. 49.
19. Personal interview with Björn Stigson, Brussels, 17 January 1997.
20. WBCSD, *Signals for Change: Business Progress for Sustainable Development*, WBCSD, Geneva, 1997.
21. Ibid.

Chapter 17

1. IPCC, *Second Assessment Report*, 1995. The Intergovernmental Panel on Climate Change (IPCC) was jointly established by the World Meteorological Organization and the United Nations Environment Programme in 1988, in order to: (i) assess available scientific information on climate change, (ii) assess the environmental and socioeconomic impacts of climate change, and (iii) formulate response strategies.
2. 'Economists Call for Carbon Taxes', *ENDS Environment Daily*, 14 February 1997.
3. This was agreed at the Kyoto Conference in December 1997. Kyoto was the Third Conference of the Parties (COP-3) to the UNFCC, the UN Framework Convention on Climate Change (also known as the 'Climate Convention'). The Convention, which aims to stabilise greenhouse gas concentrations in the atmosphere at a level which would prevent dangerous interference with the climate system, was signed by 154 countries at the 1992 Rio Earth Summit. Eighty-four nations signed the 1997 Kyoto Protocol, which is a development of the Convention containing specific targets and timetables. Thirty-nine industrialised countries under the Protocol have agreed to reduce emissions of six greenhouse gases: carbon dioxide, methane, nitrous oxide, hydrofluorocarbons, perfluorocarbons and sulphur hexafluoride. The European Union agreed to an 8 per cent overall reduction, the United States to 7 per cent, Japan to 6 per cent, while Australia was allowed to increase emissions by 8 per cent. Still far from entering into force, the Kyoto Protocol requires ratification by 55 of the Parties accounting for at least 55 per cent of total CO_2 emissions. By 15 March 1999, 84 governments had signed the Protocol, but only seven countries (the Maldives, Antigua and Barbuda, El Salvador, Panama, Fiji, Tuvalu and Trinidad and Tobago) had ratified it.
4. The Fourth Conference of the Parties (COP-4) to the Climate Convention took place in November 1998 in Buenos Aires, Argentina. COP-4 delayed nearly all important issues until the next COP. Parties adopted the Buenos Aires Action Plan, which sets a deadline of 2000 to complete work on the rules governing the Kyoto flexible mechanisms, with priority to the Clean

Development Mechanism (CDM), the financial mechanisms to assist southern countries, and the development and transfer of technology.

5. In 1998, the US Senate passed by a vote of 95–0 the Byrd-Hagel Resolution, which states that the United States should not be signatory to any protocol that excludes southern countries from legally binding commitments or that causes serious harm to the US economy.

6. Under pressure from critique by environmental groups, BP left the GCC in 1996. Shell left in early 1998. However, both companies are still members of the American Petroleum Institute (API). After having unsuccessfully lobbied the US government not to sign the Kyoto Protocol, the API now lobbies the US Senate not to ratify the Protocol.

7. 'Business Organizations Pledge Fight to Block Approval of Kyoto Pact', statement of William F. O'Keefe, then Chair of the Global Climate Coalition.

8. Global Climate Coalition web site: <http://www.globalclimate.org>

9. Ozone Action web site: <http://www.ozone.org/>

10. Letter from Robert N. Burt, BRT Chairman of the Environmental Task Force, to Stuart Eizenstat, 10 November 1998, quoted in Friends of the Earth press release 'Leaked Letter Tips US Hand at Climate Summit', 12 November 1998.

11. Ibid.

12. Quoted in Bob Burton and Sheldon Rampton, 'Thinking Globally, Acting Vocally: the International Conspiracy to Overheat the Earth', Center for Media & Democracy, *PR Watch*, 4(4), 4th Quarter 1997.

13. Björn Stigson, WBCSD President, 'Kyoto: Where Do We Go From Here?', *Earth Times*, 17 December 1997.

14. Phone interview with Daniel Cloquet, 24 October 1997.

15. Zygmunt Tyszkiewicz, quoted in '...While UNICE Attacks Plan From Inside', *ENDS Environment Daily*, 23 October 1997.

16. Phone interview with Daniel Cloquet, 24 October 1997.

17. Phone interview with Caroline Walcot, 24 October 1997.

18. Ibid.

19. Passages in international treaties under negotiation that have not yet been agreed upon are usually put in brackets. Often several alternative bracketed text versions are included in the draft treaty text.

20. Phone interview with ERT's Caroline Walcot, 24 October 1997.

21. Ibid.

22. Caroline Walcot, quoted in 'Mixed European Reactions to Kyoto Deal', *ENDS Environment Daily*, 11 December 1997.

23. The report *Refrigeration & Global Warming: An Independent Review of the Role of HFC Refrigerants* was published in October 1997 and funded by the European Fluorocarbon Technical Committee (EFCTC), a sector group of CEFIC.

24. CEFIC position paper, 'Post-Kyoto Views on Climate Policies', 12 June 1998.

25. *UNICE Opinion on the Proposal for a Council Directive on Taxation of Energy Products*, position paper, Brussels, 6 May 1997.

26. Letter from UNICE Secretary-General Zygmunt Tyszkiewicz to Commission President Jacques Santer, 6 February 1997.

27. Phone interview with Caroline Walcot, 24 October 1997.

28. Phone interview with Bent Jensen, 23 October 1997.

29. Designed by Single Market Commissioner Mario Monti, the proposal (Energy Tax III b) recycled the previous one but gave member states two

options. The first was to impose minimum excise duties on electricity, coal and gas over long transitional periods; the second, to avoid strong UK opposition to taxing domestic fuels, was to hike existing excise duties on road fuels, allowing member states to set a zero rate for electricity, gas and coal.

30. Green MEPs blamed the New Labour MEPs for having given in to the pressure of the industry lobby. Source: *ENDS Daily*, 10 February 1999.

31. *Missing Greenlinks*, Greenpeace Switzerland, 1995.

32. Given the proviso that no new taxes are levied on energy, the chemical industry has made a unilateral commitment to increase energy efficiency by 20 per cent between 1990 and 2005 in its Voluntary Energy Efficiency Programme (VEEP).

33. CEFIC introduced a set of voluntary rules to 'discourage the European Commission from inventing a European equivalent to the Toxic Release Inventory, a law passed in the United States in the aftermath of the Bhopal gas disaster that requires corporations to report their chemical releases to the public'. Quote taken from Joshua Karliner, *The Corporate Planet: Ecology and Politics in the Age of Globalization*, San Francisco: Sierra Club Books, 1997.

34. ERT, *Climate Change: An ERT Report on Positive Action*, Brussels, April 1997. The Environmental Watchdog Group is made up of directors from the environmental and health departments of ERT member corporations.

35. Ibid.

36. Phone interview with Caroline Walcot, 24 October 1997.

37. UNICE, *EU's Strategy Responding to Climate Change*, UNICE input to COP-4 in Buenos Aires, Brussels, October 1998.

38. Quote taken from 'German Elections Threaten Meltdown for Nuclear Power in EU', *European Voice*, 14 January 1999.

Chapter 18

1. Phone interview with Stefano Bertasi, coordinator of the ICC Working Group on Trade and Investment, 22 February 1999.

2. Maria Livanos Cattaui, 'UN-Business Partnership Forged on Global Economy', *International Herald Tribune*, 9 February 1998.

3. Ibid.

4. *Wall Street Journal*, 6–7 March 1998, front page.

5. Secretary-General of the United Nations and the International Chamber of Commerce, 'Joint Statement on Common Interests', 9 February 1998.

6. ICC, 'UN-Business Partnership to Boost Economic Development', press release, 9 February 1998.

7. In January 1999, Lebanese banker Adnan Kassar succeeded Helmut Maucher as ICC president. Maucher remained a vice-president of the ICC, along with Richard D. McCormick, Chairman and Chief Executive Officer of US West Inc. Source: ICC web site.

8. Olivier Hoedeman, notes made at the Geneva Business Dialogue, 23–24 September 1998.

9. Ibid.

10. Helmut Maucher, 'Ruling by Consent', guest column in the *Financial Times Exporter*, 6 December 1997.

11. Message from Kofi Annan, ICC Geneva Business Dialogue, 24 September 1998.
12. Maria Livanos Cattaui, 'Business and the UN: Common Ground', *Journal of Commerce*, 3 August 1998.
13. ICC, *Geneva Business Declaration*, Geneva, 24 September 1998.
14. Secretary-General of the United Nations, press release SG/T/2115, 4 February 1999.
15. ICC, 'Business Helps to Boost Investment in Africa', press release, 20 January 1999.
16. Ibid.
17. UNCTAD, 'Business Works with UNCTAD to Boost Investment in Africa', press release TAD/INF/2789, 19 January 1999.
18. 'No MAI, but MFI with GATS Approach, Says Fortin', *South-North Development Monitor (SUNS)*, 17 June 1998.
19. Ibid.
20. UNDP, internal document on the Global Sustainable Development Facility project, July 1998.
21. Apart from the companies mentioned in the text, the first 16 corporations that agreed to participate in the Global Sustainable Development Facility were as follows: Cultor Corporation (Finland), ESKOM (South Africa), Owens Conring (USA), AT&T (USA), Citibank (USA), IKEA (Sweden), Ericsson (Sweden) and Telia (Sweden).
22. Examples from UNDP, internal document on the Global Sustainable Development Facility project, July 1998.
23. All quotes from UNDP internal document referred to in notes 20 and 22.
24. Thalif Deen, InterPress Service, 22 April 1999.
25. 'A Perilous Partnership – The United Nations Development Programme's Flirtation with Corporate Collaboration', TRAC, March 1999.
26. 'Preliminary Guidelines for GSDF Pilot Projects'. In the preparatory phase of the GSDF project, the partners involved discussed questions such as: 'What will the result be if an additional two billion join the market economy and double or triple their income? How could these developments change corporate balance sheets? What products and services are needed? What would happen if the two billion people remain excluded from the market?'
27. Helmut Maucher, 'Ruling by Consent'.
28. 'The Voice of Business Heard Around the World', *Financial Times*, 29 December 1998.
29. Helmut Maucher, 'Ruling by Consent'.
30. Ibid.
31. *Wall Street Journal*, 6–7 March 1998, front page.
32. *Journal of Commerce*, 16 March 1998.
33. UN Department of Public Information, *Business and the UN: An Overview*, June 1998.
34. Interview with Helmut Maucher, *Financial Times*, 29 December 1998.
35. The Bretton Woods institutions are the International Monetary Fund (IMF), the World Bank and the General Agreement on Tariffs and Trade (GATT, which later became the World Trade Organization, WTO), all founded during an intergovernmental conference in Bretton Woods, New Hampshire in 1944.
36. Annan has taken every opportunity to improve the troubled relations between the US and the UN. At a conference organised by the right-wing

organisation Empower America, Annan spoke on the issue 'Why Conservatives Should Support the United Nations'. Source: UN, 'Secretary-General Confident That United States and United Nations Can Find Way to Mutually Supportive Relationship', press release SG/SM/6754, 16 October 1998.

37. ICC letter to G-8 Summit, May 1999.

38. Maria Livanos Cattaui, 'UN-Business Partnership Forged on Global Economy'.

39. Secretary-General of the United Nations and the International Chamber of Commerce, 'Joint Statement on Common Interests', 9 February 1998.

40. UN, 'Secretary-General Proposes Global Compact on Human Rights, Labour, Environment in Address to World Economic Forum in Davos', UN press release SG/SM/6881, 1 February 1999.

41. Olivier Hoedeman, notes made at the Geneva Business Dialogue, 23–24 September 1998.

42. Corporate Europe Observatory, 'Nestlé and the United Nations: Partnership or Penetration?', *CEObserver*, Issue 2, April 1998.

43. Olivier Hoedeman, notes made at the Geneva Business Dialogue, 23–24 September 1998.

44. 'Business and the Global Economy', ICC Statement to the G-8 Summit, 15–17 May 1998.

Chapter 19

1. Reference to political activities and lobby group membership is largely absent in the annual reports of European-based TNCs. No further information is provided on corporate web sites. In their annual reports, a number of companies proudly announce their membership in the World Business Council for Sustainable Development (WBCSD) and their participation in CEFIC's 'Responsible Care' programme or the ICC's Charter for Sustainable Development. But why are only the 'green' business organisations mentioned, and not the company's involvement in corporate lobby groups with controversial political agendas like the European Roundtable of Industrialists (ERT), EuropaBio and the International Chamber of Commerce (ICC)? In the summer of 1998, Corporate Europe Observatory wrote letters asking that question to over fifty large European corporations active in the ERT, the ICC and other international lobby organisations; in other words corporations indisputably involved in political lobbying. Eighteen companies did not respond at all, despite one or more reminders. Corporate Europe Observatory, 'Ending Corporate Secrecy', *CEObserver*, Issue 3, Amsterdam, June 1999.

2. 'Parliament's Register of Shame', *European Voice*, 2–8 April 1998.

3. Centre for Responsive Politics, *Influence Inc.*, Washington, DC, 1998.

4. Corporate Europe Observatory, *CEObserver*, Issues 2 and 3.

5. A tax on all international capital transactions, named after the Nobel Prize-winning economist James Tobin.

6. Community Supported Agriculture (CSA, also known as 'subscription farming' or 'linking farmers with consumers') is an alternative to the current system of agriculture, best described as corporate agriculture because of its dependence upon large agribusiness. In CSA, consumers buy shares to support the farmers' expenses during the year. In return, share-

holders receive fresh products throughout the growing season. Benefits of CSA include environmentally-friendly, local food production for local consumption, and a decrease in the enormous distances that food travels in today's globalised market.

7. LETS aim to revitalise informal local economies by enabling people to exchange goods and services using a local currency. A list is compiled of what members need and can provide, prices are set, and goods and services are paid with a local currency that never enters the official economy.

8. Joshua Karliner, *The Corporate Planet: Ecology and Politics in the Age of Globalization,* San Francisco: Sierra Club Books, 1997.

Appendix 1

1. Personal interview with John Russell, 16 December 1998.
2. Committee of Independent Experts, *First Report on Allegations Regarding Fraud, Mismanagement and Nepotism in the European Commission,* 15 March 1999.
3. European Commission, 'Intergovernmental Conference 1996, Commission Opinion', Brussels/Luxembourg, 1996, p. 20.
4. Quote from television documentary *Europa BV,* VPRO television, Netherlands, 19 October 1997.
5. Currently, there are 15 EU member states: Austria, Belgium, Denmark, Finland, France, Germany, Greece, Ireland, Italy, Luxembourg, the Netherlands, Portugal, Spain, Sweden and the United Kingdom.
6. In some policy areas, the European Parliament can reject legislative proposals which have been approved by the Council. See also note 10.
7. 'Doing the Splits', *The Economist,* 8 March 1997.
8. Ibid.
9. Personal interview with Michael Hindley, MEP, 17 February 1999.
10. Co-decision is one of the decision-making procedures set up in the Maastricht Treaty. It allows the European Parliament to suggest amendments to Council proposals. If the Council does not agree, the Parliament is entitled to a second reading. In the case that they stick to their amendments, a conciliation procedure begins that can last up to a maximum of three months.
11. 'Stanley Crossick and the European Policy Centre', *The Economist,* 14 July 1998.

Index